SHADE-GROWN SLAVERY

Shade-Grown Slavery

The Lives of Slaves on Coffee Plantations in Cuba

William C. Van Norman Jr.

Vanderbilt University Press

Nashville

© 2013 by Vanderbilt University Press
Nashville, Tennessee 37235
All rights reserved
First printing 2013

This book is printed on acid-free paper.
Manufactured in the United States of America

Library of Congress Cataloging-in-Publication Data on file

LC control number 2012033921
LC classification number HT1076.V36 2012
Dewey class number 306.3′6209729109033—dc23

ISBN 978-0-8265-1914-6 (cloth)
ISBN 978-0-8265-1915-3 (paperback)
ISBN 978-0-8265-1916-0 (e-book)

For the slaves of Cuba's coffee plantations

and for Esther, Mariel, and Alison

CONTENTS

ACKNOWLEDGMENTS

This work began over a decade ago in the provincial archives of Matanzas, Cuba, when I was a graduate student at the University of North Carolina at Chapel Hill. I worked in numerous archives and libraries in Cuba and in Spain over many years, compiling the data and stories that went into the making of this study. As is always the case, the first book of any historian is shaped through countless interactions in many venues that all contribute to the final outcome. I want to begin by asking forgiveness for any I have omitted here. Time and memory often conspire against us.

Louis A. Pérez Jr. guided my work at UNC and was all I could have hoped for as a mentor. I wish to express my deep gratitude and acknowledge my debt to him. He was always generous with his guidance and helped me find resources on the island that were invaluable to this work. John Chasteen, Kathryn Burns, Lisa Lindsay, and Lars Schoultz offered tremendous insights on preparing this study for publication. Other faculty at the University of North Carolina and Duke University have contributed to my progress and success. I warmly thank Sarah Shields for her encouragement and her example of integrity as a scholar. I valued her thoughtfulness and friendship during my years at UNC. Lloyd Kramer guided me from my first days at UNC and continued to be supportive throughout my time in Chapel Hill. John French and Barry Gaspar of Duke University helped me to become more rigorous in my thinking and to see Cuba and slavery on the island as part of a larger system situated in the Caribbean and Latin America.

Sherry Johnson, of Florida International University, and I became friends while researching in Seville. Our conversations over the years have enriched my development as a scholar and have broadened my knowledge of Cuba. She was generous with advice and in her critiques of my work. I appreciate her support and continued friendship.

K. Lynn Stoner was my mentor in the history department at Arizona State University during my undergraduate years. Her guidance drew me into the study of Cuba and the Afro-Cuban population. She has continued to encourage me and to be a good friend. I am also compelled to mention the late Kenneth Morrison, my mentor in religious studies; he deeply influenced my scholarship as both a researcher and as a teacher. His passing in 2012 was a great loss. He will be missed. I am forever grateful to Lynn and Ken for the contributions they have made to my life.

Numerous friends and colleagues have contributed to the success of this project through reading parts of its drafts and offering encouragement, critiques, and advice. Mariola Espinosa, Manuel Barcia, Matt Childs, Katherine Lopez, Charlotte Cosner, Ethan Kytle, Oscar Chamosa, Joshua Nadel, David Carlson, Dan Kerr, Laura Lewis, and Kristen McCleary have been great friends and each in their own way has helped me bring this work to its conclusion.

Grants and fellowships aided my research and encouraged my work. I received help from the UNC Department of History through Mowry Grants and a Quinn Fellowship; from the Graduate School through the Waddell Memorial Fellowship and the Off-Campus Fellowship; and from the Institute of Latin American Studies through the Tinker Grants. I also want to thank the Conference on Latin American History for granting me the Lydia Cabrera Award for Cuban Historical Studies. Their generosity permitted my work in Spain, greatly enhancing this project and my knowledge of Cuba. At James Madison University, I have received support from the Department of History, the College of Arts and Letters, and the Office of International Programs. My sincere thanks to Michael Galgano, head of the History Department; David Jeffries, dean of the College of Arts and Letters; and the staff at OIP.

I would be remiss if I did not thank the friends and colleagues I have made during my research trips to Cuba and Spain. Gladys Marel García, Gabino La Rosa Corzo, and Tomás Fernández Robaina helped me immeasurably during my trips to Cuba. I am grateful to them for their guidance and for teaching me about Cuba, past and present. This work would not have been possible were it not for the assistance I received from the Centro de Antropología. I especially thank Lourdes Serrano Peralta and Isabel Reyes Mora for their generous help during my visits. The staff at the Archivo Nacional de Cuba, notably Isabel Oviedo and Julio Lopez, were very helpful, as were the staff at the provincial archives in Matanzas and Pinar del Río, as well as at the Biblioteca Nacional José Martí and the Biblioteca Lingüistica y Literatura. I want to thank Consuelo Naranjo Orovio at the Consejo Superior de Investigaciones Científicas in Madrid for her help during my research in Spain. She not only advised me about collections of documents I should explore but also paved the way for my work in the Archivo Nacional and helped me locate contacts in Seville who facilitated my work in the Archivo General de Indies. The staff at both institutions were very professional and helpful throughout my work there.

A special thanks goes out to Eli Bortz at Vanderbilt University Press for his patience and his editorial advice as I pulled the manuscript together. His help and encouragement were invaluable. The suggestions of my two anonymous referees and copyeditor Peg Duthie have helped improve this final version a great deal. I also want to thank Gabrielle Lanier for her timely and diligent work on the maps found in this book, and David Carlson for graciously allowing me to use two of his photographs of Cuban coffee plantations.

I want to acknowledge the important contributions Patty Chase made in the early stages of the project. She was always supportive during the long research process, and her advice made me a better writer. My daughters, Mariel and Alison, had to endure long periods of me being an absent father, but their presence always enriched my life and they inspired me to get away from the desk. I am thankful for their patience, love, and support.

Esther Poveda came into my life four years ago. Her support and encouragement helped me in ways I could not have anticipated. Most importantly, she helped me to take my writing to a higher level and find my voice as a writer. We also talked through many difficult issues and ideas in the manuscript in a way that challenged me to think more clearly and articulate my ideas more directly to the reader. Our relationship started as a transatlantic romance and she agreed to marry me while I was still working hard to finish this study. The relationship and the book project have been challenges that we both have risen to meet every day. Her choice to come with me to the States attests to her love and understanding. I am deeply grateful for her devotion and support in helping me finish this project and for our journey together.

SHADE-GROWN SLAVERY

INTRODUCTION

The Crop Mattered

Over 70 percent of coffee exports were shipped from Havana in 1827. It is apparent that as many slaves were employed on coffee farms as were in sugar and that coffee cultivation was as dependent upon slave labor as the sugar sector. The number of slaves utilized on each coffee farm could be as great as on sugar plantations. —Laird W. Bergad, Fe Iglesias García, and María del Carmen Barcia

It was during the summer of 1998, as I was working through hundreds of records from plantations in the provincial archive in Matanzas, Cuba, that I became increasingly aware of large numbers of documents from coffee plantations in the region.[1] Not long after that realization, I was reading *The Cuban Slave Market, 1790–1880* when I encountered the above quote. It was these pieces, along with the lack of studies on coffee plantations and the slaves who worked on them, that led me on the long process of research and writing that resulted in this work. Throughout, I have been motivated to restore the story of those thousands of slaves to the history of Cuba and to expand our understanding of plantation life on the island.

Historians and others have told the story of slavery on sugar plantations in numerous studies and other works over the last 150 years while virtually ignoring or minimizing other types of slavery on the island and other economic activities that contributed to the growth of the colony. They have often let slavery on sugar plantations stand for slavery of all types. The retelling of the story of slavery on coffee plantations in Cuba begins against that background. Coffee and sugar as plantation crops grew up together. It was not clear in the first decades of the process that sugar would rise to the preeminence it achieved in the latter half of the nineteenth century. Sugar would come to dominate not only the economic life of Cuba but also the historical narrative. But Cuba was always much more than just a sugar island.

Coffee plantations were major contributors in expanding the frontier, populating the island, and broadening the colony's economic base. The *cafetal* (coffee plantation) loomed large in the Cuban imagination, shaping ideas of prosperity, beauty, and order. Slaves on the cafetales had a distinctive experience compared to those on other types of farms. Material conditions mattered, as they shaped experiences. Coffee slaves, like all slaves on plantations, lived a life of enslavement and hardship. But their daily lives were filtered through a particular work

1

regime, agricultural cycle, and living arrangements that affected demography and mortality, thereby facilitating social and cultural variations. To be sure, there were similarities across types of enslavement on the island, but there were also differences rooted in the crops and conditions. For tens of thousands of slaves, those distinctions mattered.

Each chapter of this study explores different aspects of the coffee plantation and the lives of the slaves who worked on the farms. The text is divided into three parts, with the first section devoted to the rise of the coffee plantation complex and the historical context of the coffee boom during the late eighteenth and early nineteenth centuries. The second section is devoted to the experiences of the slaves on the cafetales, drawing out the implications of the foundations laid in the first section. Part III is the final section, with concluding remarks and some thoughts on the longer-term implications of the coffee plantation experience.

The first chapter begins by looking at how the slave population and the plantation complex expanded rapidly. It looks at how slaves provided the labor to fuel the construction of the vast plantation complex that characterized the nineteenth century on the island. It also establishes a periodization of the coffee plantation era and shows how slaves built the plantations that would populate the countryside outside Havana for dozens of kilometers in every direction. Chapter 1 thereby establishes a framework, showing the trajectory of plantation and demographic growth that situates the subsequent chapters.

Chapter 2 looks back to the decades before the beginning of the plantation boom years to explore the groundwork that enabled the decades of sustained growth that followed. This chapter argues that the plantation boom was not caused by the Haitian Revolution; rather, the expansion of plantation agriculture was already well underway by 1791 and was facilitated by a decades-long process of structural changes negotiated between island and peninsular leaders. It also looks at the demographic consequences of the rising number of coffee plantations in western Cuba. The chapter shows how the plantation and regional population shifted over time to a more balanced population of men and women. This created the conditions for more family formation and higher fertility rates on coffee plantations. The result was a more rapid rate of creolization in the coffee zone. These factors taken together had several implications that differentiated the slaves on coffee plantations from their counterparts on sugar plantations.

Chapter 3, the first chapter of Part II, explores how slaveholders shaped the spaces, both positive and negative, of their plantations and what they hoped to accomplish as they directed the construction of their agricultural sites. The chapter also looks at how the people who inhabited the built environments redirected and resisted slaveholders' intentions. Slaves made the plantations their own in many respects and this chapter discusses how those processes unfolded.

Chapter 4 is the first chapter that looks at how slaves specifically expressed their intentions or will within the spaces of coffee plantations. This chapter focuses on religious practices, first by tracing the African origins of these practices and the ways in which they have been historically misunderstood. This is particularly important because we rely on documents from the period as well as later pieces in the historiography that reflect those embedded misapprehensions. African religious practices are often exoticized, but it is crucial that they be understood on their own terms. Armed with these analytical tools, we look at specific cases in which slaves used religious practices.

Slaves also engaged in commercial activities on cafetales, and that is the focus of Chapter 5. Slaves grew food, raised animals, and made various types of goods. They sold these items for their own benefit, as well as purchasing other goods. These activities suggest several things, including the scale of the under-studied grey-market economy, the extent of participation in the *coartación* (self-purchase system), and the role that economic participation played in fostering slave autonomy.

Chapter 6 explores the relationship between slave resistance and rebellions to cultural factors. In this section, I argue for a broader understanding of causality in incidents of slave violence and resistance. The chapter contends that rebellions were a cultural expression with African roots. Rather than attributing them to rising numbers of creoles on the farms, which I view largely as a correlative rather than causal factor, I explain how slave actions point to a dialogical process in which slaves used violence to protest and attempt to change the terms of their relationship to the slaveholders.

The final part explores the role of the cafetal in the Cuban imagination and the ways it shaped ideas of beauty and gender norms. The Conclusion also briefly discusses the decline of coffee during the 1840s.

PART I
Roots
The Expansion of Coffee
and the Slave Population

CHAPTER 1

Café con azúcar
The Expansion of the Slave Population and Plantations

Whatever the circumstances of the planter may be, in point of
fortune, I would by no means advise him to set out with a great
number of negroes. . . . Six, or at most twelve male negroes,
with one or two women, will be found sufficient to make the first
essay. —Pierre-Joseph Laborie

On a December morning in 1828, as the day dawned, the plantation
bell on the *cafetal* (coffee plantation) known as "the Paciencia" rang
out, calling the slaves to work. Pio *mandingo* and Gertrudis *mandingo*
were among the workers who came out to learn what tasks they were to perform
that day. It was late fall—harvest time—so all attention was focused on bringing in the crop, a task that required all hands available. The *mayoral* (overseer)
charged each able-bodied worker with bringing in two baskets of coffee cherries,
a typical amount on a day such as this. Men, women, and children headed out to
the fields to pick the ripe, red fruit from the coffee bushes. The men picked fruit
from the tops, the women from the middle branches, and the children from the
lowest arms of the bushes. As their baskets filled, Pio and the other men carried
the heavy loads back to the processing area for sorting, washing, and drying.
Once the quota was filled for the day, the newest harvest was put to soak so the
coffee beans could be extracted from their pulpy husks. After completing their
assignments, Pio and Gertrudis, along with their fellow workers, had time for
tasks of their own choosing, such as tending their gardens or making some item
to sell.

This was a typical day in a routine that changed with the seasons. This snap-
shot of daily life, while mundane, reveals a rich complexity and a distinctive
way of life unique to the cafetal.[1] Pio *mandingo* and Gertrudis *mandingo*, husband and wife, lived on the cafetal Paciencia during the 1820s and 1830s.[2] The
couple were among dozens who were enslaved on the farm.[3] To the casual observer, their lives seem rigorous and simple, and like the lives of agricultural
people everywhere, their existence was marked by regularity and a humble way
of being. Thus, in many ways, the typical view of these slaves' existence is ac-
curate, but a closer examination reveals lives and a social order with layers of

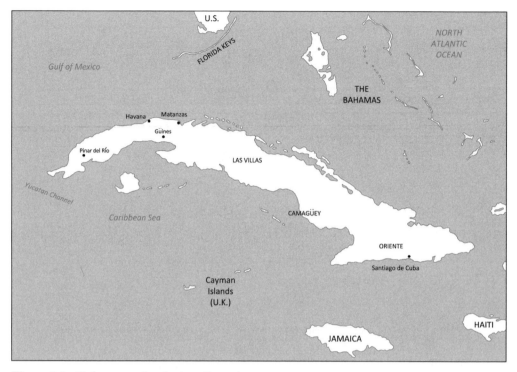

Figure 1.1. Cuba ca. early nineteenth century

complexity that were the result of the circumstances of their enslavement. The patterns they lived followed a rhythm regulated by the seasons and the crop they labored to produce; thus, their day-to-day activities shifted over the course of the year in regular ways. But their lives were affected not only by work; they also dwelled in a community of fellow workers situated within a paternalistic and patriarchal structure that defined the broader plantation experience. Collectively, they had to contend with the will and the demands of the slaveholder and his agents, who actively sought to shape the workforce both mentally and demographically, with the hope of maximizing production. All the while, Pio and Gertrudis, and others like them, attempted to create the conditions of a life with some sense of normality within the context of the plantation that was their home. To begin to understand their experiences, we need to go back to an earlier time to see how the system of plantation agriculture developed in Cuba. It was the rapid expansion of this complex of elements that swept them and tens of thousands of others like them from their African homelands onto farms across the island.

Pio and Gertrudis worked and lived on the Paciencia alongside fifty to sixty other captives at any one time. There were hundreds more on nearby farms, and still thousands of others on the hundreds of plantations that sprang up across the landscape of western Cuba during the great boom. Pio and Gertrudis's story was unique, but they also shared commonalities typical of the laborers on hundreds of cafetales in the region. They were but two souls who were part of a great rising tide of forced migration that would grow to three quarters of a million people before it began to subside. The presence of this multitude would forever change the face of Cuba, reconfiguring both the rural and urban landscapes and transforming the cultural moorings of the colony in ways that have continued to reverberate. The labor of Pio and Gertrudis helped to transform Cuba into a rich colony with a diverse economy, and the lives they struggled to define created a new and complex culture that has come to define the island and all its people.

Pio and Gertrudis were living on the Paciencia and available to work on that particular morning as a result of the actions and decisions of numerous people who had shaped the world in which they lived. The planter who claimed ownership over them, Alonso Benigno Muñoz, was the most immediate influence, but there were also countless others past and present of whom they had little or no knowledge. These individuals included officials in Havana and Madrid, the slave traders who had brought them across the Atlantic, and those in Africa who had sold them into the Atlantic trading system. Based on their reported ethnicity, the trail could even include religious and political leaders in west Africa. There were numerous struggles during the late eighteenth and early nineteenth centuries in the region known as "the Senegambia," as various factions fought to control people and territory.[4] Attempts at conversion and conquest between colonialist trading outposts, traditional religious practitioners, and Muslims resulted in many people being swept into the transatlantic slave trade. This is likely how Pio and Gertrudis were enslaved and brought to Cuba.

Muñoz acquired Pio during the 1820s to work on his cafetal as a general laborer—what was known as a *negro del campo*.[5] The work Pio and others did on the farm varied depending on the season and also changed over time in relation to the age or stage of development of the plantation. In other words, the work in constructing a new farm was distinct from the labor on a plantation that had reached production age and different still from a farm that had matured fully. The records suggest that Pio was acquired after the Paciencia had reached production stage; as a result, his experience of the farm would have been different from those who had built the farm during the period of plantation expansion. The beginnings of the so-called plantation boom can be traced to the late 1780s and it grew in magnitude through the first several decades of the nineteenth century, but the decisions that facilitated the period of rapid growth stretch back to the first half of the eighteenth century. The cafetal Paciencia was similar to the hundreds of other cafetales that had been established during the period of expansion southwestward from Havana in the region known as the *vuelta abajo*. The eastern end of the vuelta abajo was largely devoted to coffee cultivation.[6]

Coffee was also grown in hilly areas in every direction outside of Havana, although the greatest concentration of cafetales was southwest of the city. Coffee cultivators established their new farms almost entirely within the *jurisdicción* (province) of Havana. The area populated by these plantations stretched from Callajabos, a few kilometers west of the *municipio* (municipality) of Ar-

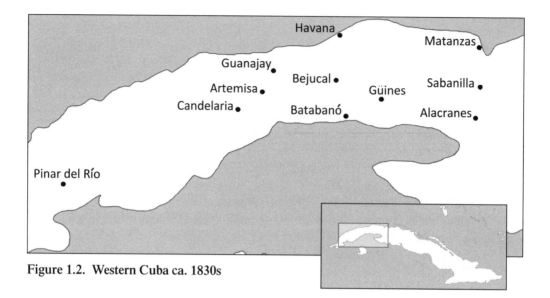

Figure 1.2. Western Cuba ca. 1830s

temisa, approximately sixty kilometers to the southwest of Havana, all the way to Matanzas, one hundred kilometers to the east of Havana on the north coast.

The core region in which planters established their cafetales and that became the often romanticized coffee zone was on a strip of elevated land approximately twenty kilometers from north to south and roughly sixty kilometers from its western extremities to the east. The informally defined district included important clusters of cafetales throughout the region, from the town of Callajabos on its western edge to Santiago de las Vegas in the east. The most well-known locale and the zone of some of the most vigorous activity was at the western end of the coffee-growing region, near the eastern end of the famous tobacco-growing territory. It was this confluence of agricultural zones that was known as the vuelta abajo. Many of the important cafetales and spaces devoted to coffee production were along the *camino real á vueltabajo* (main road to the vuelta abajo) around the town of Guanajay and in the old *corral* known as San Marcos (which later became the municipio of Artemisa).[7] Other important centers of coffee production located within the western coffee region included Wajay, Alquízar, San Antonio de los Baños, Güira de Melena, and Bejucal. This main area in which the cafetales were concentrated included approximately twelve hundred square kilometers of land.[8] There were also two notable areas of coffee cultivation, often thought of mainly as zones of sugar production, that lay just beyond the main region of cafetales. Farmland surrounding the towns of Güines and Matanzas, home to many nearby *ingenios* (sugar plantations), also held numerous cafetales and a thriving coffee element as a part of their local economies.

Muñoz founded his plantation in San Marcos and developed it in the same fashion as many of his contemporaries, drawing on the lessons of those who had established the first cafetales in the region.[9] Those earlier pioneers began the process that would develop into a coffee boom within a few decades. The conditions that led to the creation of coffee farms in western Cuba were not accidental, but generated by a concerted effort by government and commercial leaders in Madrid as well as in the colonial capital of Havana. The origins of coffee cultivation in Cuba extend back to the early decades of the eighteenth century and emerged out of the desires of both leaders in Spain and colonial subjects on the island to increase the prosperity of the colony. Each group had distinct motives but similar aims, which converged to create the legal and commercial framework that enabled the expansion of plantation agriculture on the island, resulting in the rapid growth that began in the 1790s.

Coffee arrived in Cuba in 1748, when José María de la Torre brought seeds from the French colony of Saint Domingue and founded the first cafetal in what is now Wajay, southwest of Havana.[10] Production of the bean expanded slowly and it began to be exported in significant amounts only around 1790. In that year Saint Domingue produced over half of the coffee in the world, exporting some thirty-three thousand tons, while Cuba exported only ninety-three tons.[11] From that first Cuban cafetal would grow a vast system that, for a few decades in the nineteenth century, would rival the sugar kingdom in the wealth it created and in the numbers of slaves held. In 1790 there were fewer than ten cafetales in western Cuba, but by 1804 the number had grown to at least eighty-four. Production had risen from less than a hundred tons to nearly one thousand tons in the space of fourteen years.[12] The number of plantations continued to expand dramatically, so that by the year 1841 a survey of farms counted 582 coffee estates producing beans within the jurisdiction of Havana.[13] While it may seem that this rapid growth might be attributable to the collapse of the export economy of neighboring Saint Domingue following the Haitian Revolution, which began in 1791, the reasons are actually much more complex. The development of the coffee sector can be traced to reforms that began in Spain a hundred years earlier. Cuban expansion would not have been possible in the 1790s unless planters had been ready to take advantage of the situation when opportunity presented itself. In fact, the groundwork had been laid decades before.

Following the triumph of the Bourbons in the War of Succession, Philip V began to institute a series of planned policy changes in Spain to strengthen the monarchy and centralize control of the war-torn kingdom.[14] The measures he instituted were modeled after earlier reforms successfully enacted in France. The first step was the revocation of *fueros* (specific privileges granted to the upper class and the military), through the institution of the *Nueva Planta* in Aragón, which included Valencia and Catalonia.[15] This laid the groundwork for the intendancy system and later reforms in Spain that would eventually be carried to the New World.[16] The aim of these reforms was to subdue opposition to Philip's rule by centralizing and increasing control over regions farther afield. The destabilizing of traditional power bases allowed Philip and his coterie to institute new courts and military rule, and install new leadership in the outlying districts, thus solidifying Bourbon control over a wider area of Spain. The success of those first steps led to the relocation in 1717 of the Casa de Contratación (House of Commerce) to Cádiz and to codification of the intendancy system.[17] This was necessary to wrest control of the vital overseas trade system out of the hands of entrenched interests in Seville. In 1720 Philip ordered the reorganization of the Council of the Indies, creating more centralized control over Spanish America and the wealth the colonies generated. These moves were initially successful, but their effectiveness was ultimately limited by Philip's own weakness as a ruler. Once Ferdinand VI ascended to the throne, the early reforms found a new advocate in his secretary, Cenón de Somodevilla, the Marquis of La Ensenada, and from 1749 it became clear that the restructuring was permanently in effect.[18]

When Charles III ascended to the throne of Spain in August 1759, the pace and commitment to reform increased. As his administration progressed, under the leadership of minister Leopoldo di Grigorio, the Marqués de Esquilache, there emerged a broader and more dedicated plan to reshape the empire. Charles reversed Ferdinand's policy of neutrality in the Seven Years War and entered the conflict on the side of France. This would prove to be a mistake and added to the losses Spain had suffered in the earlier War of Jenkins's Ear (1739–1741) with the British. Losses during the conflict were felt not only on the European front but also were dramatically revealed in the British occupation of Havana in 1762–1763. The years of economic difficulty that began under Philip V had continued under succeeding years of Bourbon rule as Spain absorbed serious blows during many years of war. There were tangible losses as a result of British aggression against Spanish territory on the Iberian peninsula and in the New World. The British had attacked eastern Cuba and the northern South American coast during the War of Jenkins's Ear and had returned during the Seven Years War to gain a foothold on Spanish lands, first seizing Gibraltar and later capturing Havana.

Once the leaders negotiated peace and the British returned Havana to Spanish sovereignty, Charles and Esquilache felt compelled to act decisively to improve defensive capabilities both at home and overseas.[19] They decided that the best course of action was to begin by extending the administrative and judicial reforms begun under previous administrations in Spain. As with the earlier moves, this was a way not only to increase and improve control but also to augment tax revenues flowing to the Crown. They reasoned that expanding the revenues of the state would finance necessary growth of the military and its infrastructure. What followed were the first of what have come to be known as the Bourbon reforms but in fact were the logical extensions of the reform processes begun decades earlier under Philip V at the conclusion of the War of Succession.

Following the Peace of Paris in 1763, Esquilache, with the authority and approval of Charles, began a vigorous campaign of change in Cuba.[20] The first stage was to increase security. The court dispatched the Catalano Ambrosio Funes de Villalpando Abarca de Bolea, the conde de Ricla (count of Ricla), to take control of Havana from the British under the terms of peace and to begin to remake the military detachment in the colony.[21] Ricla had proposed to the king that the garrison in Cuba be modeled after the militia system that had proved successful against the Austrians in the struggle over the Two Sicilies. As Charles had realized victory in that instance, he agreed to the plan, and Ricla undertook the task with the aid of Field Marshal Alejandro O'Reilly.[22] Within the space of two years, Ricla, O'Reilly, and Esquilache reshaped the military in Cuba, and Esquilache subsequently promulgated this new system through much of Spanish America after 1769.[23]

The second vital aspect of restructuring was the reorganization of revenue collection to finance the expansion of Spain's military presence in its New World colonies. Charles regarded Cuba as part of the extended frontier of eastern New Spain, so he agreed with the proposal to finance Cuban fortifications with monies from Mexico. Ricla advanced this idea along with a range of suggestions for increasing Crown income so that the Cuban economy could support the increased military presence. The Junta de Ministros (Council of Ministers) adopted three of Ricla's taxation suggestions, raising the *alcabala* (a sales tax) and instituting new taxes on property and *aguardiente* (a clear alcoholic beverage made from sugar cane).[24] The trio of reformers knew that generating additional revenue would not only involve imposing new levies but also mean expanding the economic base of the colonial economy. While they may have viewed Cuba as the front doorstep of New Spain, they also saw the island's potential and wanted the colony to become self-supporting. This goal meshed with that held by leading figures in Cuba, who were likewise advocating for economic reforms that would expand and revitalize the island economy. This was a self-interested local view. From the perspective of Madrid, it was vital that the Cuban economy become more productive and generate more income to support a more robust military presence in the Caribbean that would hold back British expansionism and act as a first line of defense for the mainland colonies. For the reformers the logical path of development was plantation agriculture. Their plan for growth would be realized through a series of economic incentives to stimulate expansion. Ricla and O'Reilly framed the incentives as concessions to the local elites. This was a wise strategy, as it balanced new taxes with additional privileges, which mollified local leaders.[25]

The next phase of reform was to improve management of local government so that newly derived income would move efficiently back to Spain. Esquilache proposed instituting the intendancy system in Cuba. This model of organization had been used in parts of Spain since the 1740s. The system utilized a more streamlined hierarchy of officials who answered directly to Madrid, eliminating large numbers of locally appointed offices and thus, in theory, reducing local influences and corruption. The relatively small size of Cuba, geographically and demographically, as well as its isolation, contributed to the success of the system. The intendancy model was spread to mainland Spanish America following its successful trial run in Cuba, with mixed results. O'Reilly proposed in 1764 a more sweeping change in commercial regulations to bring all the previous actions to fruition. The king, intrigued by the O'Reilly idea, established a special commission to make recommendations about commercial policies for the Spanish Caribbean. The findings of the study resulted in the Real Cédula of 1765 that established zones of free trade. With the new royal approval, five Caribbean ports, including Havana, were opened to free trade with nine major ports in Spain.[26] Allan Kuethe notes that another order the same day, also signed by Esquilache, made a number of concessions to the burgeoning sugar industry, including a consolidation and reduction of export duties. More significant was the abolition of duties on the importation of slaves, though it did not allow for unrestricted imports of Africans.[27] The additional order authorized by Esquilache would seem to point toward an early bias in favor of sugar interests, but this was not entirely the case. Kuethe fails to mention that concessions were made to the fledgling coffee industry as well, with its producers likewise gaining a waiver of export duties. If the entire package of new rules is taken into consideration, we can see that the reformers were more interested in an open-ended process of development. It is evident that they were pushing forward in a way that aimed for a specific goal, improving the economy through the development of large-scale agriculture, but they were not trying to skew the process too much toward one type of plantation over another. In other words, the process was not teleological, but aimed at producing a prosperous economy, however that goal might be achieved. Further evidence of the support for a broader base of development incentives can be seen in a 1767 letter to the king by Miguel de Altarriva, Intendente de Ejército y de Hacienda. Altarriva petitioned for an extension of the existing waivers on coffee exports and thanked the Crown for previous considerations as well as their "inclinación a fomentar esta planta" (inclination to encourage this crop), specifically referring to king's extension of tax waivers for the development of coffee.[28]

The program of reform had a tangible impact: revenues and exports increased, new fortifications were constructed, and a Cuban militia was raised. As a result of the incentives, more plantations were built and agricultural production went up. The number of ingenios rose from 120 to 478.[29] Exports of sugar began to climb slowly from 5.4 metric tons in 1764–1768 to 7.9 metric tons by 1771.[30] One of the earliest cafetales was established in 1768 by Contador Mayor (Head Treasurer) José Antonio Gelabert, near Havana.[31] Later figures suggest that other plantations were started during this early period and that coffee was exported in small quantities to Spain, but its commercial viability as an export crop was yet to come. While these first attempts at encouraging expansion of the Cuban economy showed promise, they did not produce the immediate results for which Spain had hoped. Nevertheless, they did suggest the efficacy of the idea of reducing trade barriers.

Beginning in 1778 the Crown launched, through a series of decrees, the next round of reform policies, which built on the earlier successes and would prove decisive in triggering the coffee plantation boom. These acts, generally referred to as the *Decretos del comercio libre* (Decrees of free trade), extended and expanded the earlier policies.[32] Charles III, in one of his final acts, opened the doors wide for the free trade of goods between all the major ports in Spanish America and Spain. The new regulations unlocked the ports of Spain, including those of Majorca and the Canary Islands, to trade goods freely with the significant ports of Spanish America. In addition, these harbors were now available to ships flying foreign flags as well as those bearing the colors of Spain. Vessels had to be licensed and pay taxes, but these new rules provided an orderly and profitable way for agricultural producers and traders in Cuba to openly access expanding markets for coffee and sugar in Europe and North America.[33] The opening of the Canary Islands created an important connection to Cuba that would be important in the development of the Caribbean island. This was not the last significant reform Cuba was to see.

Charles IV ascended to the throne following the death of his father on December 14, 1788, and continued the policies and trajectory of the earlier administration. On February 28, 1789, the king issued the *Decreto de libertad de comercio de esclavos* (Decree of free trade of slaves), which contained provisions planters in Cuba had desired since the beginnings of the process of reform. This decree by the Crown freed current and prospective plantation owners to obtain the slaves they needed to expand their holdings without constraint. They were now only limited by the availability of capital. The island was opened to foreign slavers and ships could trade directly between Cuba and the African coast.[34] Prior to the 1789 act, as reported in the census of 1774, there were 44,333 slaves on the island. By 1792, as result of the opening of the slave trade, that number had swelled to 84,590 and by 1804 to 180,000.[35] Clearly, the actions by the Crown had a rapid and dramatic effect in bolstering the size of the enslaved population and thus expanding the pool of available labor for economic, especially agricultural, growth. These reforms, like the earlier efforts, have often been described as targeted to promote sugar expansion.[36] A closer reading of the text reveals that the interest of the Crown was, in fact, the expansion of a range of agricultural crops, much like the earlier round of reforms under Charles III, suggesting a desire for a diversified island economy. This is especially evident in section 8 of the decree of 1789, in which Charles IV specifically mentions a range of desired destinations for slaves and imposes a tax on workers diverted to nonagricultural tasks.[37] The actions taken over the course of the 1780s laid the foundations for the expansion of the plantation economy that leaders in Cuba had envisioned. The stage was now set.

Once planters secured the legal means and the economic opportunity to construct new plantations and refashion the Cuban economy, they did so with vigor, thus launching the first period of development of the coffee plantation complex—establishment and early expansion.[38] This was the period of the construction of the first wave of cafetales and the expansion of the territory in which coffee was and would be grown. This period of regional growth and development corresponded to the stages of the life cycle of individual plantations, as we will see. Planters did not set about this new undertaking without guidance. The first growers of coffee were most certainly long-term residents of Cuba, but they were soon joined by French immigrants fleeing the violence in Saint Domingue (soon to be known as Haiti), as well as new settlers from various parts of Spain, including the far-flung regions of Galicia and the Canary Islands. The ranks of coffee growers in the first decades of the nineteenth century also included farmers from the United States, France, and Germany. Members of these groups came from diverse ecological and agricultural backgrounds and, with the exception of immigrants from Haiti, had little knowledge or experience with the tropical climate of Cuba. The understanding of plantation agricultural practices of a more general nature would have spread from more experienced growers to newcomers and from older cultivated areas out into the frontier of the vuelta abajo. As coffee was a cultivar relatively new to the island, few planters would have had extensive or even basic knowledge of the needs of the plant or how to produce and process a crop. For these reasons, the information particular to coffee and its production that was accumulated and promulgated by its advocates, especially members of the Sociedad Económica de Amigos del País, was significant and appears to have been used widely.[39]

Prospective planters learned how to build efficient, profitable, and orderly cafetales in part by consulting the collected wisdom of the Sociedad Económica. An analysis of the guides reveals select planter views on a wide range of issues, including level of investment, technological expertise, physical layout, and ways of managing slave labor. Even though conformity was not uniform and many planters may not have strictly adhered to the advice offered, it is nevertheless instructive to analyze the literature, as the guidance offers a window into the general mindset of plantation owners. In addition, an examination of instructions for developing and managing cafetales suggests the conceptual construction of an ideal model of the cafetal that informed the contributors. A further comparison of farms and their organizational elements with printed advice reveals compelling evidence that *cafetaleros* (coffee plantation owners) followed the disseminated guidelines. Their adherence to the parameters of this ideal model helped to create a typology of the coffee farm that the Cuban people internalized not only as an agricultural model but also as a cultural form, which we will discuss later.

Pablo Boloix, a member of the Sociedad Económica, was instrumental in producing the first study of local coffee plantations in 1797. He was charged with finding instructive examples of coffee cultivation that could serve as models for prospective farmers interested in starting their own coffee plantations.[40] In his report to the society, he identified five cafetales that he considered to be a representative cross-section of the first stage of plantation development and of the emerging coffee industry. Boloix surveyed the farms to determine the quantity and quality of the plants as well as the methods used by the cultivators. In addition, he examined the equipment, buildings, and animals on the cafetales, as well as enumerating the workforce of slaves. His intent was to instruct his readers on some of the important elements in establishing a farm that would be profitable and lasting. The plantations were all within a one- or two-day ride from Havana, with the cafetales Moka and Bella Vista in Arcos de Canasi being the most distant at sixteen *leguas* (about 107 kilometers). The cafetales Placeres, Limones, and Viertudes [*sic*] were in the *partido* (district) of Guanajay, ranging in distance from thirty-five to eighty-five kilometers southwest of Havana (see Figure 1.2). Four of the five appear to have been approximately the same size, based on the number of coffee bushes planted, with an average of 31,500. Antonio Morejón's Viertudes was an established plantation, with plants up to four years old, but stocked with less than eighteen thousand bushes. Three of the farms had reached or were nearing the age of production, while the other two appeared to be newly founded, as all their plants were less than one year in age.[41]

Boloix carefully recorded the numbers and ages of the coffee bushes and seedlings to explain to his readers the importance of beginning a farm with staggered plantings and to place coffee bushes in the larger fields once they reached seedling stage. This suggested that to build a successful farm one would need to have more than a single stage of planting and field preparation. One area of land would have to be set aside and planted with seed to produce seedlings. Additional fields were to be developed for transplanted seedlings that would grow into productive plants. *Cafetos* (coffee bushes) were to be planted farther apart to allow for growth in the plots designated for production. We can see evidence of this when Boloix noted the distance between plants in areas with mature or maturing bushes, signaling to his readers the important relationship between proper spacing and the health of productive plants. The author recorded that workers on four of the plantations set the cafetos out at least three *varas* (two and one-half meters) apart, adding that closer plantings were inadvisable. To highlight this factor further, Boloix points out that on the cafetal Limones, where the plants were only two and one-half varas apart (about two meters), production did not reach its potential and there was evidence of many cafetos that had died in years past.[42] The Sociedad Económica representative also emphasized the orderliness of the rows that he observed, specifically mentioning the Placeres, where he found the fields to be "perfectly delineated." On the Moka, the rows were not straight, but this fault was pardoned because the hilly terrain of the farm made marking the rows difficult. His attention to this feature on each cafetal shows that he considered it an important element of plantation management.

The machinery of production also merited mention in the report. Boloix noted that on four of the farms, workers had constructed mills to separate, clean, and winnow the beans. The Moka was the lone example lacking a mill. The author reported that the slaves on the Moka processed the coffee in small batches in basins that resembled large mortars and pestles. He added that the owner was making plans to construct a mill or mills. All five farms had sorting and drying areas, which were indispensable and found on all viable cafetales. These were large flat platforms or floors constructed of masonry that had been pounded and brushed smooth, and in these early forms, there was often a roof or awning over all or part of the surface. Two of the farms also had cisterns to collect water for washing the harvest.

Boloix paid attention to the slaves working on the five cafetales he examined. His main goal was to emphasize that large numbers of slaves, such as those required on an ingenio, were unnecessary on the cafetal, especially in the early stages of development. This point would appeal to readers interested in developing a plantation, as it meant that the most expensive investment element, slaves, would be significantly less than on a sugar cane farm. The Limones had the largest contingent, at thirty-one workers, and the Bella Vista was a close second, with twenty-eight. Boloix noted that since 1795 (during the intervening twenty-six months), the Bella Vista had grown from a farm with only five thousand plants to one with thirty-six thousand plants, while expanding its *dotación* (slave workforce) by only ten persons. The Moka had nineteen slaves in 1797, but the expansion of the population is carefully noted by Boloix. The owners started the farm with only two slaves. They added four workers in the second year, six in the third, and then finally seven more. Boloix thus illustrated for his readers the progressive nature of labor demands on fledgling cafetales as they grew slowly and steadily over successive years. His report makes clear how, along with lower investments in machinery and land, the initial capital outlay was much less for coffee than for sugar.[43] The Placeres, with twelve slaves, and the Viertudes, with eleven, were the smallest of the sample. In a time when workers were always in demand, establishing that a working cafetal could be maintained with a third or less of the numbers of slaves needed on an ingenio may have persuaded more than a few people to invest in the crop.

Boloix did not comment on the gender of the slaves on the cafetales he surveyed, though he did note the numbers of men and women on each farm. Three of the farms had only one female slave—the Moka, Bella Vista, and Limones—while the Viertudes had an all-male population. The notable exception to this early configuration was the Placeres. Its population was made up of six males and six females. The plantation of Antonio Robredo had been developed only recently, as evidenced by the young age of the cafetos on the farm—no plants were over one year in age. During this early phase of development of the broader coffee industry in Cuba, owners followed the lead of earlier and more well-established planters of sugar and, as we will see, the advice offered in the literature on coffee farm development. Owners of cane farms consistently bought slaves for their plantations with a ratio of two or three males to each female. This pattern explains why the older plantations in this survey were almost exclusively male. Robredo did not follow this approach for reasons that are lost to us. We can only speculate, but he may have been forging a new way of thinking that many planters would follow in later years. As planters began to better understand and develop distinctive management practices suited to the production of coffee, they began to balance the gender ratio of their labor forces as plantations matured. Robredo may have recognized or anticipated the specific demands of coffee labor and the suitability of women for many of the regular tasks, and bought equal numbers of men and women. Regardless of the reason, this move lowered his initial investment even further, as female slaves were typically less expensive than males. His farm, despite the different makeup of his labor force, compared favorably with the others in the survey. Robredo arguably was one of the first to realize the utility of female slaves on cafetales but, as we will see later, he was far from the last. The large numbers of female slaves who would end up on the cafetales of the San Marcos area would have great and unforeseen consequences for the growing African and Afro-Cuban population of the vuelta abajo.

Historians often have constructed general arguments about plantation life and the populace that would later be known as Afro-Cuban based in part on the notion of a population ratio among slaves of two males to one female.[44] The local areas of San Marcos/Artemisa, Callajabos, Alquízar, and Guanajay and specific representative cafetales in those areas offer a different view. In the early stages of plantation development, the structure of the slave population in locales in which planters specialized in coffee mirrored that of other districts. As others have shown and the figures earlier in this chapter demonstrate, profound growth in land under cultivation was realized through expanding imports of Africans to enlarge the slave population. As we can see in the plantations Boloix surveyed, many planters sought to acquire as many men as possible to perform the rigorous work required in establishing new farms on virgin land. But as plantations and the coffee economy began to mature, owners instituted changes within the populations of their farms that would be reflected across individual districts. One of the most important changes was the narrowing gap in sex distribution as owners evidently moved to balance the populations on their farms. The regional numbers reflected this shift, though it is difficult to detect, as the compilation of figures was determined by political geography, which meant that local counts reflected the diversity of agricultural production within any particular district.

Padrones, counts of local populations that officials undertook for a variety of differing reasons, offer a closer look at smaller segments of the population, although they present some obstacles to analysis of their own. In particular, the figures were typically aggregated for all types of farms within a district so that it is difficult, without extensive plantation inventories, to assess population distributions across types of farms. Nevertheless, padrones, with their narrow local focus, offer a better view of the contours of populations in coffee districts than broader regional counts that included districts dominated by sugar cane farms. In the San Marcos area, later known as Artemisa, the padron of 1808 shows that there were sixty cafetales and sixty *sitios de labor*, as well as nineteen *portreros*.[45] The working-age population between the ages of fifteen and sixty years was, as expected at this early date, overwhelmingly male, with their ranks numbering between 1,016 and 1,025.[46] The corresponding female population consisted of 154 women. Females constituted only about 13 percent of the group or a ratio of 663 males per 100 females.[47] The presence of a substantial contingent of young slaves, numbering 135 people, evidenced the beginnings of a second type of change that would become more visible over time among the local group—creolization. It is clear that cafetaleros followed the pattern set by sugar plantation owners as they assembled populations for their new farms, accounting for the rigors of building new plantations and therefore configuring the group to be heavily male and working-age. Nevertheless, the enslaved on the cafetales began reproducing, as evidenced by a growing population under the age of six-teen that already made up 10 percent of the group. Among these younger slaves, as might be expected, there was sex parity, as the group consisted of sixty-five males and seventy females.[48] A pattern of creolization through reproduction and narrowing sex distribution as a result of both patterns of acquisition and local births was beginning to emerge across the region. During the period of expansion between roughly 1790 and 1820, the slave population was skewed male but that changed incrementally as more plantations matured and, as we will see, planters transformed their working-age *dotaciones* (complements of slaves) with larger numbers of women and creoles. In other words, the regional population in its early stages of development mirrored that of the first stage of establishment and growth of individual plantations.

Pablo Boloix contributed to the ongoing expansion of coffee cultivation by continuing his efforts in promoting the crop and by playing a significant role in the production of a translation of arguably the most important manual on con-structing and operating a coffee plantation in the Caribbean: *The Coffee Planter of Saint Domingo* by Pierre-Joseph Laborie. This work appears to have been published first in some form in 1795. The draft or portions that were available were well received by English settlers in Haiti during the revolution and a full version of the book was printed in 1798.[49] Laborie, a creole coffee planter from the French colony, fled during the revolution and produced the final version of his manual while living in Jamaica.[50] The work, nearly two hundred pages in length, explicates for the reader every aspect of establishing and operating a cafetal on a Caribbean island. Laborie approached coffee farming and its expla-nation in a very systematic and orderly fashion.[51] As we have seen, Boloix, in his report on working cafetales, also emphasized orderliness, proper spacing, and care of the plants. His presentation of data and advice bears a striking correla-tion to the instructions offered by Laborie. The relationship between the advice of Laborie and what Boloix found and wrote suggests that both the Cuban author and the planters whose farms he surveyed were familiar with the principles of Laborie's work and had designed their plantations accordingly prior to the pub-lication of *Cultivo del cafeto* in 1809.[52] This may be attributed, at least in part, to the number of French immigrants to Cuba following the uprising on Saint Domingue. But the effects of the Haitian Revolution cannot fully account for the conditions Boloix encountered in Cuba. He conducted his survey in 1797, only six years after the initial slave rebellion in Saint Domingue, and three of the six farms he surveyed were founded concurrently with or prior to the revolt.[53] This suggests that planters in Cuba had their own variety of motivations to enter the arena of coffee production, which cannot be facilely explained as a reaction to the revolution underway on the neighboring island. There is no clear evidence that Cuban planters knew of the work of Laborie, but the report of Boloix shows conformity of the plantations to the ideas of which Laborie wrote, suggesting that it is very likely that his knowledge had been transmitted either in printed form or by word of mouth. The circumstantial evidence suggests that an exploration of Laborie's recommendations offers a reliable representation of how a coffee plantation of the time was configured and operated.

Laborie first took up the importance of carefully choosing land for a plantation. He stressed that the "proper choice" of "suitable grounds" was vital to the success of a coffee plantation.[54] This may seem self-evident to many readers, but this factor was often overlooked, according to the author. The elevation and declination of a prospective piece of land needed to be considered, as these provided insight into rainfall totals, temperature range, and the stability of the soil. The highest elevations, the upper ranges of mountains, could be useful, but bushes in colder climes did not produce as abundantly. Steeper slopes presented a different problem. This type of ground, while offering suitable temperatures, would lose much of its topsoil as a result of erosion. Lower elevations presented their own difficulty because of higher ambient temperatures. Laborie also noted that heavily forested land often had poor soil and should be avoided. This advice was relevant in the Caribbean, as many islands have areas of rain forest that would appear to the untrained eye as very fertile but as Laborie noted are in fact generally unsuitable for agricultural use. Higher elevations, such as an upper plateau, were preferable, because such locales provided a milder climate with the moderate temperatures and abundant rainfall that coffee bushes prefer and also tended to afford rich, deep soil. The author considered moderately firm earth tending toward red in color as the most desirable.[55] Laborie offered that lowland farms could be successful if they were located inland, to avoid what he viewed as the deleterious effects of salt-laden ocean winds, and oriented to the north and the west, which would provide some shielding from the worst heat.[56]

The advice of the French agriculturist had to be creatively adapted to the terrain of western Cuba. Although the land is contoured, it does not rise to the kind of high elevation he suggested. The vuelta abajo region, which became the principal coffee-growing region of western Cuba, was inland, conforming to the ideal for lowland cultivation suggested by the author, although it is unclear if planters chose the region for the reasons Laborie discussed. What is evident is that a large number of cafetaleros established their farms in a region that matched many of Laborie's criteria. Lacking mountainous highlands, Cuban planters enabled a successful growth cycle for coffee plants by developing the placement of trees to act as shade for the cafetos.[57] The overwhelming majority of advice Laborie offered concerned the type of care coffee plants required when plantations were located in higher or mountainous elevations. Considering his experience in the highlands of Saint Domingue and that his initial readership was seeking to establish farms in the mountains of Jamaica, this emphasis is understandable. Nevertheless, he did venture a few words to those who might attempt to grow the bean in lower and hotter climes.

> In hot situations, plantain trees are intermingled with the coffee trees, for the purpose of shade and coolness. These are usually placed at every fourth or sixth row, as the trees are more or less distant, and the place more or less hot. This

is generally attended with great success. but the plantain trees are sometimes placed in the intervals of the coffee trees, and, of course, too near them, so that they become entangled with their boughs, and the fall of the clusters of the plantains, and even of the leaves, may break and hurt them. It is better, therefore, that a plantain tree be placed instead of a coffee tree, and that the rows be alternately plantain and coffee.[58]

As Francisco Pérez de la Riva has shown, the use of shade to improve crop yields was debated throughout the early decades of the nineteenth century. Even while discussion continued, it is clear from the accounts of observers and travelers that the majority of Cuban coffee planters were using shade strategically during the period.[59] Planters may have developed the idea of using trees for shading the cafetos from the practice of planting *plátanos* (plantains) between the rows of plants to use the land more efficiently and produce food for their enslaved workforce. Observing the beneficial effect that shading the plants produced in increased output and healthier bushes, they may have expanded the practice to the calculated placement of fruit trees. As with many such developments, it may well have been "discovered" accidentally. Elements of this practice were outlined by Laborie, further suggesting that planters were familiar with his methods and were using and modifying them as needed to suit the local environment. We can infer from the fact that this practice does not appear prominently in the local literature until the debates of the 1820s and 1830s that in some cases planters led the way in innovation while at other times the "agricultural intelligentsia" blazed new trails.

Once a planter such as Alonso Benigno Muñoz or Antonio Robredo acquired property for his new plantation, he needed laborers to develop the land and construct the facilities of the cafetal.[60] This was accomplished almost exclusively through the use of slaves. The structure of the labor force and the types of people who performed various jobs was delineated along class and status lines in the colonial Spanish world. This meant that the rigorous manual work needed to create a coffee plantation from virgin land demanded the strength and numbers of slaves. Laborie recommended acquiring six to twelve male slaves and one or two females, noting that that the only reason to purchase a female at this early stage was to acquire a cook for the male workers.[61] It is clear from inventories and population records that fledgling cafetaleros considered men to be better suited for all these types of tasks. We can see this example in practice in the cases cited by Boloix. Laborie also noted that the planter should consider the desired level of production for the plantation and adjust the number of slaves accordingly to accommodate the growing diversity of work on the farm. He recommended that the number of workers fall between forty and fifty for a plantation yielding 100,000 to 150,000 pounds of coffee per year.[62]

The farmers and their slaves who built the cafetales of the vuelta abajo were opening new lands to agriculture. The work they undertook was arduous, pushing them to the limits of their endurance, and it was even dangerous at times.

Their tasks included felling trees and removing all underbrush to clear the land, followed by demarcating fields and breaking the soil for first plantings as well as constructing buildings. When a planter and his contingent of slaves first arrived at the new plantation site, the initial job was to set up temporary living quarters, and then to begin to clear the land to create space for fields and permanent housing. This, the author warns, was not to be taken lightly. In his view, slaves should not be permitted to sleep outside for health reasons, though security certainly may have also figured into his thinking. Putting the workers in quarters right away, he contended, would begin to foster in them an attachment to the land that would benefit the planter through their increased loyalty. In addition, Laborie cautioned his readers that slaves should be worked in pairs or groups when cutting down trees, as this work was very dangerous. By keeping them together, they could watch out for each other, and if someone suffered an injury, he would not be alone and could receive immediate care.[63]

The next order of business was constructing roads and planting food crops. Paths one to two meters wide facilitated commerce between neighboring farms, delineated the range of fields, and allowed people to move easily about the confines of the cafetal. Laborie considered this a very important feature of an efficient farm. Nevertheless, he cautioned that not all the slaves should be devoted to these construction projects; rather, as soon as there was sufficient land cleared to permit planting, some of the crew should be diverted to preparing the ground and putting in food crops. He recommended initially planting fast-growing crops, such as beans and corn, to ensure that there would be adequate provisions for the workers.[64] In addition to its practical application for the maintenance of the workforce, this strategy also would minimize both capital outlays and the reliance of the owner on outside sources for supplies. Laborie mentioned these in concert because he saw planting and roads as related. Roads were needed to divide the farm into working segments, actually defining and separating the spaces for growing food and the export crop of coffee, as well as to facilitate movement about the plantation, enabling people and equipment to move easily between the fields and the central area of the plantation. These were linked also in another way. Laborie recommended setting aside a two- to three-meter buffer along the sides of all the pathways and using this area to plant grasses, flowers, and fruit trees. Included among his recommended plantings were sugar cane and guinea grass. He especially emphasized the planting of fruit trees as a way both to beautify the farm and to supplement the diet of the slaves. In addition to typical fruit trees such as mango, mamey, tamarind, and citrus, the author also proposed the *cañafistola* (also known as "the golden shower tree," or *amaltas*) and the *güira* (calabash).[65] The flowers and bean pods of the cañafistola are medicinal, while the güira produces large gourds that could be used as bowls or containers; thus, both of these types of trees had practical uses or benefits for the slave population. It was here that Laborie also counseled planting plantains in some abundance, calling it the "delicious manna of America" and one of the "most useful" plants on the plantation.[66] Finally, the author suggests planting flowers along the lanes of the farm to create "delightful pathways."[67] Laborie offers little elaboration on why he considered creating a more beautiful space important but suggests that creating a pleasant and healthy environment will make for a more efficient and profitable plantation. This advice is related to his recommendation on housing for slaves. He implied that by treating the workers well, making their environment more pleasing, and ensuring that they are well fed and housed, they will become more passive, manageable, and less prone to run away or cause disturbances, and thus constitute a more productive workforce.[68]

The early emphasis on the orderly and symmetrical layout of the coffee farm was echoed in later publications and became the hallmark of the Cuban cafetal. Travelers in the countryside often noted that while the ingenios were impressive because of their size, they were often dull and uninspiring to behold. The cafetales, on the other hand, were a delight to the eye and became known as the gardens of Cuba. John Wurdemann, a visitor to Cuba in the early 1840s, wrote rapturously about the beauty of Cuban coffee estates. The esteemed poet Marie del Occidente (Maria Gowen Brooks) had composed the highly regarded epic poem "Zophiel" on a Cuban coffee plantation. To those wondering how this could have been possible in the midst of an "unlettered people," Wurdemann replied:

> Why! It is by a quadruple alley of palms, cocoas, and oranges, interspersed with the tamarind, the pomegranate, the mangoe [*sic*], and the rose-apple, with a background of coffee, and plantains covering every portion of the soil with their luxuriant verdure. I have often passed by it in the still hour of night, . . . [and] thought that no fitter birth-place could be found for the images she has created. A coffee estate is indeed a perfect garden, surpassing in beauty aught that the bleak climate of England can produce.[69]

This image resonated down through the decades and outlived the heyday of coffee farms in the west. The accounts of visitors to the island and literary works such as the classic *Cecilia Valdés* by vuelta abajo native Cirilo Villaverde have perpetuated this vision of the coffee plantation. These renditions of the cafetal and its charms are kept alive through the ongoing popularity of Villaverde's novel and continue to influence Cubans in subtle ways.[70] The ideal of beauty and efficiency Laborie advocated extended beyond roads with attractive and useful borders to all areas of the farm and to the people themselves, as we will see.

The second major phase of establishing a new cafetal was the construction of the numerous buildings needed for the variety of aspects related to coffee production and processing. These structures were raised by the slaves under the direction of the master or overseer, usually during the first two years of the life of the new farm. Construction projects fell into two main types: housing and related domestic structures, and buildings or projects related to the production of the crop. Laborie, as might be expected, privileged practicality and the planter in his account and gave his attention first to the necessity of gathering materials during the development of the agricultural lands. The planter or overseer should direct the workers to accumulate stones and timber during the clearing, leveling, and planting of fields.[71] Assuming the planter, or rather the workers, had sufficient materials to undertake construction projects, they would begin the work on buildings related to the main purpose of the farm.

Structures related to the production of the crop were of primary importance and needed to be erected prior to the first significant harvest, which usually occurred during the third or fourth year in the initial cycle of the cafetal. Three main types of projects had to be mounted. Every farm needed a mill house, drying platforms, and a building used for sorting, packing, and storage.[72] In addition, many farms needed cisterns built to capture and hold the water necessary to clean and process raw coffee.[73] There were typically three types of mills on a cafetal: the *molino de quitar las cerezas* (grater mill), the *molino de limpiar* (cleaning or washing mill), and the *molino de aventar* (winnowing or fan-mill).[74] Each of these were used to perform a specific step in the processing and transformation of raw coffee into a product ready for the marketplace. The labor involved will be discussed in the next chapter. The mills were often housed within a single structure, a *casa de molino*, which usually was a roofed structure with open sides for ventilation. Laborie describes a typical structure as one of twenty by forty feet in size.[75] The inventory of the cafetal Mariana describes an even larger structure, thirty-nine by nineteen varas, that included both the mills and storage space.[76] In other cases, such as on the Campana, there was a separate storage building.[77] This was a large, walled building that stored the finished beans until they were taken to market. The storehouse consisted of several rooms so that the coffee could be separated by age and grade. It is imperative that coffee beans be kept dry, so the storage facility needed to be well constructed. In addition, *tendales* (drying platforms) were required. These were large floors on which the slaves spread the beans out to dry in the sun. Laborie recommended that the size of the platform be able to hold the entire harvest of a single day. The construction of a platform took several weeks and involved numerous steps, as the surface had to withstand the acids that leached from the beans as well as the continual exposure to the elements. The surface had to be very smooth and either flat or slightly sloped so that moisture did not accumulate or pool under the beans. Slaves had to level the ground and excavate a section for the foundation of the platform, and then fill the base with rock and gravel, which had to be successively pounded down to compact and compress the layer. This was then covered over with finer gravel and then finally with *mampostería*.[78] Several layers of mampostería had to be applied, with each layer being allowed to dry before the next was added. In addition, the final layer had to be smoothed with brooms so that its surface would be very fine. The construction process had to be repeated as many times as necessary, as a farm often needed several platforms, depending

Figure 1.3. Drying platforms on the cafetal Isabelica. Photo courtesy of David C. Carlson

on the size of the plantation. In the photograph of the drying platforms on the cafetal Isabelica, multiple platforms are visible, as is the effect of the pounding and polishing on their surfaces. Also, note the notches cut into the side of the retaining wall to allow rainwater to drain. In addition, a channel is visible between and below the two surfaces; it directs the water away from the platforms.

Placement of the buildings was to be guided by complementary goals. The choices made by the planter could either contribute to or undermine the efficient production of the crop and the control of his slaves through the calibration of the location of structures and their uses with the topography of his land. In Laborie's view, understanding how to configure the layout of a plantation to take full advantage of the geography was a critical element in determining the success of the prospective farm.[79] Laborie recommended that the best possible orientation was to locate all the buildings in the center of the farm with fields surrounding and extending out on all sides.[80] This configuration allowed for close management of the crops and the slaves, as both were easily accessible from the central compound. If the main buildings were located at the extreme end of the property, some of the fields would, by necessity, have to be a great distance from the processing and storage facilities. This would require additional time and labor to accomplish necessary tasks. If, on the other hand, the buildings were centrally

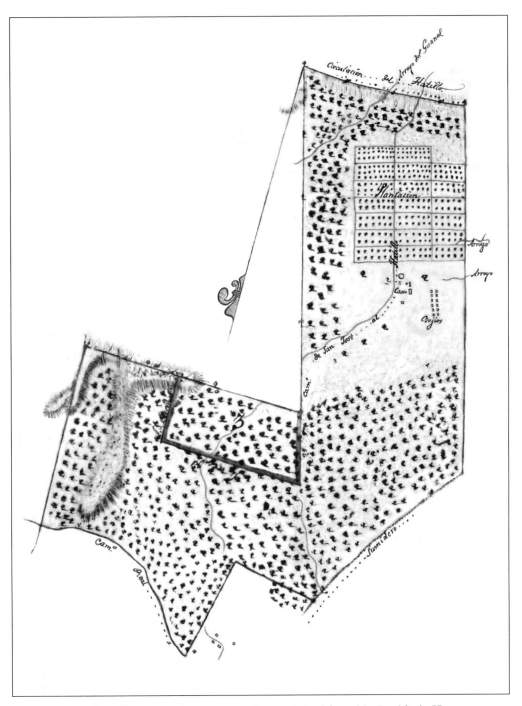

Figure 1.4. Cafetal Paciencia. Map created from original found in Desiderio Herrera, "Plano a fs. 672. . . ," 1839 (September 30), Fondo Escribanías de Ortega, Legajo 38, Número 1, Archivo Nacional de Cuba.

located, time and effort would be more uniform. In addition, the author argues that by keeping all the buildings together, the master or overseer could maintain a higher degree of order both in the execution of labor and during periods of time when the slaves were allowed to work for themselves or engage in other activities. This strategy was widely employed in Cuba and is represented in the plan of the cafetal of Alonso Benigno Muñoz, the Paciencia, circa 1839.[81] As the map shows, Muñoz designed the structure of the farm and developed it in a manner that closely conformed to the model described by Laborie. All the buildings were centrally located in the center of the fields of coffee and within sight of each other. There were additional implications of this types of plantation design for both the slaveholder and the slaves that will be explored in Chapter 3.

Laborie understood that such a layout was an ideal that was not always possible, given the varieties of terrain planters might encounter. He advised that if the declivity of the property was too great—in excess of fifteen degrees—coffee plantings should be placed at the highest elevation and the buildings below, with the pastureland and provision grounds at the lowest point. In this way, the slaves bore their heaviest burdens, such as loads of picked coffee, going downhill rather than climbing upwards. Consistent with his overall approach, Laborie offered this recommendation not for the sake of the workers but rather to promote the most efficient operation of the farm and use of the labor.

Once the working buildings were built (or there were at least functional structures) and the first coffee fields were planted, slaves began the construction of the slaveholder's house.[82] Laborie describes two methods of building that depended on the materials at hand. He suggested stone if it was available, and timbers with wattled and whitewashed walls if the supply of stones was insufficient. The material of choice on many Cuban cafetales was wood overlaid with masonry plaster, which was referred to as *mampostería*. Examples of this style of construction of the *casa de vivienda* (main house) include the grand mansion of the famed cafetal Angerona, and the main houses of the Paciencia, the Jesús Nazareno, and the Mariana.[83] Not all farms conformed to this idea; some were built more modestly, as represented by the main house on the cafetal of Zeferino de la Peña, which his slaves constructed more crudely of wood.[84]

Some planters' houses conformed more closely to the stereotype of the "big house." Situated on a hill, overlooking the fields and the slave quarters, many contained elaborate fixtures and statues, ostentatious religious icons, and expansive architectural features such as Roman pillars. The house of José Rubio Campos, owner of the cafetal Mariana, for example, had more than a dozen pieces of furniture made from cedar and mahogany, as well as several accoutrements made from silver.[85] The Reverend Abiel Abbot of Massachusetts visited the cafetal Angerona twice in 1828 and was impressed by its beauty and orderliness. The approach to the house, Abbot noted, was "by a broad and superb avenue, adorned in the usual manner, except that at the foot of the hill, on an elevated pedestal stands his sylvan deity, the Goddess of Silence, furnishing the name and emblem of the bachelor's estate. It is a fine marble statue in Roman costume."[86] The traveler also mentioned a second statue "representing a water deity."[87] The cafetal Jesus Nazareno, founded by Agustín Valdés y Pedroso, was notable for the large elevated cross that stood between the main house and the batey. It was situated so that anyone approaching the house or going to or from the batey had to pass by it.[88] The Paciencia and the Jesús Nazareno had pillars adorning the fronts of their main houses.[89]

Planters who lived on their farms, such as Andrés Souchay, owner of the cafetal Angerona, tended to build more impressive and substantial buildings, while families that owned several farms and maintained a primary residence in Havana usually erected serviceable but less expensive and less ostentatious housing. An example of the latter type can be seen in the holdings of the O'Farrill y Herrera family. According to the 1823 *testamentaria* (testament) of the wealthy heiress Teresa O'Farrill y Herrera, she owned two ingenios and one cafetal—the Recreo—as well as a residence in Havana. The main house on the Recreo, though good-sized at approximately 1,900 square feet, was a simple structure of three rooms and with few of the adornments such as those noted earlier.[90] It was not richly appointed, as it was only used as a temporary dwelling for family members overseeing operations. In other instances, it was likely that a small farmer who had to use his limited resources wisely would merely build a dwelling that balanced need with materials at hand. Such was the case of Zeferino de la Peña, who constructed on his cafetal a modest three-room structure of approximately 1,200 square feet that was furnished with functional items and largely devoid of luxury. The house served as his principal residence.[91]

There were, then, three types of main houses on cafetales in relation to owner status and use patterns. These categories also suggest some of the reasons planters chose to grow coffee and the images they sought to project to the world around them. Working from the bottom up, we find poorer farmers who built functional housing for themselves, such as in the case of de la Peña. An aspiring planter with limited capital might have chosen coffee rather than sugar cane because it required less land, fewer slaves, and little specialized equipment, and thus a smaller initial investment. We would also see this reflected in the way in which he constructed buildings on the farm. We also find planters of more means who built cafetales. These are in two categories. There were those who lived on their farms and others who lived in nearby cities such as Havana. In the case of the former, represented by Andrés Souchay, they chose to grow coffee for their own reasons and tended to own only one plantation. He and those like him made their farms showcases and comfortable places to live for themselves and their families. In the latter case, we find examples like Teresa O'Farrill y Herrera, who owned more than one type of farm and lived in Havana. Plantation owners like O'Farrill y Herrera were people of considerable wealth who diversified their holdings and built functional and even comfortable personal housing on their farms but reserved luxury for life in the city.

While it is certain that the plantation slaves did not construct every item associated with the house of the slaveholder, it is clear that it was through their labor that the bulk of the work, including most of the skilled crafts, was realized. Not only did the slaves have to construct the dwelling of their owner, but they also had to fashion a house for the mayoral. Farms of even a moderate size, on which as few as ten slaves lived and worked, had an overseer and therefore needed housing for him as well. In some instances the building needed to accommodate the family of the mayoral, in which case the structure was a more substantial undertaking, as it would then require several rooms. Casas de mayoral ranged in size from approximately 450 square feet on the Recreo to as large as 800 square feet on the cafetal Valiente (owned by Joaquín Ayestarán and Gerónimo Merlhy).[92] In most cases the casa de mayoral also included a second smaller separate structure that housed a kitchen. The building method was similar to that of the main house. Beams of *quiebrahacha* (black ironwood) were used to support strips cut from royal palm trees. Workers overlaid the wood with mampostería. In the case of poorer farmers such as de la Peña, the mayoral typically was given a room in the coffee storage building.[93]

It is important to note that while the erection of the casa de mayoral was part of the larger scheme of fabricating buildings necessary for the operation of the farm, its construction by the slaves holds a certain irony. We cannot be certain if creating this particular edifice had a unique significance for the slaves, but it was the house of the person most closely associated with their immediate condition of oppression. There was an inherent logic in utilizing the slaves to perform construction labor needed on the farm on which they lived. They were purchased explicitly for work and therefore were to be used in every task in which they could be effectively mobilized.[94] At the same time, requiring them to construct the accommodations for the person who controlled their lives doubled the effect of what Michel Foucault has called the organization of functional space that articulated not only discipline but also hierarchy.[95] Their compulsory participation in their own domination reinforced their subordinate position in the hierarchical order. By their own hands, they transformed the space of the plantation from its natural state to a structured environment meant to maintain themselves in a state of bondage. This work made it very clear to all the laborers involved that their purpose was to serve, and that they were subordinate to the will of their owner. The tasks of building the farm and especially its housing not only helped to establish a functioning hierarchy within the space of the plantation, but it also instantiated a visible representation of power, order, and hierarchy in the physical presence of the structures the slaves built and that populated their quotidian experience.

Another visible reminder to the slaves of their subordinate position was the construction and location of separate cooking facilities for the planter, the overseer, and the workers. The outdoor kitchen was a common fixture on plantations, set apart from the main living structures both for safety and to reduce heat transfer to the other quarters, an important feature in the tropical climate. In many cases, multiple cooking sites were built to prepare food separately for the slaves and the slaveholder, the overseer, and their families. Examples of this can be found on the cafetales Campana and Mariana.[96] This additional element of segregation would reinforce further the notion of hierarchy on the plantation. This would make clear to new slaves that the power of the slaveholder extended beyond the fields and into every aspect of their lives.

The work of the enslaved construction crew was not finished until they built their own housing. Typically on a new plantation they would build first some quick temporary housing and then turn to other tasks. Then at a later date they would return to the construction of more sturdy and permanent structures. For the first several decades of coffee cultivation, slave quarters consisted of *bohíos* (small huts or cottages) that workers built in a village-type setting. This style of housing would be modified later on some farms for a number of reasons, as we will see. The timing of construction—occurring after the completion of most other building projects—and the quality of slave housing—thatched roof huts with dirt floors compared to plastered and tiled buildings with smooth durable floors—further reinforced social hierarchy and African subservience.[97]

The final structure that several, especially larger, plantations contained was a hospital. Every farm needed a place to house the sick; this often was a large room set aside within the storage building or a separate hut among the bohíos. On larger cafetales, a facility often was constructed to deal with two sources of slave infirmity. Newly arrived slaves often were in a debilitated state of heath and needed space and time to regain their vigor before being put to the rigors of farm work. Life in the fields and the bohíos was hard and slaves were subject to general illnesses. They also could suffer injuries while working. Greater numbers of inhabitants on a farm necessitated an additional facility. The accommodations were minimal, as masters feared that comfortable conditions would encourage absenteeism among the workers. There were exceptions, such as the hospital on the Angerona, which Mary Peabody Mann described as containing "numerous appliances for the comfort of the sick."[98] Abbot confirms her description and adds that the hospital on Souchay's cafetal also functioned as a nursery, which contributed to the success Souchay had at raising a creole population.[99] The traveler also notes that the yard of the building was enclosed and shaded, a design he had earlier encountered on a cafetal near Limonal, which he had described as "a stone building with a yard walled in, airy and commodious."[100]

Thus, by the end of the first five or six years in the life of a cafetal, we find a fully functioning agricultural workplace with a full complement of buildings and a landscape producing sizable quantities of coffee suitable for export as well as sufficient foodstuffs to support its growing population of enslaved workers. This was mirrored throughout the coffee-growing region of western Cuba, as the broader area experienced a first stage of development in which the area saw the construction of roads and the emergence of new towns or expansion of small villages into larger pueblos, where numerous planters established dozens of plantations that went through the initial stages of growth and development at approximately the same time. The regional period of first growth was longer than the five or six years a single plantation would experience because of the staggered development of many farms being built across the broader area. Thus, this first period began during the 1780s and lasted through the first years of the nineteenth century, when the region collectively moved to the period of a mature but still growing plantation complex. The coming era would be marked by robust exports and ongoing expansion. Planters were largely enthusiastic about their future prospects and their prosperity attracted new investors and potential planters who wanted to share in the increasingly idealized life of the cafetalero.

Planters from older families along with new settlers created a new system of plantations with a new crop not previously grown in the Spanish colonies. They built this newly emerging plantation complex on the foundation of decades of reform motivated by personal and family desires for financial and social gain and also by the hopes of leaders in Cuba and Spain to create a more prosperous economy on the island colony. To bring this world to fruition, leaders and planters first had to create the cognitive framework for this new reality. They had to imagine what the needs of a greater system would encompass and develop the infrastructure to enable its construction. This infrastructure included legal and economic elements as well as practical considerations such as land and workers. It is clear that the first steps taken by this diverse group of actors created the legal and economic framework that enabled the expansion of the existing foundation, the encouragement of new crops, and the construction of new plantations. They also realized that building the world they imagined would require many more laborers. This could not be accomplished with the existing population of workers; expansion would require the importation of new hands, and the clear choice was to bring in more slaves from the African continent. As a result, those shaping events always coupled changes in the legal codes and tax laws with new and greater permissions to import more slaves. The expansionist vision facilitated changing the legal and economic structures. The changes that were made drove the expansion of the slave trade to Cuba, which resulted in the importation of thousands of new slaves who built the physical spaces imagined by the colonial elites.

The unshackling of the restraints that held back economic growth led to a plantation complex far beyond anything that had previously existed on the island, and in size and scope, it rivaled anything seen in the Western Hemisphere. As the planter class grew, so did the area under cultivation in both coffee and sugar, launching what we now know as the plantation boom. This led to the shackling of tens of thousands of new slaves such as Pio and Gertrudis. Their lives and the lives of people across western and central Africa would change forever as a massive forced migration exploded across the Cuban landscape. As we will see, their presence would have profound and unintended consequences.

Expansion also meant an increase in other elements of support, such as a network of portreros. Landholders attempted to keep pace in other areas and expanded the production of food crops to support the population. The timing of developments would prove to be important. Events in the French colony of Saint Domingue would supercharge Cuban efforts, virtually guaranteeing success and leading to the second phase of growth among the coffee farms, when significant numbers of plantations began to enter the mature production stage. This period further shaped the importation of slaves and the characteristics of the populations on individual farms. The size and structure of the dotaciones would prove to be key elements both for the slaves on the cafetales and for the Cuban culture that began to take shape during the years ahead.

CHAPTER 2

Transformations
Building Frameworks and Structures

New plantations were carved out of the Cuban wilderness by the labor of a growing force of slaves. Their labor built new plantations seemingly without end. The landscape for a hundred kilometers west, south, and east of Havana was covered with farms. It is important to understand the labor involved in building this new environment and who performed that labor, but we should also keep in mind the role of planters and officials in this process. It was planters, leaders of the colony, and investors who imagined and argued for an infrastructure and laws that facilitated the rise of the plantation complex in Cuba. These ambitious colonists sought ways to increase the economic stability for their extended families, thereby creating larger networks of contacts and connections that spread out from Havana and reached back to Spain. The intention was to increase personal and family wealth and it was this motivation that led them to imagine what was needed to build a more diverse and prosperous economy for Cuba. It would take laws, commercial connections, and cooperation from officials in Spain to create a diverse agricultural economy. Colonists began to argue steadily for what they wanted, ultimately gaining the support of king and council.

Ports were opened and ships began to deliver slaves to Cuba in increasing numbers. The numbers grew steadily and the flow did not stop for decades. The planters directed and the slaves toiled and a dynamic plantation economy was built. By the time the peak was reached, over one thousand coffee farms had been constructed. Tens of thousands of Africans were living and working on hundreds of farms within a day's ride from Havana. This chapter tells the story of how planters acquired the means to build the coffee plantation complex in Cuba, exploring the legal and logistical aspects that led to explosive growth. The chapter also shows how this legal opening fueled a massive influx of enslaved Africans that created a shifting demographic landscape.

The development of coffee cultivation in western Cuba during the last two decades of the eighteenth century and the first two decades of the nineteenth century was marked by sustained growth and consistent profits. The coffee complex emerged alongside the expansion of the number of sugar plantations, with both types of enterprises experiencing explosive growth. Other crops continued to be developed as well and ancillary systems for the rapidly growing population—slave and free—emerged. These included farms devoted to raising food crops as well as expanding port facilities in Havana, Matanzas, and Mariel. This growth in the countryside also led to new roads, and by the 1830s, Cuba's first railroad. The agricultural system that emerged was multifaceted, with planters and merchants of varying backgrounds working as integral parts. Their holdings reveal some of the complexity of the Cuban agricultural system as it developed. There were small holders, single-farm owners with larger establishments, and planters with multiple farms growing a variety of crops. They were part of a very diverse and robust economy on the island that flourished for nearly half a century. The complexity of the system has often been obscured by the later emergence of sugar as the dominant crop. How and why coffee went into some decline beginning in the latter part of the 1840s is part of this story. How the system emerged in its more complex form is a story that is not well known. Focusing on the elite planters helps us to see not only the place of coffee in the larger Cuban economy but also why the system evolved as it did and the forces that ultimately undermined its complexity.

Sugar monoculture on the island was not inevitable. Its later dominance of the agricultural economy often obscures the processes and history of its later ascendance as well as the realities of Cuba's earlier period of agricultural diversity. The "triumph" of sugar was not a natural outcome, but the result of choices made by political elites as they responded to internal and external pressures and the actions of outside actors, as well as environmental factors. As we have seen, the foundation of the plantation boom was laid during the eighteenth century and the structures that were put in place encouraged growth in a number of areas. These earlier actions created a complex and diverse agriculturally based economy. This complexity and also the processes of change were reflected in the social and family structures of Cuba during the period. Many scholars have depicted this social web as the realm of the sugar elite who drove the island consistently toward monoculture and set the stage for a later rush of foreign investors seeking to capitalize on the fast profits available in the sugar market. In fact, the so-called sugar elite were, at least in part, made up of families who acquired diverse holdings, and they actively worked to create an agricultural system that did not rely on a single crop. This is not to say that outside investors played no part in transforming the Cuban economy. Rather, there was an important foreign presence among plantation owners stretching back to the early part of the nineteenth century and it was their growing presence combined with the inability or resistance of creoles to assimilate them into the social structure that contributed to changes in island social networks. As foreign investment rose, there was a coincident breakdown of agricultural and economic diversity, resulting in the later so-called monocrop economy. Social and economic influences were intertwined in a way that the process of transformation was indeterminate and contested until sufficient momentum merged with other factors such as environmental catastrophe and world markets to trap Cubans in a world they only partly made.

Historians have created an extensive historiography of plantation agriculture in Cuba that focuses on monocrop sugar with only the occasional nod to the actual diversity that existed from the 1790s to the middle of the nineteenth century. Laird Bergad, Fe Iglesias, and María del Carmen Barcia, in their book *The Cuban Slave Market, 1790–1880*, offer a particularly compelling example of the problem. On the one hand, they state:

> Although after 1850 eastern Cuba would be associated with coffee farming, during the period of coffee prosperity prior to the 1840s, production was concentrated in the Havana and Matanzas regions of western Cuba. Over 70 percent of coffee exports were shipped from Havana in 1827. It is apparent that as many slaves were employed on coffee farms as were in sugar and that coffee cultivation was as dependent upon slave labor as the sugar sector. The number of slaves utilized on each coffee farm could be as great as on sugar plantations.[1]

On the other hand, they assert that it is clear that "sugar's labor needs determined the patterns of slaving to the island."[2] This apparent contradiction is left unexamined. The authors recognize that there were large numbers of slaves on the cafetales but then discount, without explanation, the influence that the cafetaleros who were buying those slaves may have exerted. While it is evident that owners of sugar plantations had a significant influence on slave-purchasing patterns in Cuba, such a generalization ignores the complexity of slaving on the island and the broader context of the transatlantic trade. Underlying such thinking is the popularly held typology of Cuban agricultural society reported by Cuban anthropologist Fernando Ortiz in his seminal work *Contrapunteo Cubano del tabaco y el azúcar* (published in English as *Cuban Counterpoint*). In this view, sugar planters were largely absentee owners and made up the great landed elite of Cuba. They lived in Havana and wielded considerable influence over colonial politics and the economy. On the other hand, tobacco farmers were small holders and little more than peasants. They produced an economically important crop but their farms were small in size and so individual planters had little wealth and influence. Because of the small size of their farms, slaves were not a significant factor in tobacco production. In 1944, in his introduction to *El café: Historia de su cultiva y explotación en Cuba* (Coffee: The history of its cultivation and exploitation in Cuba), by Francisco Pérez de la Riva, Ortiz extended the framework to include coffee planters, whom he saw as falling between the two poles. They were yet another wholly separate group, living on their medium-size plantations and achieving a measure of prosperity; they aspired to the greatness achieved by the sugar barons, but also embraced the new ideal of plantation life they were creating.[3] Many scholars have allowed this mythic depiction of plantation hierarchy to subtly influence them. Bergad et al. exemplify this problem by considering the sugar elite and their desires as separate from other landholders. Thus, they are able to simultaneously hold the position that sugar drove the slave trade in Cuba, even though it did not hold a predominate position during the most active years of plantation growth and development.[4]

If we put aside the musing of Ortiz and take a closer look at the development of plantation society in Cuba, what emerges is a picture of a vibrant expanding sector that included not only sugar, tobacco, and coffee but also cotton, indigo, cacao, honey, and a wide range of food crops.[5] It is clear that sugar was important and had an influence on the course of development and the patterns of slave buying in Cuba. But there were also other influential factors that as yet have not been fully considered. The role of reform and how that process was shaped by influential advocates for Cuba reveals the early interest in diversity.

As explained in Chapter 1, the 1789 *Decreto de libertad de comercio de esclavos* contained new concessions for the agricultural interests of Cuba. Francisco Arango y Parreño was instrumental in obtaining these provisions. Arango y Parreño, a figure often associated with sugar interests, was a man who devoted his life to the broad development of Cuba. His days spanned the period of Cuba's greatest growth. Born in 1765, he was a precocious youth, and his father put him in charge of the family estate at the age of fourteen. Further demonstrating his quick mind and maturity, he successfully argued an important case before the court in Santo Domingo on the island of Hispaniola despite being only twenty years old. Success followed on success as his father arranged for the young Francisco to travel to Spain to further his legal studies where he quickly earned a degree at the Academia de Jurisprudencia de Santa Bárbara (Santa Bárbara Law School). In 1787, he was named the *apoderado* (legal representative) in Spain of the *ayuntamiento* (municipal government) of Havana. Arango, now with access to the halls of power in Madrid, began to advocate vigorously for the extension and expansion of the reforms of 1765. His work at court culminated with the issuance of the decrees of free trade in 1788 and 1789 that lifted limits on tonnage, opened the ports, and allowed the unfettered importation of African slaves.[6]

In Havana, Arango was a founding member of the influential Sociedad Económica. The young advocate, along with members of the leading families of Cuba, called for the establishment of a society that would promote development on the island. The group focused its work not on the advancement of narrow interests but on the stimulation of a broad range of projects through the creation of a forum for educating members and the public on the benefits and requirements of various endeavors. The Crown approved the formation of the society in a royal decree in 1791. As a member, Arango wrote numerous *discursos* concerning ways to improve the Cuban economy and agricultural system.[7] Some of these were the outgrowth of his trips to Jamaica, Santo Domingo, the United States, and England. His works, written over the course of several decades, consistently advocated free trade and improved methods of production for a range of crops. Writing in 1792, Arango outlined seven obstacles to the development of agriculture on the island. Many have taken this document to be concerned with the expansion of sugar. Read more closely, we can see that the author was using sugar cane as a case study, as he draws on a variety of examples as evidence of the potential latent in Cuba. Comparing Haiti with his home island, he points out that the "French, from inferior soil, have taken a hundred thousand quintales of coffee. . . . Why do we look for more proof?"[8] Arango would echo those words again in 1827 following a trip to Jamaica. He acknowledged that the prosperity of the island was now dependent on coffee and sugar exports but urged expanding Cuban access to new markets and continuing to develop new exports so that the economy would not be subject to the whims of shifting prices.[9] As we have seen, one of the ways Arango and his cohort in the recently established Sociedad Económica promoted development was through the promulgation of reports and other publications. The commitment of the society and especially Arango is further evidenced by the publication of a book that described how to establish a cafetal and how to cultivate coffee.[10]

During this period of active restructuring, development, and change in Cuba, something unexpected happened: the Haitian Revolution. As has already been suggested and generally accepted in the literature, the revolt of the slaves on nearby Saint Domingue altered both markets and thinking about plantation agriculture. It is clear that the commercial production of sugar rapidly declined in the colony, thus removing a major world market supplier of product from the competitive field. But the effects of the Haitian Revolution did not affect coffee production and exports to the same degree as it did other crops. While exports in sugar declined dramatically, from 140 million pounds in 1789 to less than 20 million in 1801, coffee exports only declined from approximately 77 million pounds to 43 million during the same period.[11] Furthermore, from 1821 to 1840, Haitian coffee exports averaged 39.76 million pounds per year.[12] It is clear that exports of sugar rapidly plummeted, falling almost 86 percent, but coffee output fell only 44 percent and shipments subsequently remained stable for more than two decades.[13]

The reduction of Haitian sugar exports in the world market certainly helped ensure the success of the Cuban expansion of its sugar sector. The Haitian collapse provided new incentives in the form of rising world prices and reduced competition. This, along with Spanish incentives, created a perfect environment for a boom in sugar. The climate for coffee was somewhat different. While Haitian coffee exports declined, they were still an important part of the global market. The continued presence of Haitian coffee exports meant that the expansion of the crop in Cuba would face competition throughout its development. Prices for coffee did rise globally, though not as dramatically as for sugar, and Haitian coffee continued to have an effect on the overall market supply. The cafetaleros of Cuba expanded their estates without the same benefit of Haitian decline and succeeded in spite of the continuation of a competitive world market. The slave revolt and subsequent revolution was not a causal factor in the buildup of Cuban plantations and may have only helped sugar growers, making the later success of Cuban coffee all the more impressive.[14]

Once we understand that Cuban elites were interested in developing an agricultural economy with a broader base, it raises the question of Fernando Ortiz and his thesis of separate agricultural spheres. Ortiz emerged in the early decades of the twentieth century as one of the most influential scholars of Cuban culture and history. *Contrapunteo cubano del tabaco y el azúcar*, first published in 1940, continues to be one of his most widely read works.[15] Ortiz, despite what the title might imply, mainly was concerned with the rise of sugar, using tobacco cultivation primarily as a way to highlight aspects of sugar agriculture. He argues that each of these crops, and by extension the different forms of labor each demanded, created its own subculture with very distinctive characteristics. Ortiz contended that tobacco, grown by small farmers with few or no slaves, produced a type of peasant agricultural class, while sugar, which was deeply dependent on the labor of slaves, formed a landed elite. This broad generalization, while deeply flawed on several accounts, had enough grains of truth for his ideas to resonate. Ortiz insisted that the society and culture of Cubans was molded by the presence of two central types of landholders: the sugar baron and the small tobacco farmer. His thesis rested in part on the ideas that these were the enduring crops of Cuban agriculture and that they were organized differently, in that sugar was a crop dependent on African slaves while tobacco was the product of free white labor.[16] In this formulation Ortiz ignored coffee, the second most important crop in Cuba during the era of the plantation boom, and thereby failed to account for a substantial portion of planters and slaves during a critical formative period of Cuban history.[17] In addition, he did not consider the contradictory empirical evidence that numerous plantation owners held farms of more than one type. Third, and arguably most importantly, Ortiz failed to link those who performed the work on the farms to the cultures they helped to create, as well as overgeneralizing about the makeup of specific labor forces. In spite of these problems, Ortiz has been influential throughout the ensuing decades.

The influence of Ortiz's ideas has obscured the complexity of Cuban agricultural economy and society. Rather than divergent segments of functionality operating along class or sector lines as he described, the economy of Cuba was an interconnected system that united rural and urban interests and spanned crop-based segments through family ties that were at the core of Cuban expansion throughout the first three to four decades of the nineteenth century. Representative of this trend were the Teresa O'Farrill y Herrera and Manuel O'Reilly y Calvo families. Both families were important members of Havana's agricultural elite during the boom period of the early nineteenth century. They were part of what Oscar Zanetti has referred to as the old elite of the "Havana municipal oligarchy," which was made up of well-connected and intertwined families of equal class.[18] The old elite are most often cited as the founders of the sugar plantation system in Cuba, but even a brief survey of the holdings of these two representative families disrupts the common view. Teresa O'Farrill y Herrera, the wife and heir of Ygnacio Herrera y Pedroso, owned two ingenios; the larger was the San Ignacio, with a complement of 321 slaves. She also owned a cafetal, the

Recreo, as well as four portreros), with 107 and 68 total slaves respectively.[19] The plantations of the O'Reilly y Calvo family included the ingenio Santa Teresa de Jesús and the cafetales la Rosa and la Resurrección. Manuel O'Reilly y Calvo willed these properties to his daughter Rosa O'Reilly y Calvo and to Joaquín de Herrera, further expanding the scope of his clan by naming an extended family member as a new property holder.[20] There were at least five other cafetales owned by members of the extended O'Reilly y Calvo family during the 1810s to the 1830s.[21] Zanetti also comments on how families in this class tended to marry not only within the class but very closely within the family to protect and maintain assets, while at the same time extending the circle of the family and its holdings.[22] In the case of the O'Reilly y Calvo family, records of sales from 1832 to 1833 reveal the dispersal of income derived from the operations, with the Santa Teresa de Jesús grossing nearly 18,000 pesos on its sugar, while the Rosa and the Resurrección earned a combined 14,200 pesos for their coffee. These examples allow us to see how these families built connections through inheritance and also how they spread their investments across types of farms.

The rapid expansion of plantation agriculture beginning in 1790 was fueled by the old Havana elites developing their existing and extensive land holdings along with a rising tide of immigration from across Europe and the Caribbean. This inflow did not initially displace the traditional elite of Havana. They adapted to changing fortunes through a strategy of assimilation and alliance building that brought new blood and money into their circle and helped to solidify their position of influence into the 1830s and 1840s. The immigrants were the newly wealthy plantation owners. As noted earlier, coffee planters were represented both in Havana's municipal oligarchy and among the newly wealthy planters. Zanetti argues that another useful distinction for analysis is to differentiate between creoles and Spaniards as there were crossovers between groups but Spanish birth carried with it privileges that became increasingly important after the wars of independence on the mainland. I would add that we should also account for non-Spanish immigrants. A third important group emerged during the 1820s, made up of Spanish-born merchants who engaged in slave trading and import/export commerce.[23]

Zanetti contends that the commercial interests of these three groups were centered around the production and sale of sugar along with the slave trade. Wealth and power shifted along the creole-Spanish axis because of complicating factors of external connections and privileged access to power resulting from changes due to the Napoleonic wars, mainland independence, and the criminalization of the international trade in slaves. The old landed creole elite slowly lost power to Spanish-born immigrants and the merchant class became dominant over time thanks to the wealth that the illegal trade in slaves produced. Once the slave trade became illegal, prices for slaves soared, creating vast new profits for those who could evade the legal consequences.[24] This helps us to understand the shifting power dynamics but does not reveal the full complexity of the planter class, as Zanetti focuses exclusively on the sugar trade. As we have seen, many among the Havana municipal oligarchy actually had diverse holdings. As Zanetti shows, some among the newly rich moved into the ranks of the oligarchy over time as they acquired extensive wealth. This was an important early strategy that complemented that system and structure of power put into place by the old elites. We can see evidence of this process in the linkages between the O'Reilly and O'Farrill families and the older Herrera, Pedroso, and Calvo families. By securing alliances through marriage, the leading families of Cuba built wealth, security, and stability for their offspring. Family ties enabled acquisition of property through expansion of the agricultural base, which in turn reaped noble titles from the Spanish Crown. As expansion continued, not all who found sudden success in plantation agriculture were brought into the circle of power in Havana. Many of the newly wealthy chose sugar to build their own fortunes and a growing number of them did not anchor their accomplishments in the alliances of Havana and Spain but had their own self-interested goals.

The most significant aspect of Zanetti's argument is that the locus of profits and power shifted away from the creole landed elite to those who controlled technology in the form of more modern sugar mills and the illegal trade in slaves. This was almost entirely in the hands of outside interests—namely, Spanish merchants and foreign capital investors. This shift was also a change in direction from longer-term investment strategies to one of quicker profits, which would have a profound impact on the Cuban economy and its social structure. This had a complex effect on coffee farmers. Those who were among the old guard continued to own a variety of farms but they became less wealthy over time and were politically marginalized as creoles. Newly arrived planters often diversified into sugar and some also traded in illegal slaves. Francisco Aguirre is an example of this trend. Aguirre owned a large cafetal west of Havana during the 1830s that appears to have been both a working coffee farm and a seasoning farm for newly arrived illegal slaves.[25] He was charged in 1855 with trading in illegal slaves in a similar operation through a sugar cane farm he owned.[26]

German Cornelio Souchay is a notable example of a foreign planter who achieved great success on the frontier of western Cuba. Souchay built his cafetal, the Angerona, in the vuelta abajo during the early years of the nineteenth century. He continued to expand his operation until Angerona was one of the largest coffee plantations in Cuba, with approximately 450 slaves and 750,000 coffee bushes. The German planter, like many of his counterparts among the Havana elite, sought to diversify as conditions were changing. He therefore established an ingenio nearby that he named the Arco Iris. This sugar cane farm was smaller, but substantial, having a slave population of over 150 people. Unlike many wealthy Cuban planters, Souchay did not regularly engage with the socially and politically powerful in the capital. He did not maintain a house in Havana and did not bring his family to the island. He sent money to Germany to support his wife and educate his children. And, most telling, he developed an overland trade route to the port of Mariel to avoid the additional costs of shipping his goods through Havana.[27]

Souchay represents an important transitional type during the period from 1810 to 1840, as he was both an insider and an outsider. He was accepted and reportedly admired for his expansive and orderly plantations and was a valued member of the local militia, holding the rank of lieutenant colonel. He was supported by the Junta de Fomento (Council of Development) in his bid to ship through Mariel. Cirilo Villaverde, an author and a contemporary of Souchay, described Angerona as impressive in its beauty and efficiency and yet foreign in every way and conceptually German.[28] In other words, Souchay established good working relations with his neighbors and those in power, but he kept his main business interests outside the city, did not marry into the inner circle, and left his property to his German family. Some earlier immigrant families, such as the O'Reilly and O'Farrill families, had become full members of Havana society and successfully integrated themselves into their new surroundings. Others, such as Souchay, may have been resistant to inclusion, or the Havana inner circle may have deemed them as undesirable. As the pace of expansion quickened and the types of people building new farms proliferated, the old families of Havana either could not or would not enlarge their circle rapidly enough to accommodate the expanding ranks of the wealthy. As Zanetti points out, once the Crown reasserted control over the colony following the conclusion of Spain's struggle with Napoleonic France, creoles were suspect and this undermined the oligarchic power structure in Havana. Spaniards and some outsiders were able to curry favor more easily with the appointed Spanish officials in charge of the colony. This is why there was a growing number of planters like the German cafetalero who grew wealthy and maintained ties both to Cuba and to the outside world during the 1820s and 1830s.

Souchay was also part of a minority in Cuba, that of foreign-born property holders, that was growing rapidly throughout the period. The group was largely made up of immigrants from North America, France, and Great Britain. A comparison of the census of 1846 with that of 1862 shows an increase of the foreign population of over 500 percent.[29] Cuban scholar Levi Marrero points out that the 1860 *padrones* (local censuses) of rural areas reveal some fifty-nine Anglo and French names on the rolls.[30] Marrero adds that there was a geographical pattern of dispersal, with Anglo-Americans in the west and French in the east. The presence of a cluster of Americans in the well-developed sections of the west is suggestive. More research is needed, but preliminary evidence points to a heretofore underexplored element in the story of the transformation of Cuban agriculture. Travel accounts and census data hint that there were a greater number of American expatriates operating plantations in Cuba than has previously been assumed.[31] There were several Americans farming coffee and sugar in the vuelta abajo to the west of Havana and in the hills and plains near Matanzas and Cardenas to the east of Havana.[32] There were also a few Americans, such as the Brooks family, gaining a foothold in the Oriente, near Santiago and Guantanamo.[33]

Outsiders continued to gain ground in Cuba and their wealth attracted investors from the United States and England. The attraction was enhanced by tax

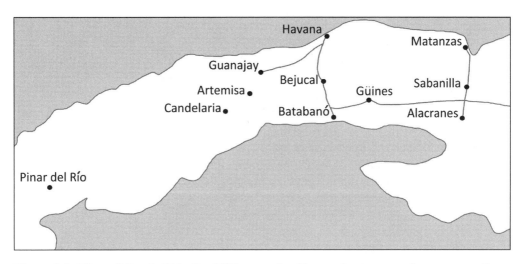

Figure 2.1. The rail line built in the 1830s served coffee- and sugar-growing areas south and west of Havana.

laws that favored foreigners. Not only were Americans and others establishing plantations in Cuba, but Cubans favoring growth continued to press into frontier areas with the help of foreign companies that controlled technology supplying needed industrial goods as well as capital. American firms also had a hand in modernizing the production of sugar with steam engines and rail lines to move goods to port more quickly and efficiently.

These developments opened the door to still more American immigration in the form of technical workers to operate and maintain the new machinery. During the 1840s and 1850s, groups emerged in the United States and Cuba who advocated annexation of the island to its northern neighbor. According to Basil Rauch, this was not simply a ploy by pro-slavery factions, as often been assumed, but was supported by shipping interests in New Orleans and by industrial capitalists in Boston who advanced a strong economic argument in favor of annexation.[34] The rising tide of pressure on traditional powers also included filibusterers in league with anti-Spanish Cubans. These factors combined to have a corrosive effect on the power of old elites with increasingly divisive consequences. In a few short years, the island was enmeshed in a destructive war that would last ten years.

The transformation of Cuba's agricultural economy from one of diversity to one dominated by sugar was not sudden, nor was it the result of mercantilist colonial policies. Rather, it was the product of transformations at the local and personal level in response to capitalist pressures that arose from outside political events. As the numbers of the newly rich—some creoles, some foreigners, and significant numbers of Spanish immigrants—grew, their power and influence expanded in proportion. The old elite lost ground as their numbers dwindled and their fortunes waned. Strategies of diversity failed in the face of falling prices, especially in the coffee sector, and environmental catastrophes, most notably the great hurricanes of the 1840s, intensified the effects of forces already at work. The historical record is clear on one point: foreign capitalists were interested in maximizing their investments through the export economy and had little interest in developing Cuba beyond their short-term goals and the perceived needs of the vast sugar *centrales* they constructed during the latter half of the nineteenth century. As this multinational faction gained a foothold, they restructured the Cuban plantocracy and moved the agricultural focus away from building a diverse economy that would have long-term benefits for the island toward the aim of quick profits found in rapidly growing sugar cane and its corollary—the illegal slave trade. The capitalist imperative for more efficient and faster production of profits undermined both diversity in general and also slower-growing and relatively less profitable coffee in particular.

Labor on a Maturing Cafetal and Its Effect on Demography

The second stage of plantation growth was marked by the shift of the farm from preparing to grow a commercial level of the crop to production of coffee at sufficient levels for shipment. On average, this occurred after five years of hard preparatory work as the workers made ready for the first major harvest. This extended period was necessitated by the long life cycle of the coffee bush. Once the first seedlings were planted, it was three years before they produced any fruit, and it was not until the fourth or fifth year that the plants reached productive maturity. This shift of the farm from preparations to produce coffee to real production meant that the day-to-day labor on the farm changed, and thus the rhythms of life became more closely connected to the cycle of the needs of the coffee plants as they were understood. This also meant that the broader region experienced many changes, as first dozens and then hundreds of plantations began to produce ton upon ton of coffee beans for the export markets in the United States and Europe.

Successful Cuban coffee plantations had two things in common: good land and suitable slaves. Once a prospective cafetalero acquired the former, he would then seek out and obtain the first slaves for his dotación. They would perform the initial tasks of carving a cafetal out of the frontier. These ten or twenty male slaves would fell the trees; clear the land and prepare the fields; build the initial infrastructure of the farm, including roads, buildings, and processing accoutrements; and establish the first plots of food crops. Land for growing food and raising animals included space for both general cultivation for the farm and plots for each individual slave for personal production.[35] This flurry of activity was male dominated and lasted through the first two to three years of the life of the farm because of the rigors described above. As this phase drew toward its close, a transformation of the cafetal began. During the third and fourth years, the plantation began to shift from a construction footing to production mode, and the planter acted accordingly by beginning to expand and reshape his contingent of slaves, primarily by acquiring more female slaves.[36] The change to production brought with it new, more regular tasks and a different order to daily life on the farm.

Under the direction of the owner or overseer, slaves established a nursery for coffee plants early in the construction phase of the farm's life, but the work associated with the seedling bed continued and became part of daily life. This important task needed to be accomplished early in the formation of the farm, as it was the first step in the long march toward production of coffee. The extended life cycle of the coffee bush meant that the work of the nursery had to start early, and it was continued throughout most of the life of a viable plantation.[37] The variety of coffee grown in Cuba during the first half of the nineteenth century was *coffea arabica* (family *rubiaceae*), a plant originating from the east African highlands. In its native environment, the woody coffee bush grows under a canopy of larger trees, a process echoed on Cuban plantations. The plants thrive in moderate rainfall and mild temperatures and can grow to heights exceeding thirty feet, suggesting some of the labor the plants required in a commercial environment. Plants that produce hundreds of seeds, such as *coffea arabica*, do so as a result of adaptation to environment and to compensate for the fragility of their seedlings.[38] The planting of seeds and tending of young cafetos by the thousands was a job crucial to the eventual financial success of the enterprise. The coffee plant is a perennial, with a long life cycle of twenty-five to thirty years. It matures slowly and does not produce its fruit in commercially viable quantities until it reaches four to five years of age, though vigorous plants as young as three years produce some salable beans. Once the plant reaches maturity, it can produce a crop every year for another twenty to twenty-five years, though in its final few years of life the output of a plant declines.[39] It could take several years for a cafetal to produce and sell its intended product, so it was vital that the investor begin the process as quickly as possible.

During the early years of a plantation, the mostly male workforce was split between those assigned to constructing necessary structures and laying out fields and roads, and those devoted to planting and tending to the nursery and vegetable gardens. Alejandro Dumont of the Sociedad Económica advised that the seedbed or nursery was the first thing to which a planter should attend and that the ground set aside should be close to water, very clean, and as flat as possible. Each individual plot should contain only six rows of seeds, with eight inches separating the rows, and each small planting should be separated by a path about two feet wide. Laborie noted that coffee could be planted with its outer shell on or peeled, and that seeds should be planted about one inch apart and covered with only a light amount of soil. A good size *semillero* (seedling bed) of eighty yards square could produce 100,000 plants. Plants sprouted within thirty to forty days and then required close care. For young plants to flourish, workers had to keep the seedlings well cultivated, watered, and free of weeds, since their vigor as productive plants was related to their health when young. Seeds could be planted at any time during the year but the best time was during rainy weather in late spring.[40] In many areas of western Africa, this type of agricultural work was typically done by women, but in the early years of the developing coffee region of western Cuba, males performed most of the labor, as they constituted the clear majority of the population. As time progressed and the region matured, the shifting demography of the area permitted the use of more female slaves to perform this kind of work. Nevertheless, the extensive use of men, doing work they must have considered to be work only suitable for women, may have had long-term effects on the reconstruction of individual and group identification that have yet to be explored.

Once the young cafetos were large enough, another task was added to the repertoire of the enslaved, as they attended to the backbreaking job of transplanting the still tender plants to the regular fields. Planters favored one of three methods of relocation and the age at which they directed the plants to be moved varied based on the chosen technique. Dumont described the three methods Cuban planters might employ. The first and least-utilized was called *plantación de barreta*.[41] Very young plants, only a few months in age, with six to eight fully formed leaves, were uprooted from the seedbed. Slaves, working in the field to which the plants were being transplanted, used iron bars to punch holes in the soil in which they placed the cafetos. This method required a great deal of labor and was risky because of the age at which the plants were moved. Another technique that was not widely practiced involved removing the plant from the nursery at an even earlier state, after about one month of growth, by digging out the earth around the entire plant. The idea was to extract the cafeto while keeping its entire root system covered in soil. This method was similar to modern approaches for transplanting seedbed plants but also was very labor intensive.

The most widely used method of transplantation was the so-called *plantío cortado* technique. This method, also recommended by Laborie, required the least skill and the smallest amount of labor.[42] Slaves dug from the seedbed young plants of about one year that had developed to the stage of having four small boughs, taking care to retain most of the taproot, which would have reached some eighteen to twenty-four inches below the surface. The central root was then cut back to a length of approximately fifteen inches and the smaller ancillary roots were trimmed. These unearthed saplings did not have to be planted immediately but could be stored under a layer of damp soil or plantain leaves for several days. Slave workers marked out rows in the field and dug holes that were nine to twelve inches wide, fifteen to eighteen inches deep, and spaced six to eight feet apart.[43] The work of planting the saplings required the slaves to be dexterous and attentive to detail. The recommended method was to suspend the cafeto in the hole by holding it with one hand, with the taproot just touching the bottom of the hole, and to use the other hand to move about six inches of dirt into the hole, packing the soil lightly. The slave then added more dirt to about three inches below ground level, so that the cafeto's bottom pair of leaves was even with the top of the hole. The worker then pressed the soil down firmly, being careful to support the plant but not to damage it.[44] The plants would suffer some shock, but with the core of their roots intact, they would rebound quickly. This was backbreaking work and could go on for many days, as it involved transplanting hundreds if not thousands of plants. Once the first field was planted, other tasks could be attended to, including planting additional fields and restocking the nursery, but weeds soon sprouted in the first plot of coffee and they required attention.

Weeds were a constant threat to the livelihood of the cafetalero and a seemingly neverending source of work for the slaves. The fertile soils and climate of Cuba meant that all manner of plant life flourished, including the undesirable undergrowth that robbed valuable nutrients from growing coffee bushes. Laborie stated that weeds left unchecked could significantly inhibit the growth of a coffee bush and also reduce the production of a crop. In some cases, weed growth could overwhelm a bush and lead to the death of the plant.[45] Completely removing undergrowth was vital for the success of new plants, but it was also important for the ongoing health and productiveness of existing stands of bushes. Weeding, then, was a job that continued throughout most of the year, but was typically assigned when other matters were less pressing, such as after the harvest in the late winter, and during the summer, between the time when new plants were set out in the fields and before the harvest began again during the late fall and winter.

Plantation managers typically organized gangs of workers to tend to the task of weeding. Mary Mann wrote that gangs for weeding or clearing brush were made up of men and women who were under the supervision of a "driver" throughout the day; the gangs were required to perform a predetermined amount of work for the day.[46] Other sources confirm this sort of work arrangement, which was a modification of what has come to be known as the gang and task labor systems. Much of the work on cafetales was organized as task labor—workers were assigned a quota of work for the day, and once it was completed, their time was their own—or as a modified version of the gang and task systems, under which a group was given a quota or fixed amount of work to be accomplished. It should be noted that on some larger farms such as Angerona, work was more regimented, as owners or managers were motivated by a perceived need for greater security. On most cafetales, though, evidence points to a more flexible work schedule.

The removal of weeds was a task that required some care when coffee plants were young, or when the terrain was fragile because of declination or soil type. In these cases, slaves had to pull weeds by hand, one plant at a time, so as not to disturb the soil or the nearby cafeto. The worker would pull out the weed, shake off the dirt, and pat down the soil to its original state. When coffee bushes were full grown, slaves typically used hoes or machetes to cut off the weeds at ground level. Both types of work were physically demanding and tedious, but they did not require a great deal of strength and could be done by both men and women.[47] There are very few direct accounts of this sort of mundane labor, but the abundance of tools used for weeding found on cafetales is evidence of the importance of weeding to cafetaleros. Large numbers of machetes and hoes appear in the inventory of nearly every cafetal in the region. The cafetal Valiente, near Güines, had in its inventory eighty hoes and an equal number of machetes, to be used by a contingent of 104 slaves.[48] On the cafetal Perseverancia, mayoral Belén de la Rosa testified that the use of machetes was so common that every working slave had a machete in his or her power.[49] Rosa's testimony revealed that on coffee plantations, both men and women performed this type of work and also that women were entrusted with the tools of labor equally with men.

In spite of its mundane day-to-day character, weeding could lead to disputes. In the late spring of 1838 on the cafetal Laborinto, owned by Diego Pintado and located in San Marcos, a major weeding operation was underway, involving more than a dozen of the males of the dotación. Directed by the mayoral, Jorge Castillo, the slaves were diligently performing their task and removing great amounts of vegetation day by day. According to one of the workers, Lucas *congo*, they had been working in fields a great distance from the central part of the farm. As the manuals of Laborie and Dumont suggested, the slaves were instructed to remove the refuse from the rows so as not to allow the pulled or cut weeds to re-root and thereby regain a hold among the coffee bushes. Since the fields in which they were working were well removed from the oversight of the owner, Castillo directed the slaves to move the piles of wilting vegetation to a nearby field on the neighboring cafetal of Ramón Charun, known as the Acierto. The slaves and the mayoral waited until dark, and then by the light of the moon hauled the weeds across the property line and into the field. Charun soon found the piles of weeds and suspected that his neighbor was dumping the waste on his property. He complained to Pintado, who assured him he was mistaken. Nevertheless, Charun was determined to catch the culprits. He began to patrol his property in the evenings with his dogs. He soon found that his suspicions were true. Charun returned to his farm and gathered some of his own men and went back to confront Castillo and the Laborinto slaves; a violent confrontation ensued. Charun testified in the investigation that followed that he was concerned about the refuse but more troubled by the damage that some of his coffee bushes had sustained as a result of the workers hauling refuse through his fields during the night. He prevailed in his case and was awarded damages.[50]

The dispute over mounds of pulled weeds testifies to the ongoing work of weeding and the practice of removing the pulled or cut weeds from the fields. The use of a male workforce in this case raises a question with several possible answers. In other contexts, mixed groups were assigned to weeding; why was this group all male? On the one hand, the dotación may have been somewhat undersized for the plantation, and they were therefore unable to keep up with the regular task. The quantity of weed refuse points out that it had been some time since the far-flung fields had been cleaned and had become at least somewhat overgrown with undesirable plants. On the other hand, it may not have been any fault of the slaves but poor management on the part of the overseer. His decision to take the easy but potentially contentious path for disposal of the byproducts of the day's labor reveals that Castillo may not have been a wise manager.

Another important aspect of plant care that slaves on cafetales carried out was the work of pruning the bushes. Trimming coffee plants involved two different processes, both of which contributed to improving crop yields. The first part of the process was the removal of what were referred to as "suckers" from the plant. These superfluous branches emerge at the joint between the main stalk and a fruit-bearing branch. They can be differentiated from desirable branches by the angle at which each grows. Branches that will produce fruit grow at nearly a ninety-degree angle to the main trunk of the bush or parallel to the ground below. Suckers, meanwhile, grow at roughly forty-five degrees and tend to turn upward. Laborie recommended that these be removed as soon as they emerged but also suggested that they could be cut off later, though this was not best for the plant.[51] Nevertheless, even if the suckers were removed, they would regrow. Thus, checking the plantation's stock of bushes for new suckers was a periodic and ongoing job.[52]

The second aspect of pruning involved cutting the top of the plant to limit its height. Planters typically directed their slaves to "top" the cafetos to improve yields and also to make the plants more robust. Slaves were sent into a field to trim the bushes when the plants reached a height of about six feet. The plant tops were still green and could be easily snapped off by hand. If the bushes were allowed to grow somewhat taller and the stalk became woody, then a special hooked machete (*machete calabrozo*) or sometimes a smaller blade would be used to cut the top to the desired height of between five and six feet.[53] The plants responded to this procedure in two ways. They grew outward, becoming larger in circumference rather than taller, and the vegetation became more dense. This had two beneficial effects for the planter. Each trimmed bush produced more fruit, and as the plants were shorter, the crop was easier to harvest. The shorter bushes did not have to be pulled and bent over for workers to pick the ripe cherries, and more of the crop was closer to the ground. This meant that younger and shorter people could be used as workers during the harvest; even young children could be put to the task. Planters also might direct their slaves to trim or top their plants to protect them from strong prevailing winds. Bushes could be cut to as short as four feet so that their tendency to grow broader would be accentuated, and their low, dense profile would then protect them from the strong or gusty winds that could damage taller plants.[54]

The other part of the year was devoted to the crop. Picking and processing the cherries—converting them into salable coffee beans—was the focus of activity on the farm. Coffee bushes bloom in the late winter or early spring; the fruit that forms from the self-pollinating flowers takes approximately eight months to ripen. Clusters of flowers emerge at the joints or nodes that occur every few inches along the branches. This means that each bush will produce dozens of cherries. The fruit of the coffee bush begins as a small green sphere that steadily grows over the months, becoming oblong and turning first yellow and then red when ripe; thus the name "cherry" for the ripened fruit. The coffee bean is the bifurcated seed within the fruit of the plant. Once the cherries began to ripen, managers sent slaves into the fields for the harvest, which took place over several months since only ripe cherries were plucked. Each slave was given a basket; the day's work typically was to fill two baskets with cherries.[55] Men, women, and children all worked together to scour the plants for the ripened fruit and to pick their quota for the day as quickly as possible. An important aspect that needs to be emphasized is that the main work of the farm, most notably harvesting the cherries or fruit of the coffee plant, was a task that required dexterity more than strength. The cherries were easily removed but had to be carefully selected so as not to disturb surrounding fruits that were not yet ready. Laborie commented that women often were better coffee pickers than men, both in the quality and quantity of the fruit harvested.[56] In the Dumont manual, the authors stressed the importance of picking one cherry at a time, so as to avoid getting too many green unripe fruits mixed in, which would result in the loss of prematurely harvested beans.[57] Laborie also warned against letting the slaves strip the branches when picking—grabbing a branch in one hand and pulling down the length of it with the other, which removed most of the leaves and all the fruit in one quick move. Workers might engage in this practice to finish more quickly, but this could damage the plant and required additional labor during sorting to remove the leaves and the unripe fruit.[58]

Once the harvest was underway, the workers handled the yield of each day in one of two ways. The goal was the same with each method, as the aim was to remove the tough outer shell of the coffee fruit and its inner membrane (the parchment) to reveal the inner seeds. The seeds or beans were then sorted and dried, and could be stored indefinitely before being taken to market. In the first technique, the slaves loaded the newly picked cherries into a mill called a *molino de quitar* (*las cerezas*) that was designed to crack open the outer covering.[59] One or two men provided the power to drive smaller mills, but animals turned the wheels of the larger versions. After the hulls were cracked, workers then moved the fruit into barrels or tanks of water to soak for twenty-four hours.[60] This softened the outer shell or covering for easier removal. After soaking the cherries, the slaves removed them from the water and spread them on drying platforms known as *barbacoas*, where they were left to dry for approximately one week. The plantation manager had to be watchful for rain or heavy dew, as exposure to moisture at this stage of the process would seriously damage the quality of the seeds. If he anticipated wet conditions, he directed the slaves to cover the beans to protect them from harm. The next step in the process was to load the cracked and dried fruit into another mill that separated the shells from the inner material. The design of the apparatus allowed the beans to fall through a grate, or ridges, while trapping the broken coverings above. Workers gathered up the beans— many still covered in parchment—and spread them out on tables or on a smaller drying platform to be cleaned and sorted. The slaves removed the thin membrane and other debris and graded the beans as they worked. Once the beans were cleaned and stable (meaning sufficiently dry for long-term storage), the slaves bagged them for sale or later marketing.

The second method did not require large quantities of water for soaking, which was preferable in some areas because of environmental differences in the availability of water; it also meant that cisterns did not have to be constructed. Those who followed the second method instructed their workers to take their harvest directly to the drying platforms, where they spread out the cherries to cure for three to six weeks. The time varied depending on weather conditions and the moisture content of the cherries. During the initial drying stage, several slaves, usually males, would rake through the cherries three or four times per day to dissipate heat and the moisture that would build up. Stirring the cherries improved evaporation of the moisture that the fruit gave off and helped to prevent the onset of decay.[61] As with the other method, if the overseer or planter anticipated rain or thought that the dew of the evening would be heavy, he instructed the slaves to rake the fruit into mounds and cover them with sailcloth, plantain leaves, or palm leaves. As in the previous example, additional moisture could harm the final product. Once dried in this fashion, the outer covering of the beans was brittle and could be easily cracked open by a mill such as the molino de quitar. Laborie recommended the first method of soaking the cherries, but later writers such as Abbot noted that planters had found that drying the beans "in cherry" yielded approximately 3 percent more in weight on average.[62] Since the crop was sold by weight, this meant that planters realized more profit from beans processed in this manner. The fact that Abbot and others observed that most planters were using the latter technique demonstrates that coffee growers experimented with various approaches and sought to maximize their profits.

During the process to crack open the dried cherries, some debris, such as leaves, twigs, and pieces of dried covering, fell through the grating of the mill and mixed with the beans. Slaves had to sort through this and remove all the extraneous material from the beans, as in the first method I described. This might be done before the shelled beans were returned to the drying platforms or, if the beans were deemed sufficiently dried, they would be moved directly to the sorting tables. If that was the case, then the debris was removed during the sorting process. Sorting the beans was a multistep process. Workers graded the produce while ensuring that the beans were clean and sound. The labor of the final sort usually took place in a building or a pergola. Some of the stronger slaves would carry barrels of beans to the sorting area and spread them out on tables where the women would pick through the produce for stray leaves, small stones, and the like, and also separate the crop into three grades for market.[63] Cornelio Souchay, the owner of cafetal Angerona, who was known as an innovator, had glass windows installed in his sorting room so that his slaves could work when it was raining or cold, thus preparing the crop for market without risk to the produce or their health.[64]

There were other types of work to be done on cafetales not directly connected to nurturing the coffee plants and producing the salable crop. This other labor fell into two main categories: work related to general maintenance of the farm, and tasks associated with the support of the inhabitants. Maintenance included repairing and sharpening tools for weeding and pruning, making and repairing baskets used in picking and carrying coffee cherries, repairing and re-fabricating the parts—posts, wheels, gears, and grating—used in the mills, and constructing and repairing fences, walls, and avenues of transportation. There is little direct evidence to verify the amount of time or the number of workers devoted to these types of tasks, though it is clear that these sorts of activities were ongoing. The presence of carpenters and masons on a number of cafetales is suggestive. In some cases the carpenter or mason was not a slave, while in others the craftsman was enslaved. If, as inventories and other records report, a farm had a *buen carpintero* (good carpenter) or an *albañil* (mason), his special skills would be not only noted in reports but put to use building farm infrastructure or enhancements, regardless of his status.[65] The acquisition and maintenance of a carpenter or mason, whether free or enslaved, implies a sufficient amount of necessary work to keep the specialist occupied and to justify the expense. Moreover, even if the tradesman was free, the projects often required the assistance of auxiliary laborers. Abiel Abbot, writing of his visit to a cafetal in Limonal, noted that "there is a great extent of wall building on this estate." While touring the farm, he observed four slaves building a wall that in the owner's vision would eventually enclose the entire plantation. Abbot also commented that some slaves were carrying limestone to the site and others were breaking rocks to the appropriate size.[66] This shows that even though there might only be one mason listed in a farm inventory, numerous slaves were often engaged in work related to a project that likely was supervised by the craftsmen on the plantation.

Large-scale projects, such as the construction of water tanks or walls, were substantial undertakings that required a sizable portion of the available pool of laborers. Such an undertaking required a commitment of time, energy, and resources that underscores a sense of permanence and command over both the land and the workers by the planters. Nevertheless, such stone structures were not uncommon, and they were often mentioned by travelers to the island.[67] The use of a large part of the workforce necessarily occurred during a time when other tasks were unnecessary or inadvisable. The case Abbot observed was during the period after the coffee bushes had flowered but before the harvest. Weeding or pruning would have damaged the emerging crop by disturbing the flowers before the fruit was well established. Weeding was also potentially disruptive to the plants because it required large numbers of slaves to work in close proximity to the bushes when the plants were in a fragile state. It was during such times that owners needed to occupy their slaves with other undertakings. This helped the process of control by keeping the slaves busy while at the same time reinforcing the visual representations of power through the construction of permanent, fortified elaborations of the plantation complex.

Individual plantations went through specific stages of growth as they matured, moving from newly established farms to established productive enterprises. For any new plantation, the first stage was the commencement of construction or establishment, coinciding with the first stages of the agricultural lifespan of the farm. This first period lasted approximately five to six years. The first period was defined by the growth cycle of the coffee plant, which typically took five to six years to reach its potential as a productive plant. The first notable harvest was on average at four years. The second stage was when the farm began to reach full production. At this stage the first return on investment was realized, as expanding harvests enabled the sale and export of coffee beans. Also during this phase the slave population stabilized, as the owner could now determine accurately the number of slaves needed to work the crop, the farm's main structures were all largely in place, and longer-term strategic planting work was implemented. The stability of the second level lasted for approximately fifteen years after the beginning of sizable harvests. Phase three was full maturity, and that often included a cycle of decline. Some of the earlier plantings began to decline in their yield, but if successful long-term planning had occurred, new fields were brought into production. If long-term planning had not been implemented, the farm began to experience a marked decline in harvests. This period began at about the fifteen- to eighteen-year mark and continued into the future, depending on management practices. With good planning, a farm could continue to be productive indefinitely, through rotating fields and staggering plantings.

Planters understood that it was in their interests to align the population of slaves on their plantations with labor and crop needs. As a result, a relationship emerged between demography and the life cycle of the farm. This can be seen on individual farms and also collectively in the region. As mentioned earlier, the workforce of a new farm was typically overwhelmingly male because of the rigors of establishing a new plantation on virgin land: trees had to be felled, roads built, fields cleared and plowed, and buildings constructed—all work done almost exclusively by men (male slaves, in this case). After the first year or two following the establishment of a new farm, a planter would begin to add to his dotación. The next stages of work included planting seeds and managing the tiny coffee plant seedlings, and then, when they were of a suitable size, carefully transplanting the young plants to the main field. The tasks also included managing the food crops for the slave workforce and cooking. Many of these jobs could be done by women and as a result more women were added. As the farms came into their maturity, the farmers came to realize that women could do much of the labor-intensive work of picking and sorting of the newly harvested coffee cherries and later the processed beans. Stronger women could also assist in the drying process, which involved raking and turning the beans on the drying platforms. Men continued to do the heavier work, such as carrying the full baskets of cherries and providing the power to operate the cleaning and milling machinery. Men also moved the crop to the drying platforms, rotated the beans as they dried, and moved, bagged, and put into storage the finished product. So, over time, the farm's population became increasingly gender balanced as a result of the division of labor and the realization by planters that this made for a productive workforce.

There was a broader trend of periodization in the coffee-growing region that roughly mirrored that of a farm. Throughout the territory southwest of Havana, dozens of farms were being constructed during the 1790s and the first decade of the 1800s. It could be said that the region was in a first stage of development much like that of a single farm—and, the population was heavily male, which was reflected in the findings that Boloix published in his survey and also in the figures from the local padrones of 1808–1810.[68] The region began to reach maturity during the 1810s and 1820s, when the first-generation farms moved into full production. To be sure, more farms were added, but the general trend was stability. The political instability of the early 1820s (resulting from the reestablishment of the Spanish constitution and liberal rule) and the subsequent return of absolutist rule under King Ferdinand VII in 1823 created turmoil both politically and economically on the island.[69] The rhythm of the crops and the desire to expand and create new wealth drove the plantation economy forward once some stability was realized. Farms continued to be built and new slaves continued to be imported. Large numbers of coffee plantations reached maturity by the late 1830s. This is reflected in increasing numbers of women in the region. In the jurisdiction of Havana, there were 188,929 enslaved. Of the nearly 190,000 captives, there were 39,606 living on cafetales. In other words, 21 percent of the slaves within the jurisdiction of Havana were living and working on cafetales. According to regional figures, the overall female population continued to maintain a 36 percent share of the total, though there was a noticeable narrowing of the gap in the distribution among those aged fifteen and under. In that group, females had nearly achieved parity and made up 46 percent of the total. Also, if only the jurisdictions of Santiago and San Antonio—those most heavily populated with cafetales—are considered, then the percentage of females in the slave population rises to 39 percent.[70]

By 1841 the partido of Puerto de la Güira, which included the town of Artemisa and the old corral of San Marcos, held 73 cafetales, 6 ingenios, and 134 farms of some other type. Sixty-one percent of the slaves in the area lived on cafetales and 40 percent of the entire slave population, nearly 3,500 individuals, was female.[71] The populace in Alacranes of the same year stands in contrast. This district was dominated by ingenios, containing thirty-four of them, while there were only fourteen cafetales. Forty-three percent of the slave population lived on area ingenios while only 8 percent lived on its cafetales. The gender distribution of the population of Alacranes reflected the sugar influence, as the male population made up 70 percent of the total enslaved.[72] These two examples highlight the strong growth of the female population in San Marcos/Artemisa and also how the district diverged from the demographic trend of nearby sugar zones. Narrowing the focus further to the level of individual plantations allows us to observe these trends more closely and, where records permit, can also add additional subtlety to the demographic picture.

The San Marcos cafetal Paciencia, owned by Alonzo Benigno Muñoz, and the home of Pio and Gertrudis, offers a look at a midsized coffee farm. By 1820 Muñoz, with the labor of his slaves, had built the farm into a well-developed cafetal that consisted of ten caballerías (330 acres) of land under cultivation, on which were planted approximately 150,000 coffee bushes. In that same year, sixty-nine African and creole slaves lived and worked on the Paciencia. Of those of working age, there were twenty women and thirty-two men, all born on the African continent. There were seventeen creole children on the farm, of which seven were girls and ten boys. Females made up 39 percent of the total slaves and 25 percent were children ranging in age from two months to five years.[73] The population of the Paciencia showed some important differences from the early padron of the area. Its female and creole contingents as percentages of the population were substantially larger than those of the earlier period. In addition, the populace of the cafetal in 1820, with its narrower sex distribution gap, closely resembled the structure of the regional population of 1841, and it had reached levels of creolization the broader population may not have reached for another twenty years.

The structure of the Paciencia dotación in 1820 was not anomalous or confined to a particular period of time or stage of production but represented an ongoing trend. An 1839 inventory of the cafetal returned similar results for the population. Nineteen years after the collection of the earlier data, the number of slaves had declined slightly to sixty individuals living on the cafetal. Those listed as working-age included thirty-one males and twenty females.[74] There were another three boys and six girls on the farm. In 1820, the entire working corps consisted of African-born slaves, whereas twenty-one of the fifty-one workers in 1839 were Cuban-born, constituting 41 percent of the workforce. In addition, creoles made up half of the total dotación. The gender gap also continued to narrow, with females constituting 43 percent of the enslaved on the Paciencia.[75] The rising number of women did not signal a cafetal in decline. In the intervening years, while the Paciencia dotación continued to experience changes in its demographic configuration, it also sustained the ongoing development of the plantation. The 1839 inventory showed that the slaves brought another caballería of land under cultivation in coffee, increasing the area of land planted to eleven caballerías. In addition, the slaves expanded the number of productive coffee bushes significantly, to a total of 275,000 plants.

Inventories from other cafetales in San Marcos/Artemisa show similar demographic profiles of their dotaciones. Cafetal Campana, established sometime prior to 1810 by Felipe Fernández de Silva, had by 1832 a significantly larger slave contingent than the Paciencia between 1820 and 1839. The property consisted of 6.75 caballerías with 270,000 cafetos plus an additional 1.5 caballerías set aside as a "portrerato" (small food crop area).[76] Upon the 1832 death of Rita Estremes, the widow and heir of Fernández de Silva, there was a protracted legal struggle over the dispensation of the farm. As a result, interested parties conducted two inventories of the cafetal; the first in 1832, followed by another more detailed accounting in 1835.[77] The inventories were consistent with each other, with the 1835 tally showing slight gains among the slave population. In 1832, eighty-five slaves made up the dotación. The group was balanced both by sex distribution and by birth with forty-three females, forty-two males, forty-three creoles and forty-two *de nación* (African-born, but also born of specific groups as understood by the planter). Ninety-one slaves lived and worked on the Campana in 1835. Creoles made up a slightly larger portion of the population, 52 percent, than they had three years earlier, while sex distribution remained nearly equal, with forty-six males and forty-five females. The evidence from the Campana shows that farms from a range of sizes had dotaciones with equal or nearly equal sex distributions. Also, the structure and changes these two examples present suggest an important effect of the larger numbers of women living on cafetales. More adult females on a farm corresponded to expanding numbers of creole children. This pattern was replicated throughout the coffee district of western Havana and the eastern Pinar del Río jurisdictions.

Officials in Cayajabos, another important coffee-producing partido, created a padrón in 1808 that revealed an area much more heavily populated than Puerto de la Güira: 6,090 slaves inhabited the local farms and towns of Cayajabos, which exceeded the tally for Puerto de la Güira in 1841.[78] The *Capitán* (captain or chief official) of the partido reported that there were 1,064 slaves on forty-seven cafetales and 1,176 slaves on sixteen ingenios in the area.[79] This meant that slaves on coffee farms constituted 17 percent of the total number of slaves in the district while the proportion of those on ingenios stood at 19 percent of the total enslaved. The female population numbered 2,350, or 36 percent of the whole. This figure was consistent with a developing area and also reflected the variety of farms in the area. If there was a higher proportion of women on cafetales in the partido, it is likely their numbers would have been masked in the figures for the partido as a result of the relative size of the cafetal population vis-à-vis the total and the dominance of males on other types of farms. The padrón also revealed that there were 1,015 slaves under the age of seven and another 900 between the ages of seven and sixteen. While there are no indications of ethnicity, we can assume that most of the former group were creoles and that a substantial number of the latter also may have been born on the island.

The census of 1841 reported that the slave population of Cayajabos had expanded to 7,114 while the region underwent a reconfiguration of its plantation structure. The number of ingenios declined from sixteen to fourteen, but the number of slaves on cane farms nearly tripled to 2,975. This suggests consolidation rather than loss of farms and that planters were expanding the amount of land they had under cultivation. Cafetales grew in number from forty-seven to fifty-five while the number of slaves on coffee farms expanded by a factor of four. Unlike their counterparts on ingenios, cafetaleros increased their holdings both in absolute numbers and also expanded land under cultivation. This can be seen in the average number of slaves on each farm. In 1808 there were approximately twenty-three slaves per cafetal, whereas in 1841 that number increased to an average of seventy-five slaves. A look at some cafetales in the area will further illuminate the shifts that were occurring and what the padrón of 1808 suggests.

The 1833 death of Francisco de Bengoechea, owner of the cafetal San Francisco (also known as cafetal Liberal), occasioned an inventory of the Cayajabos farm. The plantation consisted of six caballerías of land covered with 155,000 productive coffee bushes, along with another 240,000 younger plants. A total of 143 slaves tended the fields, 80 of whom were males and 63 females. In other words, women made up 44 percent of the total. The proportion of African-born and creole slaves was similar, with 82 slaves de nación and 61 island-born; that is, 43 percent of the group were creoles. The members of the African populace on the San Francisco were in their prime years, with an average age of 28.75 years, while the youthful creoles averaged 6.75 years. It is evident that the slaves of the San Francisco were not only agriculturally productive but also producing significant numbers of offspring.[80]

The population on the San Francisco declined as it continued to undergo change in the years following the death of Bengoechea. In 1841 a new inventory of the farm showed the slave contingent had decreased by 31 people to a total of 112.[81] As the group became collectively older and more creolized, females became the majority. The average age increased from 19.33 years to 21.25 years for the total population on the farm. The age of African-born slaves of the San Francisco increased most dramatically, from 28.75 to 40 years, while the average for creoles rose from 6.75 years to 9.5. Creolization of the group continued, expanding by 19 percent to 61.6 percent of the total. The rate of increase also rose from 2 percent to 5 percent.[82] Females constituted 53 percent of the slaves on the cafetal San Francisco circa 1841. They outnumbered males in both African-born and creole categories—23 to 20 and 36 to 33, respectively.[83] The alterations the San Francisco populace underwent reflected wider trends, including the decline of the importation of slaves during the latter half of the 1830s. It also showed some of the distinctiveness of the coffee experience. Plantation owners typically regulated their slave holdings to maximize production on their farms. Rising percentages of women indicate that planters recognized that females could be used profitably on cafetales and they therefore did not try to circumvent the natural transformation toward a sex-balanced population that the process of creolization produced on individual farms. The cafetal Mariana offers an additional look at a mature plantation in Cayajabos.

The death of the planter José Rubio Campos, owner of the cafetal Mariana, occasioned an inventory for the purpose of settling his estate in 1834. The Mariana reached maturity earlier than the San Francisco, as evidenced by the contours of its population. There were 101 slaves living and working on the farm, 60 percent of whom were creoles. The rate of reproduction, 9.9 percent, far exceeded the presumed measure for Cuban slaves of 2.1 percent.[84] The high number of creoles during a period when slave imports continued to rise indicates that the farm no longer required large inputs of labor from external sources, but was an establishment that had reached stability in both production and population. The other mark of distinctiveness was the distribution of the sexes. Cafetal Mariana also had a majority female populace, with a proportion of 56 percent of the total. Women and girls constituted 52.5 percent of slaves de nación and 59 percent of the creoles.[85] These indicators were closely linked. They represent a relationship between the way in which planters shaped their dotaciones and the requisite labor of coffee cultivation and production that enabled populations on cafetales to begin to reproduce at a rate that shifted farm demography. With a slightly narrower initial ratio of males to females on cafetales vis-à-vis ingenios and trapiches, coupled with less demanding labor throughout the course of the year, there was an important coincidence of more women and conditions favorable for reproduction.[86] Once begun, the process of creolization accelerated the shift to a balanced sex distribution as observed on the cafetales San Francisco and Mariana. The slave contingent on each farm was shaped according to the needs of the planter and how he or she understood the requirements of specific crops and the capabilities of the workers. This created a pattern of demographic development specific to cafetales throughout the region that moved dotaciones toward a balanced sex distribution and more rapid creolization, while ingenios continued to require new infusions of labor from external sources. A final regional example will lend support to the existence of the pattern of demographic divergence.

Alquízar, located southwest of Havana (between Güira de Melena to its east and Artemisa to its west), was squarely within the coffee zone of the jurisdiction of Havana. Through most of the period under consideration, the town and its surrounding area was part of the jurisdiction of Santiago de las Vegas, which encompassed a large portion of what is today Artemisa province. By 1846 a new jurisdiction, San Antonio de los Baños, was carved out of Santiago de las Vegas, which included Alquízar. In 1829 the Comisión de Estadísticas (Commission of Statistics) described Alquízar as "en terreno llano, seco, y rodeado á imitación de la Artemisa, de agradables y preciosos cafetales" (a flat and dry [i.e., not swampy] land that resembles Artemisa, surrounded by pleasing, lovely cafetales).[87] Planters continued to establish cafetales in the partido, reaching a total of 106 by 1839.[88] Even after the beginning of coffee's decline in the west, as well as the devastating hurricane of 1844, there remained 63 cafetales in the district. Alquízar, along with nearby Güira de Melena, continued to rival Artemisa as the home to the greatest number of coffee farms.[89] Early cafetales in the district included the Delicias, founded by the conde de Mompox y Jaruco, Joaquín de Santa Cruz y Cárdenas, and the Bagatela and Novedad, owned by José de Fuertes.[90] The latter two farms were inventoried during the early 1830s to establish their value for sale, providing a record of the properties and their slaveholdings.

The Bagatela was the larger and more extensively planted of the two farms, with 9.25 caballerías of land, over 200,000 coffee bushes, and a dotación of 135 slaves. The Novedad consisted of 8.5 caballerías of land but had only about

50,000 coffee bushes with a nursery for growing young plants, and an enslaved population of 20 persons. An analysis of the Bagatela reveals that the creole population was 44 percent of the total. Among the creoles were both adults (those of working age) and children—forty and twenty individuals respectively. Also, of the twenty children, seven were under the age of one, indicating an approximate fertility rate of 5 percent. There were fifty-three females on the Bagatela, or 39 percent of the total number of slaves. Of the African-born slaves, 35.6 percent were women, while 43.5 percent of the creoles were female. Creolization was moving the farm toward a balanced distribution of the sexes. The figures for the Bagatela are generally consistent with those of the earlier examples, though they do not seem entirely consistent with what I have argued was the coffee norm. The reason for this was that the Bagatela had a portion of its agricultural attention directed to sugar production, as it maintained a trapiche. Therefore, a number of the slaves on the farm were devoted to sugar cane cultivation and processing, which altered the demography of the cafetal so that it straddled the coffee and sugar configurations.[91] The Novedad offers a look at a small farm, with its twenty slaves. This group was evenly balanced, with ten males and ten females. There were three young slaves, a boy and two girls under the age of ten years, but all were listed as "de campo" (i.e., old enough to work in the fields). The dotación was 35 percent creole, with half of the male population being island-born but only the two girls under ten years old being of local birth. The Novedad is an important example because it illustrates that even very small slave populations on cafetales had high proportions of females and could reach sex parity.[92]

Implications of the Demographic Shift on Cafetales

These elements all had important implications for the slaves who lived and worked in San Marcos/Artemisa, Puerto de la Güira, and the surrounding area. Their experience of slavery more closely resembled what they might have expected of slave life in Africa, in which they were able to live and work in a stable environment, raising their own food, establishing relationships both among themselves and with the slaveholding class, and having children: in short, they lived a more "normal" life than their counterparts in other circumstances. This also would have important implications both in the short and long terms.

The single most important aspect of the demographic difference or closer gender parity on cafetales was the construction of family units. Adult slaves living on cafetales could more easily find mates and produce children than their counterparts on ingenios. Increased numbers of children reduced owner dependence on slave imports, thereby leading to a more rapid creolization of the population. This also had the self-reinforcing effect of creating a more "balanced" population. The key aspect, though, was the rate of creolization. The slaves on coffee plantations throughout much of the period under consideration experienced more stable conditions, lived in family groups, and produced larger numbers of offspring. The environment for families on the cafetal not only facilitated more children but also the production of a new creole culture. These elements also were self-supporting, containing the seeds within themselves to ensure continuation, sustaining and creating cultural forms as well as the means, in the creole children, to carry those practices into the future. This process was at work across the region, where tens of thousands of slaves lived and worked on cafetales. When this entire population is considered in light of the processes that were at work, we can begin to see the importance of understanding the complexity of the demography of plantations and to imagine the cultural impact that the development of this distinct segment of the Cuban slave population had on the development of nascent group identifications among people of African heritage and the influence they would bring to bear on the larger Cuban culture.

It is beyond the scope of this work, but one of the consequences of imbalanced sex ratios on ingenios in conjunction with the brutalizing labor regime sugar planters instituted was that there were few children on sugar farms. Conversely, this meant that the decision by planters and certain advocates in government to promote the dominance of the role of sugar in constructing an export trade led to continued dependence not only on slavery but also on the transatlantic slave trade or other sources of imported labor. This would later include the Chinese coolie trade instituted in midcentury. The path that led to increasing reliance on slave imports also left the economic fortunes of Cubans vulnerable to the dependency that resulted from a shift toward a single export crop.

Throughout the island, all plantations and their enslaved populations underwent a transformation over the course of the first several decades of the nineteenth century, from mostly African and male to mostly creole and more gender balanced. What makes the experience of owners and slaves on cafetales different from that of those on other types of farms was when this transformation took place. For the other great plantation crop of Cuba—sugar—the shift occurred after midcentury and accelerated following the first steps toward abolition in the 1870s. On cafetales, rising numbers of women and creoles were a part of the process of plantation maturation, most notably during the 1830s and 1840s, while the illegal slave trade continued to flourish and slaveholders on ingenios continued to import large numbers of African-born workers. This fundamental difference created a distinctive environment on coffee farms that shaped the lives and experiences of slaves. Labor and daily life also had characteristics specific to coffee cultivation; these were not only fitted to the particular crop but were also in a dynamic relationship with the changing slave population. As the numbers of women and children expanded, they affected how the plantation operated, which in turn altered the experiences of everyone on the farm. Cafetales and the coffee districts became islands of family life amid the male-dominated enclaves of the ingenios. That is not to say that coffee plantations were pictures of domestic bliss. On the contrary, they, like other enterprises based on coerced labor, were sites of brutality and cruelty, resistance and rebellion. Nevertheless, cafetales presented slaves with a unique environment, with opportunities for personal and collective survival through biological and cultural creativity and construction. The following chapters will explore the day-to-day experiences of slaves on coffee farms—how they worked, how they challenged the intentions of those who held them in bondage, and how they encountered life. This will broaden our understanding of slavery as well as completing the groundwork for a look at how slaves on cafetales expressed themselves "positively" and "negatively" through music, religion, and violence.

Conclusion

The rise of coffee plantations in Cuba and their subsequent expansion was fueled by desire on both sides of the Atlantic. On the eastern shore, the Spanish Crown strove for many years to create a system in the colonies that was both profitable and self-sustaining. To that end, they devised the intendancy system and instituted a series of directives aimed at restructuring and reorganizing the political and economic framework of colonial Spain—first in Cuba and then throughout the region. These efforts came to be known as the Bourbon reforms. For their part, those on the western side of the Atlantic, like their counterparts in Spain, wanted profits, but they also wanted freedom of trade or enterprise. Leaders, both in Spain and in Cuba, laid the groundwork on which planters and slaves would build the plantation economy of the island. During the legal and economic restructuring, men such as Francisco Arango y Parreño and Pablo Boloix advocated for diversity in the new economy and put coffee forward as a good companion crop to sugar and tobacco, one that could become another source of prosperity. They also worked to disseminate information and argued for a model of the cafetal that was structured and reflected a distinctive style while also being efficient. Their work, coupled with the reforms, made possible the explosive growth that was to come in the vuelta abajo. The shape of the cafetal as they imagined it would have a lasting impact on the culture of Cuba.

The founders of cafetales largely followed the advice of Laborie, Boloix, and the examples set by French immigrants to Cuba and planned their new farms to be representations of economic design and sensory appeal. The presentation of an ideal coupled with widespread realization of the model contributed to a romanticization of the cafetales as the gardens of Cuba. The verdant and orderly coffee farms, with their wide variety of fruit-bearing and flowering trees and plants situated in the lush countryside of the vuelta abajo, were celebrated on the island and in many other countries in art and literature. Acclamation of the region created a cultural legacy that has continued to inform Cubans throughout succeeding generations. One of the legacies of the cafetales was that as a part of the plantation boom, efforts by planters also put into motion all the legal and economic mechanisms that rapidly expanded the population of African slaves on the island.

As the plantation complex on the island prospered, slave traders increased the flow of slaves to the island, and cafetal owners, now numbering in the hundreds, purchased Africans in larger quantities. Thousands of African-born slaves lived and worked on the coffee farms of western Cuba and their labor brought the coffee complex to maturity. As the farms and the region became fully established, productive cafetaleros began to reshape their slaveholdings. By the fourth decade of the century, the demographic makeup of the coffee region and its farms was diverging from the island's sugar plantations. More and more women lived and worked on coffee farms, creating a more balanced sex ratio. This also led to the births of more creole children on the plantations. As a result, the region of the island creolized more rapidly—approximately twenty-five years earlier—than other developed areas. This transformation would have profound effects on the lives of the slaves on the cafetales and in the subsequent generations. It would also have a lasting impact on the development of culture and identifications throughout the island in ways that continue to resonate.

PART II

Branches

The Negotiations of Life on the Cafetal

The rhythms of life on the cafetales, like all rhythms, had points of emphasis and periods of rest, and like the music that arose out of the cultural ingredients brought together during the period of the plantation boom, some activities were directed and some were created spontaneously by the "players." Gaps in directed activities or slippage in the structure created by slaveholders opened up space for slaves to exercise agency. It was in these day-to-day moments that men and women in bondage shaped time, space, and conceptions of identifications according to their own designs. It was during these "free" times that slaves grew their own food, made goods, engaged in commerce, and practiced cultural forms such as dance, music, and religion. It was in the physical spaces of the plantation that the enslaved began to retake possession of themselves by asserting new personal and group identifications. These representations found expression in and through slave actions against their oppressors.

The primary reason plantation owners held slaves was to exploit their labor. It was the overriding aspect of the slave system as well as the chief element in ordering the daily lives of enslaved workers on individual plantations. It was through the labor of slaves that the wealth of planters, the colony of Cuba, and the Spanish empire were created. Planters and officials understood this relationship and therefore managed the larger complex in ways to elicit compliant behavior from those they sought to keep in subjugation. Fully utilizing the labor of slaves meant keeping them busy, fully occupying their time to minimize the opportunities slaves had to act in their own interests. In other words, an important aspect of managing slaves was to keep them pacified, which owners tried to do by filling slaves' time with as much work as possible. Slaveholders were able to accomplish many of their goals, as evidenced by the extensive system of plantations established in Cuba. Nevertheless, their control was not absolute, as they found it impractical or inefficient to utilize or manage every minute of the time of their slaves. Slaves, for their part, quickly seized on whatever opportunities were available. They filled up any time left to them with their own activities, creating a counterpoint to the owner-imposed rhythms of the cafetal. Growing food, raising animals, and other activities contributed to the lives of slaves materially and cognitively. The production of food and other goods enabled slaves to contribute to their own well-being and created a way into the larger system of commerce. This benefited them by improving their diets and their economy, which in turn provided hope and a way of resistance against their enslavement.

It is evident that work played a significant role in how slaves experienced life on the farm. The spaces in which activities occurred also played an important part on the cafetales. Slaveholders sought to exercise control over space in much the same way they dominated time on plantations. Masters and their agents defined where activities were conducted through a classification process that delineated the uses of both buildings and open areas. The positioning of structures and the development and cultivation of selected areas on the canvas of the farm enabled planters to shape the relationships between types of buildings and types of land, as well as between land and buildings. The entire farm was a built environment constructed through the imagined design of the owner. A product of this process was the somewhat slippery or contested delineation between areas that were well-controlled by slaveholders and those places where slaves exercised some control over their own time and activities. These areas included both housing or living spaces and the fields and wooded lots of the farm.

Slaveholders directed the configuration and style of the places of habitation, but slaves inhabited them. Bohíos and *barracones* (barracks) dotted the landscape and suggested the ordering that owners intended—but within the walls and behind the doors, slaves lived their lives. Bohíos and open barracones contributed to the lived experiences of slaves by both their arrangement or style, and by their persistence vis-à-vis *barracones de patio* (enclosed barracks), which predominated on ingenios much earlier. To be sure, slaves did not control their own activities and spaces in any sort of absolute way. Instead, their actions and these places were sites of contestation in which slaves fought with their rulers for important physical and cognitive territory that marked the boundaries of self and group identification that the slaves were refashioning. It was within their living spaces that slaves produced the accoutrements of cultural and religious practices and made plans for the future. In the fields, they not only cultivated the crops that enhanced their diets and created commercial opportunities, but they also performed acts of social significance. The ways in which slaves experienced life on the cafetal were interwoven with the intentionality of both the master and the slave, which created a complex structure of warp and woof, or give and take. As long as each position was in balance, the farm operated relatively smoothly, giving the appearance of dominant master and submissive workers. If the slaveholder or his managers overstepped the boundaries of proper behavior and demands, slaves responded with active resistance or violence.

Slaves on coffee plantations were connected to the farms on which they lived through the process of investing themselves in the construction of new lives. By forming families, raising children, and participating in group activities beyond the scope of plantation labor, slaves actively reconstructed and reconfigured their lives. Slaveholders intended that their workers feel rooted in their land to foster a compliant labor force. But by establishing relatively balanced dotaciones and leaving enough physical and cognitive spaces, planters unintentionally created the grounds on which a new creole generation and culture could emerge. The unintended consequence of cultivating an identification between the slaves and the land was to promote a sense of ownership among the enslaved that transcended the legal constructs of Spanish jurisprudence. This is not to say that slaves conceived of land ownership in the same way planters did. Rather, the inhabitants who worked the land for themselves and their masters, and who lived on the land, experienced a sense of possession or rootedness in a way that lent itself to the imagination of community.

With a sense of family and group identification or community, slaves demonstrated individual and collective claims of social values and identifications. The construction and subsequent establishment of families and group collectivities engendered a sense of possessing place. This empowered slaves to act in ways that revealed their notions of propriety. A sense of proper action included not only acting within the bounds of acceptable social behavior among the enslaved population but also included the free members of the community. Moreover, if owners or their agents transgressed these embedded codes, slaves felt justified in seeking redress through whatever means they had at their disposal. Slaves with an emerging sense of individual and collective self also were concerned with improper unseen behaviors that were understood to manifest themselves visibly through disease and in other ways. These also elicited actions by slave populations. When collective identification reached a critical mass among slaves on coffee plantations, they could act demonstrably to try to restore balance, or to reach a larger goal, such as striking a blow against the slave system for freedom.

The chapters of Part II build on the core ideas that the slaves had time for self-directed activities and a distinctive population profile and argues that slaves challenged the intentions of slaveholders in a variety of ways. Enslaved Africans recovered elements of their lives and began to shape their own cultures both intentionally and passively. These emerging local cultures began to coalesce into a nascent Afro-Cuban culture that they were able to pass on to succeeding generations, thereby forming one of the key elements of Cuban culture. Chapter 3 engages the built environment of the plantation to take up this theme. Plantation owners of cafetales and ingenios similarly configured their farms in the early development of each type of farm. As each complex matured, they diverged in organization, with each taking on distinct characteristics. Coffee farms most often retained a looser organization, while sugar farms became more regimented. Housing differed, as did slave access to land. Slaveholders designed their farms to create a compliant and productive work force. Slaves, for their part, subverted the environment they were compelled to build to suit their own purposes. They made some of the spaces of the plantation their own and these zones became neo-African. Living spaces, some of the working areas, and personal areas of cultivation became the sites of cultural production and organization. The chapter takes a multidisciplinary approach by drawing on the scholarship of cultural geography and cultural theory to understand how intentions are mapped on to local structures, places, and actions. Through the behaviors of slaves, we can see how they challenged and subverted owners' efforts to shape attitudes and behaviors. The ways slaves enacted these activities are the subjects of the following chapters.

Chapter 4 explores how a variety of religious practices were central to the lives of the enslaved. Some activities looked more obviously religious to observers while others were less transparent, such as practices embedded in music and dance. These latter actions were the subject of much debate among slaveholders and officials, which offers us an opening to understand how slaves acted and also what owners thought and hoped to achieve. Slaves on the coffee plantations of western Cuba were actively engaged in religious practices that reflected not only their diverse African roots but also their new contexts. This speaks to debates surrounding African cultural survivals and the construction of neo-African identities in the Western Hemisphere. The chapter argues for a nuanced view of slave actions, which constituted remembrances and re-imaginings of the past that were imbued with new meanings.

Slaves on coffee farms also engaged in extensive commercial activities. While it is evident that the plantations were economic endeavors, slaves were active in this arena. This has been often overlooked but will be explored in Chapter 5. Owners of farms intended for the slaves on their plantations to be productive workers who attended to the main economic activity of the plantation. Slaves also subverted owners' intentions in this area of plantation life by creating their own systems of commerce. On many cafetales, slaves grew their own food, raised animals, and at times sold the products of their labor to the slaveholder. In addition, during this period there were traveling vendors with whom slaves exchanged goods, creating a broader network of commerce as well as social interaction in the region. These commercial interactions enabled the enslaved to engage in the Spanish system of *coartación*, a system of self-purchase, in numbers that suggest an extensive commercial system. This system also created a web of interactions that facilitated other kinds of activities, such as planning collective actions.

An area that has had some attention by scholars over the last several years has been slave revolts and rebellions.[1] Very few studies, though, have linked the crop under cultivation or type of plantation with incidents of revolt or how and why rebellions occurred.[2] Chapter 6 argues that incidents of revolt were higher on cafetales in large part because of the cultural factors discussed in the previous chapters. Slaves were actively creating culture and living in ways that fostered community. They also had time and resources that slaves on other farms did not often have. What this chapter shows is that there was an inverse relationship between expectations and revolts and that conditions on coffee plantations tended to raise expectations for enslaved workers. In addition, the chapter explores the relationship between the decline of coffee in the 1840s and increasing incidents of revolt. This chapter looks at cultural, structural, and economic explanations for specific revolts and rebellions in western Cuba and offers a model for understanding other incidents.

CHAPTER 3

Space Is the Place
Intentions and Subversion of Design

In the piazza of the house, on the basement story, were forty
negroes, sorting coffee into three parcels—good, inferior, and
bad. They were fine looking negroes, lusty and muscular, and
of contented countenances. Most of them were singing in a low
tone; one leading, and several responding in chorus, as in the
water-song of Carolina. —Abiel Abbot

Slaves experienced life on cafetales in multiple ways that were shaped by
those who held them in bondage, by the physical environment—both the
built and the "natural"—and by their own actions. Slavery was first and
foremost a system of labor exploitation. And it was slaves who built the hundreds of cafetales that covered the land of western Cuba. They toiled to transform the region from its beginnings as virgin land into the fertile and profitable
showplace it would become. With coffee farms, this would not be an overnight
project, but one that required planning and patience. As we have seen, it was a
four- to five-year commitment of capital from the time a planter acquired land
and slaves, and axes were laid to trees, until a cafetal began to produce a mar-
ketable crop of coffee. The work of establishing a new farm, as described in
Chapter 2, was extensive and rigorous, but once the initial list of tasks was completed—the fields cleared, cleaned, and planted, other seedings of fruit trees and
vegetables undertaken, and basic infrastructure built—the day-to-day routine of
cafetal life began in earnest. While it was the slaves who built the physical structures of the plantation, it was planters who actively defined the spaces of the
plantation and worked to erect the cognitive structure that was an important part
of shaping the lives of their slaves. As productive cafetales emerged, owners
expanded their slaveholdings, reshaping plantation demography, and instituted
management practices that governed the time and labor of their dotaciones.

The presence of women in increasing numbers on coffee plantations underscores the nature of work on these farms as well as how coffee labor was understood by slaveholders. Many tasks associated with the commercial production of
coffee beans for export required stamina and dexterity rather than sheer physical strength. Women and even children often excelled at harvesting or picking
the fruit of the coffee bush, cleaning the harvest, and sorting the dried beans.
These three aspects of the production process, along with weeding, were the

chores that required the greatest number of workers. It is evident from the shifting demography of the region that planters realized that women could be valuable contributors to a productive workforce and that they did not need to rely on a predominantly male dotaciones. This realization was reflected in the steadily expanding ranks of female slaves on cafetales.

The daily regime on coffee farms created a distinct rhythm to life. The bell that marked the beginning of each day, the review and assignment of work by the overseer, working together in groups large and small—all these created patterns of habit among the subaltern. Masters and their agents had developed an understanding of the demands of the plants their slaves were cultivating. Slaveholders and the needs of the crop, as they were understood, together shaped the day-to-day routine of workers in both intended and unintended ways.[1] The types of jobs managers scheduled to be performed located coffee labor between the poles of the task and gang labor continuum.[2] Some of the toil on coffee farms was executed using gang labor while other work allowed for the use of the task system. This marked another divergence from the more highly structured environment found on sugar cane farms, which featured an almost exclusive use of gang labor. Daily work was in large part formulated and regulated through its interaction with the yearly cycle of tasks that constituted the productive organization of coffee plantation agriculture.

It is evident that work played a significant role in how slaves experienced life on the farm. The spaces in which activities occurred also was important in the lives of those bonded on cafetales. Masters instructed their workers in the creation of highly structured and fully articulated areas of cultivation and production. In addition, owners delineated the zones for slave habitation and self-directed work. Most cafetaleros allowed their workers to continue to live in bohíos or modified types of barracones throughout the period under consideration. The earlier shift toward barracks housing on ingenios underscores the distinctiveness of the coffee experience. Masters within the coffee enclave created their own paradigm of labor management, which was manifested in the physical spaces of the plantations, exemplified in the ongoing use of bohíos, and embodied in their dotaciones. They pursued what they considered to be the most effective ways of controlling their laborers with the aim of constructing and maintaining a compliant workforce. Controlling time, space, and physical bodies all contributed to the larger goal of profit and stability.

The contours of the plantation constrained and shaped the lives and minds of slaves in many ways. Labor and environment interacted in ways that molded consciousness to inscribe the limits of action and the possibilities of personal and group identification. Planters actively pursued a variety of methods of control, as they understood that their success in creating and managing a compliant workforce depended as much on the effective deployment of psychological power as it did on the use of violence. That is not to say that the efforts of slaveholders were seamless in application or effectiveness. Their manipulation of the work regime and farm environment also created openings and opportunities. While much of daily life was controlled and supervised, there were always gaps the enslaved could fill with activities and imaginations of their own designs. Any time or space that was not actively engaged by masters or their agents was contested or controlled, at least in a limited way, by slaves. These possibilities for action created the opportunities for expression and creation that will be explored in subsequent chapters. This chapter will investigate the structural elements of the coffee plantation system and aspects of life during the boom years in western Cuba that molded, constrained, and opened spaces in the lived experience of slaves. In the end, one of the most important areas of struggle was the contestation of space. Spatial control marked the coercive slave/master relationship.

Disease, though not a human-created or imposed element, was nevertheless a powerful variable in structuring the lives of slaves both at the individual and group levels, and it played a role in interpersonal dynamics. The problem for planters and slaves alike in accounting for disease was that it was a constant concern while being unpredictable and irregular in its frequency and the intensity of symptoms. Slaves were disproportionately affected by illness as a result of their limited diet, long hours, and living conditions. The effects of pathogens were amplified within the population as a consequence of their interaction with the structures of slave life erected by the slave-owning class. The most important widespread example of the impact of disease during the period was the cholera epidemic of the early 1830s. Thousands of deaths at all levels of society resulted from the widespread outbreak, but patterns of mortality suggest that housing arrangements significantly altered the spread of the disease. The persistence of the bohío on cafetales had an important ancillary consequence for slaves.

The spaces of the plantation outlined the tensions of the master/slave relationship. Slaveholders designed plantations to function in particular ways and to shape their slaves' behavior and attitudes. This was realized through the types and arrangement of structures on the farm and also by defining how these enclosed and open spaces of the farm were to be used. Permissible and desired actions were communicated and enforced. Tensions within the relationship arose because of slave resistance to the intentions of the slaveholder. Slaves lived and worked in the spaces masters sought to define but through their occupation and use they made those spaces their own in many ways. Slave resistance to slaveholder intentions found many expressions but it began with redefining spaces and actions and making physical spaces their own and refusing to surrender the cognitive space that slaveholders sought to control.

Structure beyond Labor

An important way in which the lives of slaves were shaped by the plantation experience was through the spatial organization of the farm. In other words, slaves experienced plantation life through their interaction with the physical structures and spaces of the cafetal. Slave housing was arguably the single most important material element ultimately controlled by masters that constructed the contours of slave life. Two aspects pertaining to housing were most significant: the type of housing, and its location vis-à-vis the other buildings on the farm. By directing slaves into bohíos, and later, modified barracones, masters created conditions that allowed for a refiguring of African norms in a number of important ways that would have far-reaching consequences both for demographic change and for the reimagining of personal and group identifications as well as cultural practices. The location of the slave quarters was also significant in that the proximity and orientation to the gaze of oversight contributed to the internalizing of the limits and strictures of control by slaves.

The concerns of owners, as well as local common practice, drove the choice of housing on plantations. The use of provision grounds, while initially not peculiar to coffee farms, was more closely related to the type of housing used on a particular farm. The evaluation by an owner of the balance between the benefits derived from slave food production, on the one hand, and the lower level of control of slave movements and time, on the other, figured into the decision. Slave production of food crops will be discussed further later. Plantation housing fell into two types: bohíos, which were either huts or individuals' cottages, or barracones, barracks as slave quarters. On most plantations in Cuba during the early years of the plantation boom, the bohío was the preferred type of housing. Owners required slaves to build their own quarters and provided only limited time and materials for the task. A slave-constructed bohío, often described as a "crude shack," was typically built of stakes (cut from the thin branches of available trees, or from bamboo) that were interwoven with leaves and covered by a thatched roof. Unfinished earthen floors were the norm. In addition, a door was often present.[3] Slaves, for their part, built shelters and organized them much as they would have done in their homelands, given similar materials. In the ensuing decades, as owners and their plantations became more firmly established economically, owners instructed their slaves to erect structures of greater durability and permanence—from limestone, if it was available, or from wood. These new buildings evolved in one of two ways. In some cases, they continued to be separate dwellings. In other cases, they were individual dwellings built in long rows and connected by common walls. This latter type was an open-style barracón. Planter Edwin Atkins described the open barracón as "long double rows of stone huts with streets between."[4] The cafetal Perseverancia, with a dotación of seventy-three, fits the model of a plantation increasing in size and development, for by 1842 it had an open or modified barracón.[5]

Housing choice, dictated by the masters, was a significant way in which slave owners shaped the lives of the people they considered their property. Their aims were efficiency, profit, and security. This was true for plantation owners of all types, but how they sought their ends differed in ways that correlated both to the type of crop and the size of plantation. Coffee farms on average were smaller than sugar farms and larger than tobacco *vegas*, contributing to their distinctive configurations.[6] The continued use of bohíos and the slower transition to barracones was a choice made by owners for a variety of reasons. The expense of constructing a fortified barracón may have figured most prominently in the decision, but the benefits of lower cost and greater opportunity for slave food production as well as the relatively lower risks engendered by the smaller dotaciones of the cafetales were certainly significant. Above all, though, planter actions tended toward creating conditions to produce wealth while generating a compliant and loyal workforce, which reveals their concerns and also their recognition, at least in part, of the humanity of their enslaved workforce. Fredrika Bremer directly observed such sentiments in her travels in Cuba. A planter named Phinney and another identified as "señor D." both told her that they felt it was necessary to treat their slaves "justly" to elicit a more compliant response from their workers.[7] This comment seems to go beyond the typical framing of slavery by slaveholders as a beneficial institution for all involved—including the slaves—in which slavery is depicted as a moderate and mild institution aimed at controlling uncivilized peoples.[8] Rather, this appears to be a more self-reflective comment that shows an understanding of the range of treatment slaves suffered at the hands of slaveholders and their agents, and an awareness that more evenhanded tactics will produce more productive slaves and in turn create more profits for the slaveholder. Managing the labor of slaves and their time (both work and "free") as well as the structural elements of the plantation was an important aspect of the systems of control planters and their agents exercised on the coffee farms of western Cuba.

Slaves living in bohíos had more freedom of movement, both by design and as an effect of the types and arrangement of the structures. From an owner's perspective, this situation facilitated slave access to *conucos* (provision grounds), enabling the workers to transition easily from the assigned work of the day to the tending of their food crops. This openness, though, also created more privacy and freedom to move beyond what was proscribed. Slaves were often reported to visit other nearby plantations or cities and towns. Their travels were for a variety of reasons, including socializing, engaging in religious practices (including drumming and dancing), engaging in commerce, and on occasion plotting and carrying out revolts. These activities will be explored in later chapters. For slaveholders, this was clearly a trade-off in a number of ways, but more often than not, cafetaleros maintained open housing systems well into the nineteenth century. Examples are abundant and include cafetales such as the Recompensa, the Perseverancia, the Salvador, the Catelina [*sic*], the Juanita, and the Valiente, just to name a few.[9] The persistence of bohíos also was noted by many travel writers, such as Fredrika Bremer, Mme. Calderón de la Barca, Mary Gardner Lowell, and Mary Peabody Mann.[10]

As plantation populations expanded, some owners began to experiment with closed barracks housing as a more secure means of sheltering their slaves. Also known as the *barracón de patio*, enclosed barracks were built around an interior courtyard with a single gated opening into the enclosed area. The single point of ingress and egress permitted the overseer to lock the slaves in at night and monitor their movements more closely.[11] The shift to the closed barracón was more frequent on sugar cane plantations than on coffee farms because of the relative size and attendant perception of a greater need to control the growing numbers of enslaved. Coffee farms, meanwhile, were typically smaller than cane plantations, with an average dotación size in the vuelta abajo region of slightly less than fifty slaves for the period under consideration. On most of these farms, the bohío system continued in use until the latter half of the 1830s, when the use of open barracones began to grow. The owners of cafetales that turned to the barracón did so for reasons similar to those of their counterparts on ingenios, as a means of controlling their expanding population. As this usage expanded, especially during the 1840s, it seems to have been in response to wider pressures rather than population on individual farms, since most cafetaleros did not favor the enclosed barracón—with only a few notable exceptions. As the coffee district became more densely populated along with the broader region, more owners became concerned with the potential problems posed by systems of control that could be perceived as lax.[12] Farms that grew to a size that rivaled the largest ingenios constructed barracones de patio. Angerona, with over four hundred slaves, used a barracón that included a watchtower, revealing the understood motivation of security. Contemporary Cuban author Cirilo Villaverde remarked that the barracón construction of Angerona reminded him of a prison with its enclosed walls and guard tower.[13]

A creative response to growing population was simultaneously using a closed barracón and bohíos to house the approximately 350 slaves of the cafetal Salvador. Francisco Aguirre owned the Salvador, a mature coffee farm near the town of Banes, north of the vuelta abajo region along the road leading to the port town of Mariel. The dotación of approximately 125 slaves had been living and working on the Salvador for some time, and these longer-term workers lived in bohíos. Aguirre also had acquired nearly 225 new slaves who were living on the cafetal in August 1833. These recently arrived slaves were housed in a barracón, nearby but separate from the bohíos. While there are numerous questions concerning this unique population, it is evident that Aguirre considered these new slaves a potential risk to flee or rebel, or both. This is evidenced by their separate housing and the actions of the mayoral in locking the slaves into the barracón at night while allowing the long-term population to continue to live in the more open environment of the bohíos.[14]

The physical structures and their use were symbols of the control exercised by the master and his agents. Slaves interacted with these representations of power every day. Moreover, the relationship of the structures with one another actively created the space in which the objects of domination, both the buildings and the slaves, resided. James A. Delle and B. W. Higman both argue that the location of buildings on a plantation had an underlying rationale of control of space.[15] Delle advances two important concepts in the articulation of plantation systems of control. These ideas are what he calls the "spatiality of movement" and the "spatiality of surveillance."[16] The spatiality of movement, according to

Figure 3.1. The guard tower at cafetal Angerona.
Photo courtesy of David C. Carlson

Delle, consists of two types of actions by slaves: sanctioned and illicit. The control an owner exercised through his overseer of work hours constituted spatial domination in that the slaves were required, through threat of force, to move into particular areas, such as the plant nursery or fields, to work. Also, granting slaves access to provision grounds extended the control of plantation spaces beyond the production zones.

The spatial control of slaves even extended to areas that were a mixture of sanctioned and unsanctioned actions. Delle's argument differentiates between these two types of actions, with sanctioned actions as those directed by the slaveholder or overseer (*mayoral*), and illicit actions as those undertaken by slaves on their own behalf outside of the control of sanctioning powers. But there are also cases where slaves were used as actors in potentially illegal activities on behalf of the slaveholder or mayoral. These actions potentially would bring the slaves into confrontation with competing or higher powers or authorities who would render their supposed sanctioned actions as illicit. The dispute over slave actions between the owners of the cafetales Acierto and Laborinto, though a small incident, illustrates the difficult situation in which slaves could find themselves. As described in Chapter 2, the mayoral of the Acierto, Ramon Charun, directed its slaves to dump refuse on the neighboring farm, the Laborinto, under cover of darkness. The mayoral of the Laborinto staked out the area, and a confrontation ensued when he encountered the Acierto's slaves. The authorities were informed and investigators subsequently interviewed all those involved, including the slaves. Their testimony reveals several things about slaves' negotiation of power dynamics. At first, some refused to answer questions, while others responded that what had happened was their fault, stating that it was late and they simply had made an error in where they dumped the refuse. Apparently the investigators were suspicious, because they pressed on, and with further questioning, some of the slaves implicated the mayoral. It seems that there was a dispute between the mayorales and the landholders over property lines, but this confrontation put the slaves in a difficult and potentially dangerous situation.[17] Charun used his power to control space and action in his direction of the slaves of the Acierto. The slaves, for their part, initially deferred to Charun's legitimating authority when confronted. But as the investigation progressed, the slaves realized that the authorities from Havana were more powerful and deferred to them. This raises some additional questions about how slaves challenge control and exercise agency. For Delle and Higman, all actions that move beyond the spatial and cognitive control of the slaveholders or their agents constitute moves by a slave or slaves to an illicit space. I contend that this is the type of opening in which slaves as subalterns were able to plot their relative position or proximity to power. This understanding allowed them to navigate between two spheres of domination in order to play one against the other. As an exercise of agency, slaves could situate themselves in a sanctioned space but take an illicit stance vis-à-vis the presence of various authorities.

The demarcation of space by the slaveholders, defining the functions of particular spaces and actions taken in those spaces, was akin to the external inscription of personal or collective identification. In other words, one self-inscribes identifications but is also inscribed by others. The spatial organization of the plantation was defined or inscribed by the slaveholder, but slaves also contested those definitions, meanings, and inscriptions. The same was true for testimony before an authority figure, as in the case of the dispute between the Acierto and the Laborinto. The mayoral defined the actions of the slaves and they accepted the task and its meaning and location as instructed. When called before an authority, they initially used that inscription as cover, but when pressed, they changed their position and contested the previous order. Slaves testifying in an official inquiry most certainly felt constrained out of self-interest to tell those present exactly what they wanted to hear. Such testimonies would therefore constitute resistant texts. Actions and speech by slaves against their masters or of those in power in this context also make these texts of resistance. The slaves of the Acierto, through their rejection of Charun's story, were enacting a performative act of relocation and resistance. The works of Andrew Parker, Eve Kosofsky Sedgwick, and Homi Bhabha may provide clues as to how to understand these situations more clearly.

In examining the performative it is important to establish the idea that saying and doing are coequal as actions of resistance and contestation. This is the conceptual ground of performativity studies, where scholars have grappled with the questions "When is saying something doing something? And how is saying something doing something?"[18] In addition, when is doing something saying something? Parker and Sedgwick, building on the works of J. L. Austin and Jacques Derrida, argue that not only are speech acts and actions interchangeable, they are also clearly tied to expressions of identity. I contend that identification and spatial conceptualizations are intimately connected and mutually constitutive. Significantly, the authors position themselves between Jean-François Lyotard's postmodern notion of efficiency as performative and the radical deconstructionism of Paul de Man, who conceptualizes performativity as a disjuncture between the actor/speaker and the referent. Parker and Sedgwick balance this tension by emphasizing it, pointing to Derrida's reading of Austin and the idea of a distortion between referent, intent, speech act, and reception by the hearers. Derrida's notion of this perversion is based in part on the iterability of a particular speech act. If a performance is to be received as believable, then it has to fall into a frame of reference that the audience can locate and understand; in other words, the act has to resonate with the intended audience in a way that renders the act believable or credible. This idea may be particularly helpful in the context of the trial testimonies of slaves. They had to speak within the parameters acceptable to their slave-owning interrogators for their speech acts to qualify as iterable and credible. These speech acts also had to effect self-affirmation and ring true to fellow slaves in the same context.[19]

Illustrative of the concerns of Parker and Sedgwick is the account of the inquiry into the accusations of a captured *cimarron* (runaway), Manuel *congo*. Upon his capture, Manuel claimed that he had fled his master out of fear of the mayoral, for, he continued, the mayoral had killed one of the slaves, his friend Alejandro. Manuel and several other slaves of Don Pedro Sedano were questioned to determine if Francisco Sosa, the mayoral, had acted inappropriately. The character of their responses shows how they felt compelled to frame their answers within the parameters of credibility acceptable to their interrogators. One of the slaves, Joaquin, would not directly accuse Sosa of abusive behavior. First he located the violence in its appropriate context. He testified that if Sosa had hit Alejandro, it was related to incomplete work. Later, almost as an aside,

Joaquin says that "the mayoral is not a friend [of the slaves] for he strikes people often."[20]

Between these two positions we can see how a slave might accomplish several goals within the context of testimony. On the one hand, he could protect himself by not speaking directly against those above him. This could be achieved by equivocating the actions of their oppressors and placing them near acceptable norms. In this fashion, a slave might indirectly confirm abuse but deflect attacks on himself through an ambivalent response. On the other hand, he can speak credibly to other slaves by locating actions in relation to the entire group, in this case those of the mayoral toward slaves in general. In this way, the slave does not engage the changes directly, but through a secondary comment can ensure his own credibility while subtly confirming the bad character of the accused.

The work of Homi Bhabha penetrates into the workings of colonial power and discourse and the construction and construal of the colonial subject, in this case the enslaved people of colonial Cuba. As slaves worked to reimagine themselves in a new context, they were subject to the power and discursive world of their masters. Bhabha has argued that the display or presence of power is a key element in the ideological collaboration between cultural, political, and economic elements of the colonizer. The particular facet of this relationship that is significant is that the symbols of the colonizer—government authority, church, or plantation—were visible, while the connections between them were obscured by their distance from the source of power. From the slaves' perspective, for example, the church could be viewed as beneficial while the plantation, its master, and his agents were looked on as incursionary. Likewise, the plantation might not have seemed as ominous as an official hearing because of the imminence of power. The symbols of power—the Spanish language, Catholicism, and the law—became "fetishes, spectacles of a 'natural'/racial preeminence."[21] It is precisely the interconnection between visibility and distance that objectifies and normalizes power in the colony, to the subjected. In the courtroom or the setting of an official interrogation, the gap between symbol and source was narrowed and slaves may have perceived more clearly the impact of their own words; thus, they acted more circumspectly. Bhabha's insights would help explain seemingly compliant testimonies and actions in which slaves seemed to accept their status and generally align with authority figures' testimony or with their expectations. This is contradicted by the fact that slaves continued to bring legal actions against masters as well as by the continued presence of cimarrones and the constant fear of revolts exhibited by planters.

Again, the case of the inquiry into the actions of the mayoral, Francisco Sosa, shows the utility of Bhabha's ideas. As the testimony progressed, the questioning veered away from the issue of Alejandro to the issue of what transpired on the morning Manuel fled. Another slave, Cayatano *carabalí*, spoke directly to the question of power, revealing that there had been a test of will between Sosa and Manuel. Cayatano also framed his account with a familiar strategy, claiming that Sosa resorted to violence because Manuel was using *palo monte*, an African-based religious practice, which was why he had defied the mayoral.[22] This tactic of using the discourse of power seems to have been designed to defuse the potency of Manuel's challenge by relegating it to the masters' category of the illogical while at the same time affirming the violent actions of Sosa. In addition, Cayatano used another method to distance himself from this exchange of power. He qualified all his comments by stating that he'd heard this from someone or that from someone else. He never testified that he knew or saw anything himself.[23] This careful maneuvering in the presence of the instruments of power is not as evident when the slaves are further removed from the source—only as they are drawn in closer. It is in this spatial relationship that power is mobilized and challenged in a variety of ways. The contestation of spatial relationships and definitions was the key contested element in slave/slaveholder relationships.

Another element connecting physical space and control with attempting to shape cognitive space was the observation of the slaves. An overseer monitoring the actions of slaves was exercising the spatiality of surveillance. The location of the living quarters of the overseer and the plantation owner was arguably more important than the type of housing. Delle contends that the locations of these structures reflect the ideas discussed by Michel Foucault in *Discipline and Punish*.[24] Foucault, writing about the historical development of the ways prisoners could be controlled, argues that the Benthamite notion of panopticonism, or the organization of space and control to facilitate observation and surveillance, was a key element in conceptualizing architectures of control. By locating observational areas in places where those within could always see those they sought to control and, more importantly, where those under domination thought that they could always be observed, the "functioning of power" would become internalized and "automatic." The uncertainty of not knowing but thinking one might and could be watched caused prisoners to replicate the rules of the prison and remove the need for constant vigilance, since they themselves had become the reproducers of the system of their own control.[25] Likewise, locating the main house and the means of production at the center of the cafetal with the living quarters at the highest point—either on a hill or on the top floor of the storage facility—enabled owners or their agents to watch their slaves at all times or, more importantly, to give the impression that they *could* be watching and all-seeing. Theresa Singleton extends this argument to include the construction of walls that restricted and directed the ability of slaves to move throughout the space of the plantation. She shows that this also facilitated observation.[26] Laborie recommended locating the main house in the center so that it was in view of the coffee works as well as the slave quarters, even if this meant sacrificing some ease of access or resulted in some difficulties in construction.[27] Planters followed this advice to a fault. Few records of cafetales locate the central complex outside of the center of the farm. The Welch cafetal is an example of one that followed the rule of exception outlined by Laborie. He counseled that one ought to take into consideration the location of roads vis-à-vis the slave quarters when designing a plantation layout. Welch situated the building complex away from the center of the land because of the irregular shape of the property and the proximity of a road. The plan of the farm shows a road passing diagonally through the estate. The main house and production complex lay southeast of the road and stood between the avenue and the slave quarters.

There is abundant evidence that plantation owners considered central location and elevation an important factor in spatial organization of the plantation. Bremer notes in her description of the cafetal La Industria that the main house was situated on the highest point, looking out over the slave quarters below and the fields that extended beyond. In addition, she mentions that from the front of the house, and even from within, she could observe the workers passing by to attend to their work for the day.[28] This sort of organization is echoed in the description offered by Ramiro Guerra Sánchez of the cafetal Jesús Nazareno. Guerra Sánchez wrote that the slave quarters were situated so that the workers had to pass in front of the central dwelling whenever they entered or left the *batey* (slave quarters area). He also added that the slaves received their daily assignments by assembling each morning before the house in front of a large crucifix the master had erected.[29]

The most notable case of an exercise of coffee plantation security is on cafetal Angerona. Its tower, as shown in Figure 1, stood before the gateway into the barracón and loomed over the wall that enclosed the slave quarters. The tower, open on all sides, acted as a platform for observation of the slaves both within and outside of the barracks. Mann, in her thinly veiled account of her visit to the Angerona and observation of the workings of the farm, wrote that

> the rules of his [Souchay's] plantation were very rigid, the work he exacted very severe, the punishments for delinquency very terrible when they came. With true Anglo-Saxon sagacity, he saw that slackness of government produced slackness of service in the gentle race he domineered over. If he had tried the plan of giving them some interest in their labors, he might have struck something out of human souls, which hold all germs of motives, that would have made them labor with a will and serve his interests too, but he had not made that innovation with the rest, and even comfortable hospitals and picking rooms did not preclude the necessity of using force to extract the amount of labor he required.[30]

Most likely because of the vast numbers of slaves on the Angerona, Souchay felt the need to exercise his power to articulate a system of control through violence and the threat of violence represented by symbols such as the ever-present guard tower. The use of towers became more common over time in Cuba, especially on large plantations, as has been noted by others.[31]

Planters exercised control not only over the time and work of those in bondage but also by directing the construction of the physical spaces in which slaves lived and worked. Both the design and use of structures acted as limits of action on the workers on coffee farms. Moreover, the spatial relationships of land and structures were manipulated by owners to create a malleable group of laborers for their own exploitation. The various aspects of structure on the farm were used as elements in a system of social control. Articulation of labor, from daily duties to seasonal tasks, and the material spaces in which the enslaved lived their lives went a long way toward the goal of creating a compliant workforce. The system that masters and their agents constructed rested on an ever-present threat of violence. Nevertheless, all of the measures slaveholders used to shape the world of their slaves, which created an underlying force or momentum that made resistance difficult, lacked sufficient persuasive power without the lingering knowledge and fear of swift and brutal reprisal. The complex conditions on cafetales thus created conflicted spaces and discourses. On the one hand, planters used powerful structural elements and force to create systems of control. On the other hand, they also often relied on open housing structures and allowed slaves to direct their own activities for several hours a day, thus creating spaces for contestation of slaveholder order. This systemic contradiction is evident in the production of food by slaves on the plantation.

Food Production as a Structural Element

On most cafetales the evidence points toward slaves growing crops to feed themselves. This model of food production was promulgated by Laborie in his idealized vision of a well-designed coffee plantation and echoed throughout the limited literature that addressed the cafetales. Slaves were given space and time to produce food for their own consumption, thus in one way replicating the conditions many experienced outside of bondage. At the same time, as this was production enforced by their conditions, it was both a hegemonic act of consumption but could also act as a site of resistance. For the planters this model served a dual purpose. It both reduced capital outlay for provisions, as mentioned in Chapter 2, and also served to further articulate the labor regime on the farm. Owners sought to keep their workers busy both to utilize their labor fully and to minimize their unstructured time, thereby reducing opportunities to plan acts of insubordination. Laborie argued that slaves who were required to grow their own food would gain an attachment to the land on which they lived and worked. This connection would benefit the owner by creating a loyal workforce who felt they shared in the mission of the farm and were sharing in the benefits of their labor.[32]

If owners required their slaves to produce their own food, this meant that the plantation managers had to allot land and time so that slaves could establish and tend crops on provision grounds, as food production land for the enslaved was called. This also implied that slaves had to have freedom of access to the fields. In addition, land was also often made available for keeping animals such as chickens and pigs. These elements were facilitated by the open village-style housing system represented by the bohío. The use of individual dwellings, bohíos, in an open setting provided slaves with unfettered access to fields and livestock that needed daily attention. Long-term use of bohíos allowed cafetaleros to realize cost benefits, though at the risk of reduced security. Owners must have calculated that the positives outweighed the possible negatives, as reflected in the ongoing and persistent use of bohíos on cafetales. The use of bohíos continued on many farms throughout the period, but as some farms expanded or as concerns about security grew, there was a shift to open barracones and in a few cases enclosed barracones, such as on the Angerona, as mentioned earlier. Security and monitoring the slaves always was balanced by other necessities. The motivation for owners to reduce costs and productively keep slaves engaged usually was the deciding factor in housing arrangements. Thus, food production by the slaves was the norm.

Kenneth Kiple has argued that Cuban planters "more or less" dedicated "almost all the land to sugar cultivation and import[ed] the bulk of the slave provisions."[33] The qualification contained in his statement seems to allude to owners allowing for some use of provision grounds by slaves. Kiple does not acknowledge the presence of the tens of thousands of slaves who did not live on ingenios, though his thinking on the subject does not preclude their inclusion.[34] José García, in his overview of coffee and tobacco in Cuba, wrote that the land on cafetales was not solely occupied by coffee bushes but was planted with a variety of fruit trees, plantains, and other food crops that were interspersed with the export crop.[35] His findings support the idea that the contemporary design recommendations of Laborie and others were implemented by planters. Of the records of 188 coffee farms that I have surveyed, nearly all list among their assets plantains and fruit trees. Examples of this trend include the cafetal Paciencia, with 6,000 plantains and 400 fruit trees, and the Recreo, with 38,000 plantains and 978 fruit trees.[36] Many inventories also listed a portrero attached to the farm that was used for growing other food crops such as beans, though the records from the cafetales do not specify the contents of the portreros.[37]

Some planters may have sold some of the produce rather than use it to feed their slaves, but there is little evidence to support this proposition. What is more likely, at least in some cases, such as that of the Recreo, was that the owner of a cafetal also owned a sugar cane plantation and used the available land and slave labor on the cafetal to support the workforce on the other property.[38] That this source of food was available to the enslaved on the cafetales is supported by the observations of numerous travelers who consistently commented that slaves on cafetales appeared better fed and healthier than their counterparts on ingenios. Fredrika Bremer noted that "the slaves on this cafetal [la Industria] . . . were well fed and contented."[39] She made this comparison following her visit a few days earlier to the ingenio Santa Amelia.[40] Other evidence points to the use of produce grown on the cafetal, supplemented by purchased meat. Records for the cafetales Rosa and Resurrección show that during the months of October, November, and December 1832 and January, February, March, April, June, and August 1833, various quantities of *tasajo* (jerked beef) were purchased. The plantation manager purchased no other substantive quantity of comestibles during the period, suggesting that the slaves were consuming locally grown food along with the purchased meat.[41]

Kiple, on the other hand, argues that slaves in Cuba did not receive as much protein in their diets as has been alleged by planters or by scholars such as Manuel Moreno Fraginals. Working from import records that indicate lower levels of imported beef and fish than expected, and medical and other accounts which show that Cuban slaves were shorter on average than some of their counterparts on other islands, Kiple concludes that previous works have overestimated protein intake. Rather than consuming three pounds of jerked beef, salted pork, or salted fish per week, it is more likely that Cuban slaves ate only one pound of animal protein per week.[42] What Kiple appears to have uncovered is another striking difference in the lives of slaves on coffee farms compared to those on sugar plantations. As often has been the case, Kiple derived his conclusions from data taken from slaves on sugar plantations and generalized it to the entire enslaved population.[43] As I have argued earlier, the configuration, demographic makeup, and experiences of slaves on cafetales were significantly different, so generalizations taken from slavery on ingenios is suspect at best. Furthermore, considering reports by travelers that slaves on the cafetales appeared to be better fed and healthier than their counterparts on sugar plantations, it seems likely that Kiple's findings should not be extrapolated beyond the ingenios.

Coffee planters, in their efforts to be profitable and also to control the daily routines of their enslaved workers, created the time and space for them to grow their own food. This helps explain the low incidence of purchased foodstuffs as well as the observational evidence of slaves' health. This also had the added benefit to the planters of occupying more of the slaves' time, thus avoiding potentially problematic unfilled time. The benefits of slave food production were obvious as long as the population was manageable. Taken together, these elements produced a workforce that created substantial wealth for its owners within a controlled environment designed to limit the range of responses available to the enslaved. These factors were important in sustaining a system of power by the white elites over the increasing numbers of African workers but they were not the only elements of the plantation environment that the master class controlled.

Another Factor

Planters and their agents controlled many aspects of the lives of their enslaved workers, but there were other factors directly related to the spaces in which slaves lived and worked that neither the owners nor the slaves could manage; nevertheless, these factors had a major impact on plantation life. One such element was disease. The health of enslaved workers and their vulnerability to pathogens was a function of the larger society in which they were embedded but also was related to housing, diet, and workload. The factors that influenced the impact of epidemics were distinct on cafetales, creating a differing imprint on the coffee cultivation region. Outbreaks of yellow fever and cholera were common, and devastating to men and women, slave and free. Slave populations were often particularly hard hit as a result of large numbers of people living in close quarters, which thus eased the transmission of pathogens. Enslaved workers also suffered disproportionately because of nutritional deficits and debilitating work regimes.

Two significant epidemic events occurred during the years of the plantation boom. In the years following 1815, the incidence of yellow fever began to increase, reaching a peak during the years 1820 and 1821. Death rates rose from a baseline coefficient of 30 per 1,000 inhabitants to a peak of 57 per 1,000 persons. By 1823 life returned to normal with respect to the disease climate.[44] The cholera epidemic of 1832 and 1833 hit the region around Havana with great effect. Some owners lost as many as half of their slaves.[45] The rate of death as a result of cholera rose very rapidly and, as in the yellow fever outbreak, returned to normal levels quickly. In 1831 the rate was at a base of 31 deaths per 1000 persons, rising to a peak of 72 per 1000 in 1833, and returning to normal by 1835.[46]

During the early nineteenth century there were competing ideas about disease. The origins of disease, how it spread, how to prevent it, and how to treat it were all subjects of debate at all levels of society. It was clear that some methods of prevention such as vaccination were effective, although dangerous. What would come to be known as "germ theory" was gaining currency in the scientific and medical communities, but only slowly. These two epidemics highlight the differences in the diseases and the ways people reacted. Yellow fever is a pathogen for which long-term immunity can be developed. If a person contracted it and survived, they had immunity. This was recognized by some, and so the risky process of vaccination began to be used to combat the spread of the disease. At the same time, some officials were arguing against quarantine, as such a policy would impinge on trade, especially the broader movement of people and goods. Cholera, on the other hand, is a social disease. People did not develop immunity and it was well understood that the illness moved quickly through a population. Cholera is a particularly nasty disease caused by the bacterium *Vibrio cholerae.* This bacterium usually enters the body orally and attacks the lower intestines. It thins the lining, causing rapid fluid loss from the bloodstream. The symptoms include vomiting, diarrhea, and rapid dehydration. A person with a severe case can experience a very rapid decline, especially if he or she is already in a weakened state, and go into hypovolemic shock, a life-threatening condition ensuing from drastic reductions in total blood volume. In up to 10 percent of cases, death can occur in as few as twenty-four hours after the onset of symptoms.[47] Massive cholera outbreaks are typically caused by a common water supply becoming contaminated by fecal matter; once started, the disease spreads from person to person through subsequent exposure to the pathogen. In 1831 there was a large outbreak of cholera in Arabia, as well as in several central and eastern European cities (notably Berlin and Vienna). From this early outbreak it spread throughout north Africa, reaching London and Paris by 1832. This was followed quickly by outbreaks in North America, including Mexico. The outbreak traveled down the Mississippi and reached Cuba by late 1832.

Recent research in Mexico has suggested that cholera outbreaks can happen as a consequence of El Niño and La Niña events related to hurricane cycles.[48] This may have been a factor in creating favorable conditions for the spread of the disease once it arrived via infected ship passengers. This points to another environmental factor that also shaped the lives of slaves—hurricanes. Massive storms that scarred all the islands of the Caribbean took many lives during the course of the Cuban plantation boom. The aftermath of hurricanes was often felt most by plantation slaves, as crops and fragile slave housing were destroyed. Despite their privations, it was the enslaved who had to rebuild their own lives as well as the lives and fortunes of their owners. The ecological damage left in the wake of tropical cyclones may well have contributed to a higher incidence of disease due to contamination of water supplies and dietary deficiencies as a result of crop loss and failure. It should be noted that a hurricane struck western Cuba in 1832, just a few months prior to the beginning of the cholera outbreak in February 1833.[49]

In early March 1833, Mariano Ricafort, governor general of the colony, reported to officials in Spain that five people in Havana had succumbed to a disease with symptoms that appeared similar to cholera. Such a report reveals the vigilance of officials with respect to such potentially deadly outbreaks.[50] But Ricafort was just beginning to grasp the gravity of the situation, which by May had clearly become a crisis. In a report dated May 31, Ricafort revealed a newly adjusted total for late February for Havana and its environs: 199 deaths. He also reported that 7,911 people had perished in the region during March; 6,500 in April; and another 2,975 in May.[51] These figures would be revised monthly as the death toll continued to rise in the weeks ahead. By the end of October, Ricafort stated hopefully that the disease was beginning to abate but that the total loss of life between February and October had reached 22,705 in western Cuba.[52]

A closer examination of the figures reveals that slaves were struck down by the disease at much higher rates than the white population. Chart 1 illustrates the elevated rate of death among the African population. The rise and decline of incidents of cholera is similar in the two population groups, but the impact it had on the enslaved population was much worse. Ricafort acknowledged as much in his report, though he focused on the economic loss that the death of the slaves represented, both in capital investment and in the loss of productive workers.

The slaves of the cafetal Paciencia suffered significant losses among the adult population between 1822 and 1833. A count of the dotación in 1822 revealed that there were fifty-two adult African-born slaves on the farm, of whom thirty-two were males and twenty females. Of those, twenty-one appear to have died by the end of 1833. Of those no longer on the rolls, thirteen were men and eight were women.[53] This was a rate of decline equal to 40 percent, of whom 40

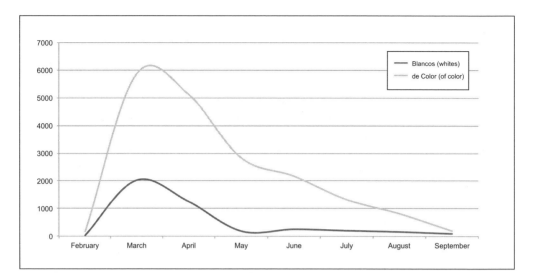

Figure 3.2. **Cholera death totals for Havana and surrounding areas during 1833. Mariano Ricafort and Ramón de la Sagra, "Informa sobre el estado de la epidemia . . . ," 1833 (October 30), Fondo Correspondencia de Cuba y Puerto Rico, Legajo 6374, Número 44, 1 and 2, Archivo Histórico Nacional (de España). This chart is derived from the figures Ricafort provided in his report to officials in Spain.**

percent were women. Among the larger regional population, men died at nearly twice the rate of women. This would seem to indicate that deaths from cholera struck at a rate equal roughly to population distributions. On a coffee plantation such as the Paciencia, where the female population was higher than the island average, higher numbers of women were affected, whereas throughout the broader region, the population was skewed male because of the expanding sugar industry; as a result, more men were infected by the contagion.

Planters and the general public feared for their lives, but plantation owners and colonial officials were also concerned for the welfare of the human capital on farms throughout the area. In the newspaper *Diario de La Habana* (Havana Daily), the public was kept informed and later enlisted to suggest remedies for the illness that was sweeping the region.[54] Readers responded with ideas for cures, including one offered by Sebastián Fornes y Guma. Fornes suggested a tonic made from flowers, herbs, and water, brewed together over heat until the liquid was the color of *vino de malaga*.[55] It is also evident that plantation owners were spending money for such cures. The account books of Manuel O'Reilly y Calvo reveal an expenditure of one *real* for "un método curativo del cólera mórbido" (a method to cure cholera).[56] O'Reilly also contracted the services of Francisco Javier Hernandez, described as a *médico accidental*, at a cost of two hundred pesos, to treat cases of cholera during the months of April and June 1833.[57] These incidents show that those in power were seeking to control the crisis through the means at their disposal.

Slaves were disproportionately affected by the cholera epidemic, as noted earlier, to an extent that cholera was sometimes referred to as a black man's disease. Kiple has shown that this effect was caused at least in part by the crowded and unsanitary conditions in which slaves lived. The susceptibility of slaves to the disease was also increased by dietary deficiencies.[58] Kiple points out that slaves who ate a nutritionally deficient diet or were malnourished would have had a lower acidic balance in their stomachs. This enabled the food- or water-borne contagion to survive the normally toxic passage through the stomach and reach the intestines, where it infected those in an already weakened state.[59] Plantation conditions would have an effect on rates of infection among slave populations.

Kiple's view is supported in records from the time. José Yarini, a doctor and sugar planter who owned a cane farm in the Guamacaro valley southeast of Matanzas, wrote a detailed and at times harrowing account of his experiences during the epidemic. He describes how planters sought out medical practitioners for help, revealing the diversity of those in the field as well as the methods employed. He mentions an English doctor and one from Poland, as well as a Chinese practitioner. He is very critical of his fellow planters, saying that "la fuerza, la violencia, el sordido interes, el insaciable deseo de las riquezas triunfa de todo."[60] Yarini describes conditions on the ingenio in ways that echo much of the literature, but with great care and detail. He blames lack of food and sanitary conditions as contributing to the ill health and vulnerability of the slave population. Interestingly, he comments on the differences he has observed on nearby cafetales. He reports that about the same number fell ill, but the rate of death was significantly different. Yarini reported that on the cafetal, of the fifteen who fell ill on the cafetal, two died. On a nearby ingenio, the same number fell ill, but about half of the total number perished.[61]

While the evidence of differentiation in rates of death between cafetales and ingenios is incomplete, it is reasonable to conclude from accounts such as Yarini's that such a difference existed. In general, slaves on cafetales lived in less crowded conditions as a result of the continued use of bohíos and open barracones, as well as the smaller average size of dotaciones. The evidence also points to the conclusion that slaves on cafetales ate better than slaves on ingenios. The relationship between open housing and the use of provision grounds would suggest that slaves on coffee farms had a greater and more diverse supply of comestibles. In addition, the earlier and faster rate of creolization compared to slaves on ingenios points to better health, resulting from more favorable diet and labor conditions among enslaved women and children. These factors would also figure into lower rates of cholera contraction. Following the lead of Kiple, one could theorize that slaves who were better fed and healthier therefore would have lower rates of infection. These elements taken together would indicate that slaves on cafetales were, in general, less affected by the epidemic than their counterparts on ingenios.

Masters and slaves alike had to cope with the devastating effects of disease outbreaks such as the cholera epidemic of 1833, which reshaped the human landscape of western Cuba by killing over twenty-two thousand people. This not only had an emotional and economic impact, but also led to renewed efforts to encourage white immigration to the island and brought a new wave of illegal imports from Africa. This occurred at a time when events in Africa created a newly deepened pool of slaves that traders drew on to fill the demand created in Cuba. The trade was enriched by the collapse of the Oyo empire in the region known as the Slave Coast of what is now southwestern Nigeria and southeastern Benin. It was in the aftermath of the disease outbreaks of the 1820s and 1830s that increasing numbers of Yoruban people, known in Cuba as *Lucumí*, were brought to the colony. As a result of their forced migration, the trajectory and development of Cuban culture was forever changed.

Conclusion

The owners of plantations were more than slaveholders; they were the masters of time and space. They sought and largely succeeded in contouring the lives of their workers. They exercised control over the quotidian and cyclical tasks that slaves performed, defining what labor was executed and when it was to occur. Planters designed and ordered the structures slaves would build. They directed the uses and activities to be contained within each part of the physical representation of the cafetal. Moreover, they ruled the realm of abstraction through the realization of the ideal plantation made manifest across the Cuban landscape. The physicality of the farm included not only the structures but also the spaces defined by and between the buildings. The sum of all the parts and the objects, human and inanimate, constituted the sphere of planter dominion.

Planters created a structure of control toward a specific end—to create a secure, efficient, and profitable farm. One of the most important elements necessary to accomplish that goal was the creation of a productive and compliant workforce out of a potentially dangerous collection of enslaved Africans. It was therefore paramount that slaveholders developed a coherent structure that demonstrated to the captives the power of their master and their subordinate place within the system of the plantation. The articulation of power by the master class, at the apex of its calculated and ruthless efficiency, constructed workers who accepted their lot as their natural place in the order of life. When slaves internalized the paternalism their masters projected, they became the tools of their own domination.

This chapter has sought to explain how the system of control was created in each of its constituent parts. The structure masters and their agents created was similar in many ways to other plantation systems, but there were important differences that marked cafetales as distinct, such as differential uses of labor found in the modified task system, and the extended use of bohíos. The chapter has also suggested that there were elements that shaped slaves' lives that were outside the scope of master influence and control. Catastrophes such as the 1833 cholera epidemic had profound and lasting influences on Cuban society in ways that went beyond the capacities of intended consequences. Events such as the epidemic also marked the limits of elite power. While slaveholders sought to extend the reach and scope of control over their workers, they were unable, in the end, to completely dominate their slaves. Enslaved Africans and their descendants resisted the imposed structure of the master class and found ways to exercise agency within the confines of their bondage. Chapters 4, 5, and 6 will explore the ways in which slaves on the cafetales of western Cuba exploited the gaps in control they found.

CHAPTER 4

Under Cover of Night
Religious Practices

The African soil, from which they were torn, still clings to
them, neither washed off in the font of baptism or the stream of
knowledge. —Robert Jameson

Religious practices were central to the lives of the enslaved all across the
island. As the previous chapters have shown, slaves on coffee plantations
lived within the context of a set of conditions that offered some limited possibilities for personal and collective expression. On the coffee plantations of western
Cuba, the rapid expansion of the enslaved population, the geographic arrangement of the district in which the cafetales were situated, and the structural organization of the farms enabled Africans and their descendants sufficient control
over their time and space to engage in practicing many of the forms of their
belief systems. Slaves engaged in religious activities in a variety of ways. Religious actions and objects were often reported in connection with uprisings, for
example. Other religiously significant practices were embedded in activities such
as music and dance and cooking. This chapter explores these types of expressions among Africans and their descendants on the coffee plantations of western
Cuba, connecting African origins to Cuban experience.

Religious practices within a population serve many functions—creating cultural cohesion, structuring knowledge systems, and ordering the social system,
just to name a few. Both the enslaved and their enslavers were religious practitioners, but this system functioned in ways that are not easily explained. As Fred
Solt et al. have recently argued, religiosity and economic inequality correlate
closely throughout the world. This also crosses class lines, as both the upper and
lower classes are more religious in societies where there is greater disparity of
wealth.[1] But in the work of Solt et al., the religion practiced is typically shared;
in other words, the upper and lower classes are practicing the same religion.
This makes it easier for those in power to use a commonly understood religious
discourse to maintain the status quo. This was not the case in Cuba. The slaveholding class and the enslaved were not typically practicing or adhering to the
same religious systems. This resulted in a gap in knowledge and limited the effectiveness of discursive measures of control and persuasion. This raises questions about conversion and also about what sort of hegemonic discourse or

power the master class was mobilizing, the ways it could institute in order to dominate the population, and how effectively Africans could resist. The environment of the cafetal allowed dotación members to reconstitute parts of their social worlds, effectively demonstrating that they could resist complete subjugation. The ongoing religious practices of slaves attest to their ability to resist and reestablish their own social structure.

This chapter will show that collective actions were intimately intertwined with cultural connections. Slaves needed networks to survive and it was through the practice of cultural activities that they created and nurtured these types of contacts. Coffee plantations provided an essential environment for cultural continuities as well as reconfigurations and propagation. Engaging in cultural practices in the context of a plantation economy or complex was of necessity an exercise of pragmatic accommodation and measured resistance. The actions the enslaved took were always in tension between these two poles. For Africans to maintain some of their relative autonomy, they had to navigate successfully the master/slave relationship.

The slaves of the cafetales of western Cuba not only found ways to subvert the construction of time and space designed by slaveholders, they also found ways to challenge the cosmological world that planters and their agents sought to impose. The spaces that slaves occupied—their housing, whether bohío or barracón—were sites of contestation between members of the ruling class and those they sought to dominate. Slaveholders controlled where slaves lived, but the enslaved shaped how they inhabited those spaces. Coerced laborers inhabited their housing in ways that served their own interests and challenged the exercise and instrumentality of power. They did not merely occupy space as laborers on demand; they rebuilt their lives within the walls of their quarters. Through their actions, in fields, in open areas of the farm, and by accessing intra-plantation networks, slaves worked to establish their own axis of power. By conducting religious practices behind closed doors, cooking their traditional dishes, drumming, dancing, and keeping their indigenous languages alive, enslaved workers fought for their collective and individual sense of self. It was through the exercise of slave agency in contesting the definitions of and activities within space and place that slaves reestablished and redefined personal and group identification—reconstituting and reshaping the cultural practices to transcend the limitations embedded in the geographic realities and definitions of their former lives. Enslaved workers, by exercising their own cultural identifications and by claiming and asserting control over the power to define who they were and would be, contravened, or at least contested, the power of the master class to shape them to be compliant plantation laborers. One of the most significant ways that Africans challenged slaveholders, maintained and adapted their cultures, asserted their own identities, and built social networks was through religious practices and living in their own cosmological worlds.

In any discussion of religious practices in African diasporic communities it is fundamental to begin with African origins. The origins of peoples and what cultural understandings they carried with them are keys to unlocking the ways in which diasporic peoples lived and expressed their cultures.[2] During the expansion and flourishing of plantations in Cuba, the trade in slaves accelerated and then remained at a high level, as there was continued demand to fuel the hunger for labor on the farms. Two broad geographic areas provided the vast majority of slaves to the island—west Africa and west central Africa. These areas can be further broken down into specific areas or points of origin defined by cultural communities, language groups, and trade networks. John Thornton has argued persuasively that the major slave-trading regions of western Africa can be divided into three zones: upper Guinea, lower Guinea, and central Africa.[3] Lower Guinea and central Africa are what I am calling "west Africa" and "west central Africa" in this study. In western Cuba, the two largest groups, as labeled by slaveholders and traders, were the *Lucumí* and the *Congo*. The Lucumí roughly corresponded to the Yoruban people of present-day southwestern Nigeria, Benin, and Togo, while the Congo group were from the territories north and south of the Congo river.[4] It remains a point of debate among historians and other scholars of Africa and the slave trade, but many have concluded that while these regions contained diverse groups within them, they did also share commonalities or at least some similarities. One such aspect was languages that were related; in some cases there were trade languages that allowed for cross-group communications. Many groups also shared similar cosmological orientations within their religious thinking and practices.

Resistance by enslaved people took many forms, but one of the most powerful and least understood was religious practices. Africans and their descendants in Cuba exercised forms and adaptations of religious practices that had their roots in their African homelands and cultures in ways that engendered hope and community, which enabled both people and their lifeways to survive. Spirituality created bonds that were unseen by the slaveholding elite and could not be broken. It was through these connections that other forms of resistance were created, facilitated, and actualized. The interplay of religious practice and cafetales was crucial, as the structure of life on coffee farms allowed the varieties of religious experiences to occur. Also, the demographic contours of the coffee complex, with its larger numbers of women and children, provided key elements both for the practice and long-term survival of systems of belief.

One of the most important ways that people make sense of their world is through religious practices. People of all cultures use religious systems to create cognitive frameworks that provide explanations for the struggles and triumphs of life. The social aspects of religious practices provide the context for collective actions that bind the community together. This was true of the diverse peoples of Africa who constructed dynamic religious systems based on ritual practices. Their ritual work reflected a cosmological framework that articulated a complex social structure within an elaborate personal universe. In Cuba, two of the most important examples of this type of religious system were among the groups of African people known as Congo and Lucumí. These two groups, understood broadly, were among the most heavily represented of people brought to Cuba as slaves. Among the people of the Congo region, who were from a number of different though related kingdoms of kimbundu- or bantu-speaking peoples in west central Africa, the *nzambi mpungu* and *nganga* religious practices predominated. The Yoruban speakers from the city-states of the Oyo Empire in western Africa were part of the *orisha* complex in their homelands. Both enslaved Congo and Lucumí people continued to develop their practices following their forced migration to Cuba. These religious systems, though their practitioners were separated by thousands of kilometers on the African mainland, shared an underlying logic, which found a shared capacity for community building and resistance in the New World. The underpinnings of these diverse religious frameworks was a rootedness in efficacious ritual or the use of ritual to define themselves and control the world around them. Control was exercised through defining power and knowledge. In other words, Congolese and Yorubans interacted through ritual with their ancestors and powerful nonhuman persons who had influence over everyday affairs, including human interactions and the physical environment.[5]

Religious practices in the Congo or Kongo region have long been misunderstood, as early observers and scholars viewed African practices through a Christian lens. They either sought to convert Africans to what they saw as a superior religious system or they looked to rehabilitate negative views of Africans by locating a supreme god analogous to the Christian god.[6] This is problematic in a number of ways, as it does not provide us with a clear understanding of African religious practices on their own terms and it distorts particular elements of African religious thinking.[7] James H. Sweet contends that there have been three significant misconceptions derived from Judeo-Christian ideas with respect to central African concepts. First is the notion of a single universal supreme god figure. Such an idea did not exist previously, as the creator was understood to be the creator of a particular people—a sort of first ancestor and not universal. This misunderstanding has also led to lack of appreciation for the place and role of other spirits in central African cosmology. The second problem is in the conceptualization of the high god figure as having qualities akin to the Christian god of unknowability and being distant or removed to a realm known as heaven. In the Congo the majority of spirits were known and knowable regarding their names, nature, and even location. The notion of a heaven awaiting in the afterlife was also an imposition, as many people in Africa had a view different from Christians regarding what happens after death. Many of the people from the cultures in the region had a horizontal or dimensional view of life and existence rather than the vertical view held by Christians. That is to say, most Africans understood the spiritual or unseen world to be adjacent, accessible, and imminent rather than distant, high above, inaccessible, and transcendent. When they died they would join their ancestors who lived with them in the same temporal space. This brings us to the final problem, regarding the aim of religious practice. Religious practice among the Congolese was pragmatic in answering questions and dealing with problems such as sickness, drought, and the harvest, rather than promoting the notion that religion was salvific and intended to prepare one for an afterlife with a remote and all-powerful being.[8]

One of the key concepts of central African cosmologies that was shared across cultures in the region was the permeability between the invisible spiritual realm and the visible world. This was understood and acted on in two complementary ways. One the one hand, many cultures held that there was a gap between the realm of the living and that of the spirits, and that space was conceptualized of as water. Water is not an impassable barrier, so these two domains were experienced as overlapping, meaning that the ancestors and spirits were present and accessible to people in their daily lives. People understood these two views as complementary, as it was clear that there was a difference between the two realms and the persons who inhabited them. While traversing water can prove to be difficult at times, it was passable and thus the two could interact in a variety of ways. The spiritual realm has often been characterized as the sacred and this overlapping characteristic as the sacred penetrating or informing the secular or profane world. I contend that this is a Western imposition of cognitive categories not unlike those outlined above. This distinction had little meaning in west central African life, as the spiritual world and the people who inhabited it were continually present in the world of the visible living. Disease, agriculture, weather, business success or failure, politics, and family dynamics were understood as subject to the influence, both positive and negative, of the ancestors and other spirits. The idea of the so-called sacred had little valence, as what others deemed as "sacred" was actually a central part of daily so-called profane life. What was meaningful in their world was power. Powerful people, regardless of the realm they inhabited, needed to be treated with respect, and when encountered, they needed to be treated with deference and care. Ritual specialists were often engaged (or enlisted) to facilitate appropriate demonstrations of respect or mediation when offense had been given or taken.[9]

In central Africa, ritual specialists were most often diviners who could, through the use of appropriate ritual work, interact with the spiritual world. People would consult with a diviner to determine the underlying cause or causes of a variety of problems and learn suitable remedies. Problems could include such things as sickness, infertility, a bad hunt, failing crops, or disagreements between neighbors or relatives. The list goes on, but in short the problems were of the everyday sort that all people might encounter. The diviner would reveal the causal agent that in turn suggested the appropriate remedy. Remediation often involved a sacrifice, a ritual feeding, or a gifting of some kind to address or mitigate the problem. Sometimes witchcraft was suspected and found, but this was a special case requiring differing solutions.

The ways in which diviners addressed problems through exchange and mediation highlights another core value or concept of west central African cosmology: reciprocity. The idea of reciprocity between people can also be understood as mutually beneficial interdependence and as the foundation of social relationships. Shared obligations can function effectively in relationships in which those involved are of equal status as well as in hierarchical contexts. The core value of beneficial exchange can be maintained. This was also true for relationships between the living and the dead or people living in the spiritual realm. As long as all involved felt like they were receiving value for what they gave, social harmony was maintained. It was only when one or many felt they were receiving bad for good—in other words, an unequal exchange—that social relations were disrupted and a diviner would be called on for advice.[10]

Witchcraft or power exercised for evil or malevolent purposes is a special case in central African societies. When a person has been doing their part in society, performing their ritual work of feeding and honoring the ancestors, and nevertheless falls ill, endures some misfortune, or encounters bad luck in an endeavor, witchcraft is often suspected. Western cultures have historically viewed witchcraft as real, so in that respect they did not differ from African cultures, but, broadly speaking, what constituted witchcraft did differ between Europeans and Africans. For Europeans, witchcraft or sorcery was a human attempt to intervene in the course of events or someone's life through the use of spiritually powerful objects, words, or potions; this often implicated healers, for example.[11] In spite of official censure, there were conflicting attitudes about the use of magic or witchcraft in European societies. On the one hand, official and orthodox society—political and church hierarchies—condemned the use as contrary to Christian principles. This gave rise, at least in part, to the Inquisition in Spain.[12] People we would consider part of the popular culture, on the other hand, while often fearful, nevertheless utilized the services of witches for help with love, crops, infertility, and many other common problems. They also feared evil witchcraft was at work when some unexpected calamity occurred. But at the most fundamental level, all exercise of what was understood as magical power was problematic. This view persisted into the twentieth century in Cuba, reflected in laws, documents, and scholarship that refers to Afro-Cuban religious practices as *brujería* (witchcraft), and sanctioned or discussed it as contributing to criminality in the population.[13] In many ways, the European view seems very similar to the African view on the surface, but there are some important differences. In west central African cultures, the existence and interaction with powerful persons who inhabit the invisible world was normative and not inherently problematic. Also, the use of spiritually powerful substances was a part of everyday life. These things were understood as an element of the natural order of things. As long as people interacted and used power at their disposal in socially productive ways, the use of what Europeans called magic was considered positively. Problems arose when people used power in antisocial ways—disrupting the social order, violating social norms, or harming individuals. Causing crops to fail, for example, would create social tensions because the loss could result in serious consequences such as famine. A person, either visible or invisible, taking such an action would be considered a witch and subject to judgment and social sanctions. Only when the evil was rooted out and dealt with appropriately could social order and balance be restored.

Ritual was also an element of west central African societies in regularized positive ways that went beyond dealing with problems in the lives of people. Ongoing rituals involved daily or regular feeding and maintenance of so-called fetish or ritual objects. Such objects were inhabited by spirits and therefore required or desired regular attention and devotion. In the cult of the spirits known as *nkisi* (sometimes referred to as *prendas* in Cuba), the spirits resided in vessels and religious specialists interacted with them. The vessels needed to be regularly attended to and maintained for the residing spirit or spirits to remain cooperative as well as to sustain the reciprocal relationship between human and spirit.[14]

There were some striking similarities between the cosmologies of the Yoruban people of west Africa and peoples from west central Africa. In addition, some of the same problems or biases regarding central African cultures and religious practices have plagued our understanding of Yoruban and other west African expressions of religious thought and culture. These religious systems were not revealed religions as in the Western traditions but were systems of practice that evolved over time and generations of action and interaction. The lack of written text and claims of revelation impeded or prejudiced Western scholars and others to view Yoruban cosmology as primitive, or at the least less developed than Western religious thought.[15] Possession rituals were another facet of Yoruban religious practice that some have struggled to understand.[16] More recently, Yoruban culture has been the object of several recent insightful studies and as a result our historical knowledge has benefited from new approaches and further scrutiny.[17]

Jacob Olupona notes that Ifá had long been understood, even by Christian missionaries, as "a system of explanation, prediction and control."[18] Olupona highlights some of the same sorts of problems that Sweet and Horton explicate, but his work also shows significant advances in our understanding of Yoruban cosmology.[19] At the same time, Olupona quotes the influential work of John Mbiti, which shows a bifurcation of sacred and profane.[20] While his work does shed additional light, the use of Western categories of analysis is problematic. When Olupona writes that there was a sacred grove between a village and the forest where the spirits lived, that designation of the grove as "sacred" does not shed any additional light on the matter and in fact may obscure more than it illuminates. Yoruban peoples lived in a world that was enlivened by the orishas. The origins of the orishas are varied: some are ancient, as they existed before the creation of humans, while others became orishas after notable lives and deaths on the human plane. All are considered ancestors in some way, either being among the first ancestors or having actual human lineage. As Mbiti pointed out, the worlds that humans and nonhuman persons inhabit overlap and intersect; they are not separate, as the idea of sacred and secular spaces would imply. By recognizing that the cosmological world of the Yorubans was dimensional, layered, and nontranscendent, we can begin to appreciate fully the significance of their quotidian practices, which reflect religious ideas and are situated within this particular type of cosmological world.[21] I am not arguing that such spaces—places where orishas lived and where ritual work took place—did not exist. What I contend is that these were not sacred spaces in the Western religious sense of sacredness. Rather, these were interstitial spaces in which the orishas or ritual specialists could bridge the gap between the dimensional planes of existence. Orishas could appear anywhere, but each orisha chose when and where to manifest. This quality of spatial permeability had larger implications that would carry over to the New World.

Understanding the cognitive mapping of the Yoruban world also leads us to shift our thinking away from the dialectical to the dialogical.[22] This shift is important because it is crucial to understanding the shared world and language of the Yoruban people and the orishas. In Western cosmologies, God is wholly other from humans and has ways and language that are unknowable. This sort of division did not exist for the Yorubans or many other west Africans. The gods were like them or they were like the gods. Their ways were knowable and what motivated them to act or not act were the same sorts of passions, hungers, and desires that drove their followers. The thing that marked orishas as different from humans was a matter of degree. While this is somewhat differently conceived, it is not unlike the west central African view of the spiritual world that was marked by relative differences in power. In the Yoruban case, people understood power as a universal life force known as *ase* (*ache*, in Cuba).

The relationship between Yorubans and the orishas was characterized further by mutual support and interdependence. Each needed the other to act on their behalf in their own spheres and through interaction. For example, humans needed the orishas to help them develop further in the ways of civilization—e.g., technology, agriculture, and political development—and help them mediate conflicts and other forms of social interactions. The orishas typically each had their own religious specialists and followers, and each orisha had his or her own history, myths, and rituals. The high god figure of the Yoruba world was and is Olódùmarè, but this orisha is removed from the human plane and has no altars or ritual specialists. Some of the orishas, such as Ọbàtàlá and Odùduà, came directly from Olódùmarè, while others like Ògún, Ṣàngó, Ọya, Yemọja, and Ọṣun had human lineage. Also in the spiritual world were the *Egúngún*, the spirits of the dead or ancestors. In practice, there were differences in interactions with the orishas. Ògún, for example, did not possess his followers, whereas Ṣàngó was an orisha who took possession or mounted his followers.[23] The followers of an orisha considered themselves to be its descendants of that orisha or the orisha's children.[24] Orishas helped Yorubans learn the art of war and other technologies and to become a prosperous and powerful people. The orishas needed the people to venerate them and feed them so that they could continue to live and be prosperous in their own realm. The understanding of this interdependent relationship between the people and the orishas resulted in reinforcement of reciprocity as a core value in the culture.

While followers of the orishas considered themselves descendants, they nevertheless regarded orishas as different from immediate ancestors. The departed immediate ancestors made up the spiritual people known as the Egúngún. Egúngún rituals were separate acts that were distinct from the veneration and offerings dedicated to the orishas. Masked or masquerade secret societies carried out the remembrance of the ancestors at major festival occasions in elaborate dances and other types of ritual performances. The honoring and remembrance of the ancestors was of vital importance to the harmonious life of the community. As the dead, the Egúngún, are members of the community, a breach against them through failure to interact properly with the ancestors, venerate them, or consult with them appropriately can and did lead to anxiety and stress. This in turn could lead to a sickness that would further raise the stress level in the community.[25] Godwin Sogolo argues that in Yoruban thought, disease has two causal elements—primary and secondary.[26] Secondary causes conform structurally to Western notions of germ theory and environmental causality. Primary causes are spiritual and social, which he argues are understood as creating social personal and collective or communal stress. Thus, the healer would seek to determine the primary cause as well as any secondary factors and treat the illness holistically.[27] As a result of the social and spiritual conceptualization as a primary causal factor of disease, people were careful to remember the ancestors and consult them concerning important issues as well as to observe the Egúngún rituals regularly.

The concept of disease also reemphasizes the importance of ritual specialists and divination and possession rituals. Divination was important in solving quotidian problems but it was also used to determine underlying causes or primary factors in an individual or wider outbreak of disease. In some cases, specialists would recommend a ritual that would result in possession by an orisha rather than divination so that the orisha could communicate more directly with the person through one of the ritual participants. In this way, we can see that possession rituals were related, at least in part, to divination practices. In both cases, the goal was to determine the underlying or primary cause of illness. The casual factor or factors were invariably social in some way. There were two basic scenarios with variations in the realm of spiritual causes for illnesses. On the one hand, the person or persons who had fallen ill had wronged, either inadvertently or intentionally, a spirit or ancestor or had breached some social norm, creating a social upheaval or disturbance that need to be rectified through an offering or some other form of propitiation or reconciliation.[28] On the other hand, there was also the possibility of witchcraft or evil actions taken by someone else against the person. This was important to uncover so the evildoer could be confronted and the action they had taken be remedied. It is important to reiterate that this idea of witchcraft within the African context was different than the ideas about witchcraft held by Europeans. The west African view was that witchcraft was at its roots antisocial behavior. It was about intent rather particular actions. In other words, the same action could be done for good or ill and it was the intention that made it witchcraft in the west African view. Europeans tended to view the actions themselves as problematic regardless of intention because of their own particular religious framework.[29]

The Congolese and the Yorubans made up a significant proportion of the slaves on cafetales. Understanding the basic concepts of their religious practices is central to grasping the cultural expressions of slaves on coffee plantations in Cuba. Some things slaves did, such as rituals that involved sacrifices, were more identifiable to the outside eye as religious, while other activities such as dancing were not as obvious. Members of the slaveholding class often did not understand what they were seeing and either feared or tolerated such activities. This reaction seems related to anxiety about how to manage large groups of slaves as well as Spanish attitudes about what they understood as witchcraft or magic. This vacillation of attitude toward religious practices by slaves resulted in responses that varied from debates and repression to a climate that allowed for more widespread religious expression. Not surprisingly, we can see religious activities occurring in ways consistent with practices in Africa centered around sickness, disease, and social disruptions.

The distinct practices of rituals and related music and dance as well as associated material objects raises questions about African cultural survivals, which have been the subject of much debate in the scholarly community for many years. Scholars of enslaved Africans took two distinct positions in older debates. Some advocated the "blank slate" view, which argued that traumatized slaves arriving at destinations in the Western Hemisphere had lost their cultural moorings and absorbed new cultural practices from the surrounding slaveholding culture.[30] Others contended that resiliency was an overriding characteristic of arriving slaves, enabling them to reconstitute their local cultures in their new contexts. Two poles of debate have emerged more recently that refine the "resilient African" view. Current perspectives reflect ideas of rapid versus slow creolization, recognizing that African cultural knowledge survived the Middle Passage but cultural expressions changed over time because of local conditions.[31] There also has been some recent scholarship, notably that of James Sweet, contending that there were some examples of the survival of complete African systems of knowledge in the New World. Sweet argues that African cultures—especially religious practice and cognitive maps—survived in their entirety and that they then began to evolve with their own historical trajectory in their new contexts. This position is contrary to the neo-African position akin to what Mintz and Price argued a generation earlier.[32] Baron Pineda is exemplary of scholars of the neo-Africanism approach, which contends that identities are at their core contingent and situational. In other words, for slaves and their descendants, being African or not was a consequence of local pressures and personal perception. Africanisms could be mobilized as the need arose, but so could other cultural expressions.[33]

It was clear to outside observers visiting Cuba during the plantation years that enslaved Africans continued to live lives informed by their cultures. One such visitor was Robert Jameson. Jameson's thoughts and observations are insightful, though tinted with the racial biases of his time.

> The African soil, from which they were torn, still clings to them, neither washed off in the font of baptism or the stream of knowledge. As to the last, indeed, it purls round without touching them. . . . It is true that the negro is taught the ritual of religion—(and religion here is a ritual only)—strongly and practically lessoned to despise this world and look forward with hope to a better; but his *fetiche* is only laid aside for a *relique*—(so far there is a *change* in his religion)—the barbarism of superstition remains—the mist is not removed from his intellect—it is but agitated by the intrusion of new ideas and soon settles thickly around them. That he should preserve, even after the lapse of generations, all the features of his former state, is not to be wondered at. Little is done to remove them; they are, as it were, but partially hid under his new habits. The different nations to which the negroes belonged in Africa are marked out in the colonies both by the master and the slaves; the former considering them variously characterized in the desired qualities, and the latter joining together with a true national spirit in such union as their lords allow. Each tribe or people has a *king* elected out of their number, whom, if they cannot enthrone in *Ashantee* glory, yet they *rag* out with much savage grandeur on the holidays in which they are permitted to meet. At these courtly festivals (usually held every Sunday and feast days) numbers of free and enslaved negroes assemble to do homage with a sort of grave merriment that one would doubt whether it was done in ridicule of memory of the former condition. [34]

There are several points that stand out in Jameson's comments. It was evident to him that Africans were not affected to any great degree by the religion of their captors and continued with their African traditions. He noted that slaves were regularly exposed to at least the forms of the Catholic faith. He also observed that the enslaved were interacting with free people of color and assembling in groups according to their African origins (*naciones*). This is significant, as it shows that some slaves had freedom of movement at times and some freedom of association. This in turn led to slaves seeking out and interacting with those with whom they had something in common. This would be crucial in creating social networks as well as reconstituting African religious and other cultural practices. This is also evident in Jameson's letter when he writes that each group held regular meetings and crowned a local leader according to their customs. These leaders were most often both political and spiritual leaders within the context in which they lived. He also mentions their singing, playing music, and dancing at these weekly festivals. Keeping in mind that African religious practice often involved group dancing and music, we can surmise that these so-called festivals were in fact serious business in the minds of the African participants. It was just these sorts of gatherings on and off the plantations that created the space of reconstruction as well as reconfiguration of cultural practices.

Religious practices that echo those of important slave-origin regions such as Yorubaland and the Congo basin—practices known in Cuba today by various names such as *Santería, Regla de Ocha, Regla de Ifá, Abakuá,* and *Palo Monte* or *Mayombe*—continue to be widely practiced on the island today.[35] These practices were kept alive by slaves in Cuba through their determination not to let a significant portion of their personal and collective identifications be suppressed. This, then, was an important form of resistance to slaveholder attempts to shape the lives of slaves. It was also a way in which slaves created collective bonds and alliances between each other on the same farm and across farms and even with Africans and creoles living in nearby towns and cities. There are several forms or cultural expressions in which we can see evidence of the religious practices of slaves on coffee farms. For African people, material culture (objects of practice), music, drumming, and dance, as well as divination and other rituals, were ways to express their individual and collective cosmological consciousness.

The cafetal Recompensa was located in the area known as San Marcos that Abiel Abbot described as the center of coffee plantations in western Cuba, estimating that there were six coffee plantations for every one sugar farm in the area.[36] During an investigation of a rebellion by the slaves of the Recompensa, it became clear that they were performing such rituals of religious significance within the confines of their bohíos. The mayoral, following a revolt, searched the bohío occupied by Damián (or Damiano) *carabalí* and Juan Nepomunceno *lucumí,* finding items such as "some sacks filled with vile things in the form of relics of [the kind] that the negroes believe contain magic and also a headdress that was extensively adorned with precious stones [*pedrerías*] and feathers of birds."[37] The conspirators had invited Federico *gangá* to the cafetal to perform a series of rituals to drive off the mayoral, telling Federico that the mayoral beat them frequently (*daba mucho castigo*).[38] Federico lived in hiding on the farm in the bohíos of Damián, Hilaria, and Petra. They moved him from one to another, keeping him hidden so that he could perform the work for which they had enlisted him. On the night when events came to a climax Federico gathered the dotación in the street that bisected the rows of the bohíos and called the people to sing and dance. Federico danced with a *muñeca* (a ritually constructed doll) and, according to the testimony of Onofre, a criollo, led others in a chant of "llanllá jaramingá gumbá há!"[39]

There are a number of important elements in this account that illustrate aspects of life and religious practices on cafetales. The slaves of the Recompensa evidently had contact with slaves on other farms, as they enlisted the assistance of a slave, Federico, from a neighboring farm. The use of roads to interact with slaves on other farms often was debated among owners and officials. The social intercourse between dotaciones was discouraged by officials, but some owners saw it as a way for slaves to find mates and defuse tensions. The general consensus, though, was that slaves moving around unsupervised was undesirable.[40] This case offers direct insight into one of the reasons that slaves sought to interact with those on other farms.

Those living on cafetales like the Recompensa had relative control over their bohíos. They were able to create goods for themselves and maintain those items. In this case they had constructed an elaborate headdress and some other significant religious objects. This clearly involved time and effort, both to search out and acquire materials as well as to assemble the items. Damián and Federico also were able to conceal Federico for three months without detection. It is not clear from the testimony that the "relics" were made on the Recompensa, but considering the length of time Federico was on the farm and the type of rituals he was performing, it would be consistent for him to have made them on the site.[41]

This case is not the only example of slaves fleeing sugar cane farms to live on cafetales. In 1837 twenty runaway slaves moved onto cafetal Santa Ana de Biajacas and were integrated into the dotación. They were eventually discovered and reported by the mayoral.[42] This case is notable in that the slaves did not flee to the forest but rather to a coffee plantation. They must have had some expectations of being able to hide or being absorbed into the population of the farm. The evidence suggests that the owner of the farm was willing to take on these slaves, but the mayoral reported it out of fear that the slaves would be discovered and that he would be blamed for harboring them. This example illuminates much about the slaves' perceptions of the differences of life on coffee plantations as compared to that on sugar farms.

On the Recompensa, the actions of Damián, Juan, and Federico show that slaves had some ability to control their time and use of space on the cafetal. The mobilization of collective action, which included members of other ethnic identities and genders, reveals that slaves were willing to cooperate across potentially divisive barriers. They showed a recognition of the efficacy of ritual acts that originated outside the sphere of their previous knowledge, which was based in their own particular experiences within specific African contexts. In this account there were, among those named, people from several different areas in Africa, based on the ascribed ethnic markers. There were several people who were, like Federico, from west central Africa, but there were also people such as Juan who were Yoruban, and Damián, who was possibly Ibo.[43] It should also be noted that the slaves of the Recompensa were engaging the services of Federico for a fee, further exposing the scope of the local slave economy.

There are two final elements of the Recompensa incident that need to be emphasized. The ultimate ritual performance of Federico was a collective ritual undertaken outside the protective and concealing walls of the bohíos. The religious specialist led the ritual action, centered around drumming and dancing, in which many members of the dotación participated. The move from inside the bohío to out in the open indicates that there were most likely so many participants that proceeding inside was impractical. It may also suggest that the slaves felt sufficiently empowered to act openly. In addition, this could be an indication of a general lack of oversight, at least at predictable times, on the Recompensa. The involvement of a large number of people contributes to the notion that there was cross-cultural appeal to the religious activities led by Federico. The widespread interest may also attest to the broad attraction of the basic form of many African religious practices from throughout the slaving region—drumming, singing, and dancing.

The intent of their action also relates to west African religious thought—their ritual act was to remove the mayoral, whose actions were problematic; he was beating people excessively or unjustly. I am not implying that some beatings were just. It is clear that people would tolerate beatings that were not excessive and were clearly linked to a grave transgression. In other words, everyone understood the rules, and if you broke them, you could expect to be beaten. When the punishment was excessive or the infraction was slight or unclear, however, the enslaved often saw these castigations as unjust or unwarranted. Furthermore, when this was the case, they saw it as grounds for action. In the west African cognitive world, such excessive actions would have been viewed as socially divisive and likely as evidence of some sickness or even witchcraft. The response to such a problem would be a ritual to remove the spiritual and visible cause of the problem.

As the example of the Recompensa shows, movement and music were central to ritual action.[44] Together, they provided participants with a collective voice and expression and they "suppl[ied] a vehicle for entering into the state of consciousness that allow[ed] an extraordinary mode of perception."[45] Drumming and dancing were regular activities on cafetales on Sundays and on days of celebrations (*festivos*). Juan Pérez de la Riva noted that the tradition of dancing and drumming stretched back to at least 1764, when a group of Africans danced and drummed for the *capitán general* in the courtyard of the Palacio.[46] Robert Jameson observed during his 1820 visit that slave and free of the same nación would assemble and play music and dance: "The *gong-gong, cows-horns*, and every kind of inharmonious instrument, are flourished on by a gasping band, assisted by clapping of hands, howling and the striking of every sounding material within reach, while the whole assemblage dance with maniac eagerness till their strength fails."[47] Jameson had little appreciation of the "noise" Africans made during their activities, but his observation of the regularity of such performances, the ethnic solidarity exhibited, and the interaction between slave and free is notable.

The ubiquitous presence of drums during African celebrations and rituals elides the question of the origin of the performers' instruments. On the plantations, slaves made the drums, and they often used the trunks of yagrumas trees for the bodies of their instruments. The craftsmanship involved in creating even rudimentary drums was time-consuming. A suitable tree had to be located and possibly felled. The trunk then had to be cut into appropriate lengths and hollowed out. The exterior had to be shaped and smoothed and was often also carved decoratively. For some types of drums, animal skins had to be acquired, cut, and attached.[48] Another important aspect of drum construction was the religious nature of the action. The drums were to be used in rituals and therefore had to be created by religious specialists.[49] These factors all suggest that the control of time and space was paramount in sustaining the ritual complex and its musical accompaniment. The consistent performance of dancing and drumming on cafetales testifies to the abilities of slaves on these farms to exercise agency. Other elements in the dynamic of the cafetal, noted earlier, imply that the performance of music and religious activities was possible and probable.

As Jameson documented, drumming and dancing occurred on all types of plantations and in urban areas, among free and enslaved Africans. His observation supports my assertion that these activities were especially significant on cafetales and to the coffee experience. Bremer points out that dancing and drumming were widespread, but she also notes that slaves on ingenios never danced during the *zafra* (harvest), and that they were worked so hard throughout the year that they danced infrequently.[50] Her comments point to the notion that dance and music—and, by extension, collective religious practice—were more frequent and more consistent on cafetales. Consistency is the important factor here, as the regular performance of rituals was crucial to establishing and maintaining a ritual complex. This was also essential to passing the traditions on to the next generation. At their fundamental level, religious practices, including dancing and drumming, constituted the performance of personal and collective or group identification by African and creole slaves.

It is my contention that slaves were engaged in a multifaceted process that both maintained and remade culture and identifications. They found time and space to reconstitute their cultural practices on the cafetales, but at the same time, they were interacting with people from other cultural backgrounds in Africa, as well as members of the slaveholding class, who were culturally Christian. This created a climate of innovation and adaptation that fit well with the pragmatic cosmologies of many African peoples. This meant that there were a variety of responses to enslavement and factors to consider in analysis. The refashioning of identification was a multifaceted and complex process, but two factors stand out vis-à-vis slaves on cafetales. The tension between owner-imposed structure and slave agency was an irritant within the system that provoked or motivated the slaves, which led to their exploitation of the gaps in the exercise of power so that they could consistently practice cultural forms. On cafetales, slaves mustered enough control over themselves and their surroundings to carve out the time and space to perform cultural activities. At the same time, their enslaved condition and the attempts by the master class to mold them created a climate of resistance that spurred the slaves to act against the masters within their own cultural norms and expressions. The evidence of ritual action or cultural expression in acts of resistance was related to the idea prevalent in the cultures of many west African peoples that understood social problems as indicative of spiritual conflicts or transgressions. The actions and motivations of the slaves suggest persistence of a world view rooted in west African cosmology. The 1835 uprising on two cafe-tales near the town of Aguacate shows evidence of this type of thinking.

In the early morning hours of July 17, 1835, on the cafetal Juanita, owned by Juan García, a large number of the slaves rose up in revolt. The uprising also involved some slaves from the neighboring cafetal of Miguel Duarte.[51] The slaves killed the mayorales of both farms, José de la Luz Pino and Francisco Sanchez, as well as Pablo Rabelo. They also seriously injured a number of other people, including the *contramayoral* (assistant overseer) of the Juanita, Pio *carabalí*.[52] García reported that most of the slaves on the farm were involved; that the majority, including the leaders, were Lucumí (Yoruban); and that many were *bo-zales* (recent arrivals).[53] Several of the slaves of Lucumí origin were hanged or killed during the suppression of the uprising, while others surrendered or were captured, and were subsequently questioned as part of the investigation to determine what had happened and why. The slaves who surrendered were of other backgrounds, save one Lucumí named Carlos. Most of the other slaves named were of Carabalí origin. One of those involved was Pablo *lucumí* from the neighboring farm of Miguel Duarte. The authorities had a particular interest in determining why slaves from another farm became involved. As we will see in Chapter 6, officials were apprehensive any time a revolt spread off the grounds of a single farm. As a result of this concern, Pablo was questioned extensively regarding why he had traveled to the Juanita. He testified that he had intended to meet or get together with four people on the Juanita who were of his nación. He continued that they had killed the mayoral and invited him to flee with them. He referred to the four as his "kin" (*parientes*), and that there were twenty altogether who had been going to flee, but they all had died.[54] Pablo's testimony reveals several important elements of this story. First, it shows that there was frequent and regular interaction between slaves on nearby plantations. This is evidenced by the fact that he knew these others and referred to them as kin. That there was a bond is also reflected in the invitation to join the flight from the farms and his willingness to accompany them. Pablo's use of the word "kin" here suggests several possible explanations. As many of these slaves appear to have been recent arrivals, it is possible, albeit remotely, that they were actual kin or potentially from the same town in Africa. Alternatively, this could be an example of the expression of fictive kin between slaves who had traveled on the same ship during the Middle Passage. It is also possible, and I would argue more likely, that Pablo was invoking a different idea of fictive kin based on ritual association. The term he used, *parientes*, conveys a very strong sense of kinship and connection. This, coupled with his initial comment that the other slaves were of his nación, rather than naming them in some other way, suggests a created kinship. These types of bonds, as I've argued elsewhere, can be formed through ritual acts and were often seen in Cuba in *cabildos de nación* (African ethnic associations that also included African-descended persons). With ties to homelands severed, connections to kin (both living and dead), identifications of kin, and notions of kin became more fluid. Associations or new local connections based on various commonalities such as language, religious practice, and similar background allowed people to create new ties and to recreate their culture in a new context. This also presented opportunities for new common or collective identifications. Slaves formed associations based on these new ethnicities in Cuba and throughout Latin America. These cabildos de nación became crucial to the propagation of African-based religious practices.[55]

Further evidence that the slaves on the two plantations were engaged in religious practices is present in the words of another slave, Miguel, from the Duarte plantation. In his testimony, he elaborated on the slaves' engagement with "devilish acts," which had climaxed in a proclamation that when the mayoral, José de la Luz Pino, appeared on horseback, they would attack him. When De la Luz Pino returned to the farm, the slaves fell on him with machetes and then set fire to his house.[56] Nicolas *lucumí* explained that they had killed both mayorales and burned down the buildings because the men were bad and had refused to give slaves water.[57] The motive for killing the mayorales is consistent with west African ideas on addressing problems, particularly antisocial behavior. Excessive violence and unjust, irrational actions were considered evidence of evil that was spiritual in origin.

The way to determine the cause of this type of evil was to consult with a religious specialist, who would perform a divination ritual. He would then pronounce his findings and what should be done. The events on the Juanita appear to conform to this sequence of events. Pablo *lucumí* was summoned from the neighboring Duarte cafetal, and after he arrived at the Juanita, he and others engaged in "devilish acts." African religious practices were typically associated with so-called devil worship and witchcraft in Spanish documents. Following their action, the ritual specialist—who appears to have been Pablo, although he may have been assisted by Trinidad *lucumí*—proclaimed that upon the return of de la Luz Pino to the farm, they would carry out the necessary remedy. This included killing not only the responsible person but those he may have infected, such as Pio *carabalí*, and burning the effects and the house of the affected person. Trinidad affirmed in his testimony that the act of arson was not an impulsive measure; rather, the slaves had gone and collected firewood and returned to the compound to burn down the buildings.

Trinidad *lucumí* was a slave from the Juanita who had managed to escape the initial roundup following the uprising. Investigators asked all the other slaves about him during interrogations, as they believed he was one of the people responsible for the uprising, but no one was forthcoming about his whereabouts. He was finally captured some two weeks after the revolt and officially questioned on August 2, sixteen days after the revolt. Trinidad implicated some other slaves in the uprising, but was not given a chance to respond to questions regarding the treatment of slaves on the farms, for at that point in the interview the authorities decided that Trinidad's condition would not allow him to proceed. Trinidad may well have been a leader, as he revealed details of the slaves' actions that others either did not have or felt constrained from sharing. All the slaves who were asked about Trinidad said they knew nothing about him, suggesting either protection or fear. More significant, though, is the testimony of Juan García, owner of the Juanita, who lists all the male slaves in his discourse and describes Trinidad as a ladino.[58] This shows that García considered Trinidad to be relatively acculturated, and yet the interviewer notes in the preface to Trinidad's statement that he was not a Christian and was clearly a practitioner of his African traditions, having "no idea of any other religious belief" beyond his native convictions.[59] These pieces offer us a clear example of a person tenaciously keeping his culture alive in a difficult circumstance. This incident also shows that enslaved people did find a sense of community, building connections within and between plantation populations. It was no accident that the slaves on two farms acted together in what they saw as a moment of crisis. They also exhibited a high degree of solidarity in response to the suppression of the rebellion. It is interesting that no enslaved women were mentioned in this account. This is inconsistent with nearly all other accounts of slave revolts or rebellions, as we will see in Chapter 6.

The full significance of the environment on coffee farms and the cultural activities of enslaved workers comes more clearly into focus when we take into account the demography on the farms and the larger coffee complex. As we have seen, the demographic changes on coffee plantations created a dynamic transformation of the population on cafetales during the 1830s. As the larger plantation system expanded and the population of slaves grew apace, the slave populace based on cafetales moved toward a balanced ratio between the sexes, becoming creolized at a much faster pace than on ingenios.[60] It may seem self-evident, but to emphasize the point, these two phenomena were related: there were increasing numbers of women on coffee farms and they were bearing more children. These two elements are also crucial to cultural survival. Cultural continuity, which includes the process of adaptation or change over time, depends on the transmission of practices through primary social units (kin) to the next generation. The ability of slaves on cafetales to consistently perform, practice, and reimagine culture within the context of evolving social and ethnic alliances that included growing numbers of children meant that the forms perpetuated and created on these farms through creative refashioning could survive into the future through the lives of the creole young.

Another aspect of this process was that of combining forms so that new expressions emerged as a result of interactions between peoples of differing backgrounds. The interaction with slaves from other cultures in this climate of oppression and resistance spurred cross-cultural understandings and cooperation, leading to cultural borrowings. Dancing, drumming, and other ritual acts were a form of resistance against the slave system in which they were enmeshed. The continual rehearsing of the forms of expression was a restatement by and for the participants of who they were and how they saw the world in spite of enslavement or repression.[61] The more clearly African collective or group dancing observed during the early nineteenth century would be transformed into a circle in which a man and woman danced by the 1850s.[62] In the Oyo kingdom, orisha practice was singular. The people of a smaller town might venerate a single orisha; in a larger city, individual specialists ritually engaged a single orisha.[63] In Cuba, these practices were combined into a system of religious practices known as the *Regla de Ocha* or *Santería*.[64] The process of transformation also affected the individuals involved. As the population became increasingly creolized, the emergence of a neo-African and Afro-Cuban identification was beginning. This identification was less connected to but clearly derived from African roots and ways of thinking, and also firmly grounded in Cuban experience. Slaves on cafetales were not only performing, as Bremer put it, "the rhythm of the sons of Africa; the real music of the creoles of Cuba," they were also creating the creoles and a new culture.[65]

CHAPTER 5

Buyers and Sellers
Work and Economy of the Slaves

Of this branch of revenue the negroes come in for a share, and
there is scarcely a male or female adult slave, that has not his
hog. —Abiel Abbot

L abor was the central defining point of the slave system on coffee plantations, as it was on other types of farms. Work most certainly dominated
much of the time and therefore the lives of slaves. The labor they performed for their masters, though, did not consume their attention completely.
This can be seen in the diversity of activities, including various kinds of work,
that slaves performed for themselves. While there are numerous accounts of the
toil extracted by slaveholders from their workers, the base of information regarding the self-directed labor of the enslaved is fragmentary. As a result, scholars
have given little attention to the labor slaves engaged in outside of the domain
of their masters, which they entered into for remuneration.[1] Often the assumption has been that slaves did not enter into the monetary or trade economy and
that most of their time was controlled by slaveholders, who used them for forced
unpaid labor. Rebecca Scott argues that contrary to earlier views, slaves participated in the economy through their labor and production on provision grounds
(*conucos*).[2] Some of the most compelling evidence that slaves were creating their
own economy and also participating in the wider system is the reported accrual
of money by slaves.

Many of the works on plantation economy have focused on broader aspects
of the system, such as the sugar or coffee complex, railroads, or imports and exports.[3] As a result, many of the ways that the enslaved interacted with the formal
economy do not appear in these accounts. Furthermore, much of the slaves' economic activities went unrecorded. The economic life of Africans on coffee farms
was varied, as they bought, sold, and traded with passing merchants and with the
farm owner or supervisor, as well as with fellow slaves. Their interactions were
often off the books, and as a result, their contributions to the economy have been
difficult to document and thus overlooked. Though their individual contributions
may have been small, collectively they contributed to an internal economy that
was more vibrant than has often been understood. For slaves to create this secondary informal economy, they needed time to grow or make goods to sell, and
also time to engage in trading. As we have seen, the cafetal provided slaves more

time than many other environments on the island. As Scott notes, one of the main foundations of slave economy was the provision grounds. It should also be noted that the conucos contributed not only to the slaves' economy but also the general economy of the cafetales, as they reduced owner operation costs. This chapter will explore the coffee economy and the provision grounds in context, and discuss food production and consumption as well. Slaves made choices about what to grow; these offer some additional insights into the culture slaves were building. The chapter will also look at a few other examples of trading nonfood items.

One of the other ways we can see the effects of the slave economy is in the accounts of slave participation in the system of coartación. This system of self-purchase has often been dismissed as inconsequential to the story of slave freedom struggles. While I will not argue that the system freed significant numbers of the enslaved, I will show that it was more significant than has been previously been assumed. The information we have on participation in the system is important, as it shows evidence of the slave economy, and also that slaveholders and officials took seriously the participation in coartación by slaves. I am also convinced that the ability to work toward freedom created hope within the community of enslaved Africans. Taking all these things together, the chapter will demonstrate that slaves created their own economy and participated in the larger economy, thereby gaining hope and acquiring some measure of autonomy, as well as in some cases accruing sufficient capital to buy freedom.

The economics of the coffee plantation is a study in contrasts. On the one hand, it was seen as the ideal of plantation life for a number of reasons. Coffee plantations typically had a wide variety of plants creating a varied landscape in contrast to the vast fields of sugar cane on an ingenio. Owners often lived on the farm, contributing to an idyllic image. Planters also cultivated this image by building attractive houses and adorning their homes and even properties with artistic objects such as paintings, nice furniture, sculptures, and fountains. Richard Henry Dana described the cafetal of Don Juan Torres, near San Antonio de los Baños, as a garden, noting that "shade is a great object in growing coffee, the grounds are laid out in lines of fruit-trees. The coffee-blossom is just in its perfection, and whole acres in sight are white with its flower, which nearly resembles that of the small white jasmine. Its fragrance is said to be delicious after a rain."[4] William Henry Hulbert also painted an admiring portrait of the cafetal:

> On one of the loveliest (cafetales) in the island, I spent a season, the brevity of which I shall always regret. Early in the inspiring morning, my friend Don ____ used to summon me for a drive. A dozen negroes would appear, to harness one little lively horse, into a light American wagon, brought by my friend for the purpose of driving over the thirteen miles of sugar and coffee estates, on which he has made good broad roads. A whole pack of dogs started off before us, yelping, leaping, and darting in all directions, and then we dashed away at a brisk pace, through the seemingly endless cane fields. The heavy dew, glittering on the waves of green, gave them a soft brilliancy; the cloudless skies, the buoy-

ant air, beguiled the way, till we drove into the cool shades of the plantaneria, or plantain grove, the unfailing adjunct of all estates in this land . . . [passing through the plantains] into the statelier sanctuaries of the cafetal. There the full-leaved orange, the thrifty, dark, glossy foliage of the mango, the tall elm-like aguacate, the coneshaped mamey, cover the land on both sides as far as the eye can reach. Everywhere you see the light, shrubby outlines of the coffee plant springing up beneath the taller trees. Avenues, miles in length, lead to the different quarters of the estate, and formed as they are of the full exuberant mango, or the branching aguacate, planted alternately with the towering royal palm, become forest aisles of surpassing beauty. . . .

The cottage of the cafetal was an elegantly proportioned little tropical mansion, cool, dark, floored with marble, wainscoted, and furnished with rich deep-hued Indian woods. A garden filled with heavy blooms, of jasmine and roses, and the gorgeous purple Carolina, and a hundred drooping odorous flowers, made the air faint with fragrance.[5]

Rev. Abiel Abbot visited the cafetal Angerona in 1828 and mentions several of its opulent features, such as the elevated statue of the "Goddess of Silence, furnishing the name and emblem of the bachelor's estate. It is a fine marble statue in Roman costume." Furthermore, in the house of the owner, he found

an elegant hall, floored with wood . . . glazed and painted. . . . In one of the windows was an Æolain harp of great power and sweetness. . . . The last three apartments are hung round with pictures, many of them in fine taste. The piazza at the eastern end of the building serves for a dining hall. In this is a fine piece of statuary, representing a water deity, with a cask on his knee and the bung out, filling a marble vase with water for washing hands before and after dinner.[6]

It is clear that cafetaleros invested in the appearance of their farms, suggesting that the farms were profitable and they had enough disposable income to finance such accoutrements. Agustín Valdés y Pedroso, owner of cafetal Jesús Nazareno, exemplifies the successful cafetal owner. He amassed enough wealth to gain a title from the king of Spain in 1816, becoming Conde de San Esteban de Cañongo. He also reportedly used his slaves to build "ornate embellishments" at the entrances of the plantation.[7]

On the other hand, planters and other interested parties debated the differences in profitability between cafetales and ingenios during the period. They often concluded that raising sugar was more lucrative, although coffee could be profitable. One of the most striking cases of the contradictions of coffee growers is that of Joaquín Santa Cruz y Cárdenas, Conde de Santa Cruz de Mopox, y de San Juan de Jaruco. Santa Cruz was well known and respected during his life. Santa Cruz y Cárdenas led a botanical expedition to Cuba (organized in Madrid in 1797) and later held extensive properties on the island, including three cafetales.[8] Following the death of the Conde de Mopox, his financial problems began to come to light through a series of lawsuits filed against his estate. In the end his family was left nearly bankrupt once all the debts had been adjudicated.[9] During the 1820s and 1830s, scholars and government officials debated differences in plantation profits, arguing that coffee farms were, on average, less profitable than sugar plantations. This line of argument lends itself to a particular interpretation of the decline of coffee in Cuba. An example of this is the recent work of Daria González Fernández, who builds on the work of Ramón de la Sagra (ca. 1831). González Fernández contends that the main factor in the rise and fall of the coffee plantation complex in Cuba was the incentives and pressures of market forces. In the early years of the expansion during the late eighteenth and early nineteenth centuries, there were reduced taxes from the Crown as well as reduced competition from Saint Domingue as a result of the Haitian Revolution. The expansion of coffee plantations in Cuba also coincided with higher prices for the crop in the market.[10] While the argument is factually correct, it fails to take into account some other relevant factors and leads to a problematic explanation of the decline of coffee farming in western Cuba.

While it is evident that coffee was not as profitable as sugar and that planters did respond to markets in some ways, explanations for their collective actions require a broader approach. González Fernández centers her argument on the lower profitability of coffee that in turn would make it more vulnerable to market fluctuations. She assumes, though, that planters would understand the fluctuations in market prices and respond in "rational" ways according to a capitalist logic. This assumption undermines the argument, as it is evident that planters during the 1830s did not respond in ways that twentieth- or twenty-first century logic would suggest. It also does not account for the slow growth cycle of the coffee bush. Planters could not respond quickly to market changes by rapidly increasing production, for example. The decline of coffee cannot be reduced to a simple market-based decision, as this fails to account for the strong pull of culturally based factors of value and quality of life. This approach also does not take into account three other factors: the tariff dispute between the United States and Spain that damaged the ability of Cuban producers to export their crop to their largest market; rising international competition, especially from Brazil, which lowered commodity prices on the international market; and the devastating hurricanes that struck the coffee-growing region of western Cuba in 1844 and 1846. These storms destroyed many farms and untold thousands of coffee bushes, as well as the shade trees that facilitated their growth and productivity.[11] Many farms during the period were part of larger portfolios, as many owners sought to diversify their holdings to ensure family prosperity. The viability of individual farms always was subject to many factors and cannot be inferred from island-wide export figures and global prices. I am convinced that many planters understood how to make their farms profitable and engaged in various measures to try to control expenses. Even wealthy owners worked to reduce costs to improve profitability. Valdés y Pedroso actively worked to reduce costs on his profitable farm, using his workers on many projects and to produce other crops for sale or to make the farm as self-sufficient as possible.[12] One of the main ways that planters were able to reduce costs was to require their workers to produce their own food. This enabled Africans to shape their diets and maintain some of their cultural practices related to food cultivation and consumption. It also meant that they had to be given time and space for cultivation, and it created for them opportunities to make money.

Cultivating conucos and keeping animals were the primary forms of work that slaves engaged in for themselves. P. J. Laborie wrote in his manual for establishing a coffee plantation that care should be given to provide the enslaved workers with space to grow food: "There should be a space for buildings, pastures, provisions grounds, grass grounds, and coffee fields . . . setting apart parcels of Ground for his first Negroes [*sic*]. Property of this sort is what most attaches them to the estate, and enables them to reap comfort from their own industry. . . . Every lot ought to be twenty-five paces square, allowing sixteen negroes to the square of land [provision grounds]."[13] Laborie says that planters should be sure to set aside land for every one of the workers. He also makes two important points on why it is important that the Africans make use of conucos or provision grounds. First, he is convinced that letting Africans till the soil on their own behalf will create a bond between them and the earth on which they live. Second, he contends that this work should be so that they can reap some of the benefits of their own labor. Together these will create more compliant workers, in his view. As in other aspects of plantation building, there is clear evidence that planters heeded the advice of Laborie.

The direct testimony of slaves toiling on their provision grounds during this period is limited, but there is substantial evidence that slaves were farming productively. They were using the produce they grew to create an economy among themselves based around their personal agricultural production. The basis for this claim is twofold. First, the presence of land set aside for food production, including fenced areas for livestock, shows that sizable amounts of food were involved. A representative case of land usage can be seen on the cafetal Mariana. Of the four and one-half caballerías of land that constituted the farm, two caballerías were set aside for food production. Of that area, eighty-two *cordeles* were fenced or enclosed for pasture.[14] In addition, there were eighty chickens (in two coops) and nearly two dozen pigs on the cafetal.[15] Many plantation inventories list land set aside for food production, with some explicitly mentioning areas for slaves to grow their own food. The cafetal Campana, for example, lists one and a half caballerías of land for food crops.[16] The inventory of the cafetal Bagatela mentions at the end of the passage describing the property "grassland for the animals and provision grounds for the negroes."[17]

The example of the cafetal Campana reveals some surprising insights into slave autonomy. Following the death of the owner of the farm, Rita Estremes, her heirs engaged in an extended fight over the property that began in 1832 and lasted until 1835. During the period of litigation over the will, there was lax management of the farm, but the workers continued to labor. The slaves planted and harvested and supported themselves without much supervision or help.[18] This is not the only example of this type of behavior. In a similar story, following the death of Benigno Muñoz, his heirs struggled among themselves over the dispensation of the cafetal Paciencia for nearly the entire decade of the 1830s. During the course of their litigation, there were several assessments of the farm and the dotación. These documents reveal that the slaves were productive, bringing new land under cultivation with new plantings of coffee as well as an eighth of a caballería in *boniato* (Cuban sweet potato).[19] They survived the cholera epidemic of 1833 without extensive loss of life. The population of slaves on the farm declined slightly between the 1820s and 1833, with the males falling from forty-two to thirty-four and females decreasing only by one, from twenty-seven to twenty-six.[20] We can see that the population was becoming more balanced between the sexes, but it also became more creole. According to account records, the only monies expended on the slaves were for purchases of *tasajo* (jerked beef) and replacements of some tools.[21] It is evident from the documentary record that enslaved Africans, when they were able to manage their own lives in large part, were productive in ways that benefited themselves.

The second type of evidence supporting private agriculture as a major aspect of slave economy consists of the implicit and explicit accounts of purchases by management of slave-produced goods. Implicit indications are found in the lack of purchases made by coffee planters of comestibles in any sizable quantities, other than the tasajo for the Paciencia. This is evident on many other farms, such as on the cafetales Rosa and Resurrección.[22] If slaveholders were providing rations for their slaves, there would be records of external purchases of various staples. As we have seen from the descriptions of farms, there were abundant fruit trees and plantains on cafetales throughout the region. Fruit, along with produce and animals raised on the farms, accounts for the absence of other types of external purchases. Another possible explanation is that slaves were being directed to farm food crops as part of their regular enforced work. This may have occurred at times, but other evidence offers additional insight into the question. It becomes clear that slaves were producing foodstuffs, as we can see evidence that mayorales were purchasing goods from the enslaved. This practice was widely known and was viewed negatively by the authorities. Concern over the practice resulted in discussions in 1825 and an eventual ban of such commerce.[23] Despite the ban, it is clear that the practice continued, and that it also involved other buyers on the farm. The traveler Abbot observed that the slaves on the plantation of "Mr. M . . . have certain privileges, as much land as they choose to till well, and the whole produce to sell in corn or pork, or what they please. I have myself seen a negro's hog worth $50."[24] On his tour of the vuelta abajo, Abbot commented extensively on the variety of food available to the slaves on the cafetales, taking special note of the abundance of meat:

> Swine are raised on the island with great ease, especially in connexion [*sic*] with a plantation. The immense quantity of plantain raised among the coffee, and the

superabundance of the mango fruit, which bends down the boughs of that large and beautiful tree, rows of which shade the extensive avenues of the plantation, to say nothing of smaller matters, afford a rich, a delicious, and fattening food for swine, almost inexhaustible. Corn also, in two, sometimes three, crops a year, comes in to fatten the animals for the market. Of this branch of revenue the negroes come in for a share, and there is scarcely a male or female adult slave, that has not his hog. Yet they are always in demand, and sell at a high price, from $10 to $50.[25]

Enslaved workers were also selling their products to others. Leon, a slave on the cafetal Paciencia, was selling pigs he raised to buyers in nearby San Marcos. He had earned forty-one pesos as of September 1834, a sizable sum.[26] Slaves on cafetales were raising crops and animals for their own consumption, as well as using their produce to create the foundation of a small-scale monetized economy within their ranks.

A related set of simple activities that affirmed and created bonds between Africans and Cuban-born slaves consisted of the social acts of cooking and eating. Slaves, as we have seen, were involved in the production of their own food. They were also often responsible for the preparation of their sustenance. Larger cafetales had dedicated kitchens and *cocineros* (cooks) to prepare at least some of the food slaves consumed. The cafetal Recreo had a slave kitchen near the quarters of the workers and listed three cooks in the inventory of the dotación: Simón *primero*, María del Pilár, and Encarnación.[27] Whether meals were cooked and consumed individually or collectively, African traditions could be maintained. The survival of recipes that show the adaptation of African cooking to local conditions in Cuba is evident in the work of Natalia Bolívar Aróstegui and Carmen González Díaz de Villegas. They show that not only did cooking traditions from various regions survive by being passed down from generation to generation, but the relationship between specific preparations and religious practices also was maintained.[28]

Coffee was not only the crop that the enslaved grew but was also an item they consumed. Afro-Cubans integrated coffee into their culture as a result of the multifaceted interaction they had with the crop. One of the most common ways we see food used, including coffee, is in religious ritual feeding of the orishas. This is evident throughout the literature and sources. Lydia Cabrera writes in her *Cuentos negros de Cuba* (published in English as *Afro-Cuban Tales*) in several stories of coffee as a way to relax and socialize.[29] She also notes in *El Monte* (The wilderness, or backwoods) that "coffee is a comfort and a necessity that God gives to the poor . . . without coffee life is worthless . . . [and] in the offerings that honor the dead, never forget to include the cup of coffee they always desired."[30] Bolívar Aróstegui and González Díaz de Villegas detail the relationship between food and ritual within Afro-Cuban religious communities. They show how foods take on various meanings through sanctions and through adding value by association with powerful orishas. For example, the consumption and offering of coffee is connected with the path of Oggún. Oggún was and is considered one of the more powerful orishas in the Regla de Ocha, arguably the most common system of Afro-Cuban religious practice on the island.[31] Coffee has been an important commodity in the Afro-Cuban community from the period of the plantation boom of the nineteenth century, when coffee production was a key element in the Cuban colonial economy, down to the present.

Beyond the sale of agricultural goods, slaves found other ways to earn money and expand their microeconomy. One such method was performing a service for remuneration. Federico *gangá* secretly came to live on the cafetal Recompensa after he fled from the nearby ingenio Calisto. He was taken in by the members of the dotación because he was a *brujo* (ritual specialist).[32] This was important to the slaves of the Recompensa because they wished to harm the administrator of the cafetal. They agreed to pay Federico twelve pesos to perform some religious acts to drive off or harm the despised mayoral in a way that would conceal their involvement. The deal was struck, but his actions of intervention in the plantation conflict led to an uprising against the overseer.[33]

Another important economic activity of the slaves was their participation in the system of self-emancipation known as *coartación*. As we have seen, Africans not only performed forced labor, they also worked for themselves, accruing sums of money that, for some, created hope, but more broadly constructed an entry point into the wider economy of the region. Visitors to the island often observed slaves in possession of money. Abbot notes that on the Angerona, Cornelio Souchay, the owner, wanted his slaves to have money. He stated that "it is a maxim with the proprietor that negroes should *have* money, and should *spend* it."[34] To that end, Souchay established a shop on the cafetal in which slaves could buy all manner of goods at subsidized prices. Abbot mentions that Souchay offered goods for purchase so that traveling salesmen could be barred from the estate. Limiting access to the workers was part of a larger system of control exercised by owners. As Scott points out, "plantation slavery as a social system depended to a large degree on isolation—as planters themselves acknowledged, for example, when they set up and explicitly defended plantation stores as instruments of social control."[35] Not only was the use of the plantation store a way to control the internal population, it also shielded slaves from outside contacts that were potentially disruptive, from the perspective of the owner. Those perceived of as threats included abolitionists and free people of color and, to a lesser extent, slaves from other farms. Abbot does not inform his readers how slaves on Angerona earned their money, but it is reasonable to assume that they worked for their currency. The example of the Angerona raises two central questions. On the one hand, where and how were slaves earning money? A related set of questions includes how much were slaves earning and on what else might they have been spending their money? On the other hand, considering the concerns of the owner, Souchay, the central issue seems to be his fears. Abbot notes that there were several groups of people from whom the owner was trying to shield his dotación, but it is not clear if his anxieties were the same for each group.

There also may have been some pragmatic motivations for isolating the group. As we have seen, slaves could and did earn money growing and selling their own produce and animals. This is the most likely way in which they earned money. There was also the possibility that they were making items to sell or trade with passing peddlers and slaves on other farms. This was seen on other farms, where a few slaves made items of religious significance and sold them.[36] It is not yet clear the extent of slave-earning power or the size of the economy they engendered, but the question of what else they might be purchasing may be related to some of the slaveholder's concerns. Abbot reported that the slaves on the Angerona bought cloth, beads, and other trinkets, as well as small cooking pots.[37] This points to the idea that the store was well stocked with items that the Africans were interested in buying. It also suggests that Souchay was interested in capturing the market his workers represented rather than letting those pesos leave the farm in the hands of passing merchants. Souchay developed this system on his farm in response to the presence of peddlers traveling a regional circuit of farms and villages, selling goods to slaves. His response implies the existence of a network that was both commercially viable and extensive enough to warrant a complex of salesmen. The success of such a commercial system would have relied on the ongoing acquisition of disposable income by a significant number of slaves living within the district. He may also have wanted to limit the viability of the coartación system by extracting capital from the hands of those with such an inclination. While there is no evidence to support this assertion, there is little evidence to suggest that his slaves participated in the system even in its heyday.

There are also records of slaves with mobility spending money in nearby towns and taverns. Abbot noted that many complained about slave drinking, but little seemed to be done to prevent it:

> In traveling in Cuba, I have heard the remarks of many planters on the subject of aguadiente, or ardent spirit, and its effects on negroes. As it is sold for half a bit for a junk bottle of it; as taverns are thick all over the country, where it can be bought; as few negroes are without money, and most of them are passionately fond of the liquor, it follows pretty naturally that they drink it, and the usual evils, physical and moral, are lamentably frequent.[38]

Two things stand out in this observation. The first is that from what he has seen and been told, there are few Africans on the island without money and they chose to spend it in part on drink in taverns. The second point is that there were taverns scattered all over the countryside, which implies slave mobility. This also suggests that slaves had an opportunity to meet other Africans who lived in their district and to interact with them in taverns. More work needs to be done to ascertain the locations and concentrations of taverns; Abbot's travels were largely in areas with high concentrations of cafetales.

The slaves of the Angerona were clearly spending their money on goods, but there is evidence that some among the enslaved on other cafetales were spend-

ing their precious resources on more than small items. Some workers were ap-
plying their earnings toward their freedom through the system of coartación.
The system of self-purchase evolved over the course of two centuries of early
colonial rule as a customary system with a set of practices and agreed-on rules.[39]
These included the formal establishment of a price for an individual's freedom
set by assessors. If there were differences in assessment, the dispute could be
arbitrated in court. Payments were accepted in installments and the *coartado*
or *coartada* (the slave buying his or her freedom) had the right to force a sale
to another slaveholder at his or her discretion. In the case of a slave who had
begun payments and subsequently his or her master died, or a slave who was
sold to another slaveholder, previously paid monies were credited to the slave's
account and carried forward. These were limited rights, but they were important nonetheless. Slaves had access to the courts and used them to complain of
mistreatment and to request the opportunity to be sold to another slaveholder.
Thus, a slave had some degree of leverage in his or her relationship with a slaveholder. This could be used in a variety of ways, but it provided some modicum of
self-protection. The right to coartación was more significant than the protections
provided by court action, in that it offered not just a change of situation but a
removal from the slave system itself, thus offering the enslaved some avenue to
self-determination. This possibility offered hope to the enslaved.

The opportunity to participate in the coartación system was dependent on access to the economy. To buy one's freedom, one needed money or an income to
be able to make regular payments. There is evidence that slaves on many types
of plantations were coartados or coartadas, but the access to time and resources
suggests that slaves on cafetales were overrepresented. The evidence is uneven,
but there are many examples of coartados and coartadas on coffee farms. On
the cafetal Paciencia, for example, there were a number of slaves who were de-
positing money with the manager of the farm toward the eventual purchase that
would secure their release from bondage. These included Nicolas (90 pesos),
José María (237, toward a total price of 800 pesos), and Ysabel (200 pesos).[40]
William Hulbert observed many slaves who had gained a quasi-free state in
which they had several days a week away from the supervision of their masters
as a result of the coartación system.[41] Rafael *gangá* of the cafetal Resurrección
may have been a slave such as those described by Hulbert, for he had earned a
substantial amount of money by 1832. Plantation records indicate that he had
paid five hundred pesos to secure his liberty.[42] The number of slaves who gained
their freedom from slavery through the coartación system was limited. Nevertheless, it is my contention that many more slaves participated in the system than
actually saw the process through to the end. Large numbers may have not completed their payments because of a variety of reasons, including sickness, flight,
death, or the loss of opportunity to earn significant amounts of money. The record of slave deposits is substantial and testifies both to the hope that coartación
represented and to the extensiveness of the slave economy that it encouraged.

The enslaved on coffee plantations created an economy within their own constrained sphere of activities. Often at the insistence of plantation owners, slaves raised food crops and animals that they consumed, thereby contributing to the profitability of the farms on which they lived and worked. They also sold some of their produce, earning money for themselves. Moreover, it is evident that some slaves produced goods such as religious objects for sale or exchange for services with other slaves. The money that Africans and their offspring earned made its way into the larger island economy through the purchase of goods from passing peddlers, in nearby stores, or on the plantation. They also spent money at taverns and likely on other sorts of entertainment. Another way workers spent money was in participating in the system of coartación, working toward buying their freedom from bondage. All these examples of economic activity suggest a functioning economy within the world of the slaves.

More work needs to be done on this topic to determine with precision the scope and size of the slave economy, as well as how the coartación system fed into the free black population. The evidence suggests that the system was more vibrant than previously assumed. According to the records from the censuses of 1827 and 1841, the free population of color grew at a rate of approximately 43 percent during the fourteen years between the two counts. This rate of expansion was faster than that of the white population, which grew 34.5 percent over the same period. It should be noted that the enslaved population expanded even more rapidly, some 52 percent, during the same period.[43]

The creation and expression of economic life by enslaved workers shows the resiliency of the Africans in the face of repression. They grabbed whatever opportunity they could to assert their humanity. The shape of this economy reflects not only their circumstances but also their culture. Culture helped people to survive cognitively by reestablishing some sense of normalcy in a few spaces of their lives. Building new social ties and family connections was a cultural act, but it also facilitated new cultural productions and the networks needed to foster economic activities. Economic life helped slaves to survive physically by enriching their diets and their social sphere. Together these could help people to begin to find a way to find some measure of autonomy and in some cases even liberation. This growing sense of autonomy and ability to act in many normal or normative ways would also ultimately contribute to slave resistance more broadly, as we will see in the next chapter.

As with many aspects of slave life and action, the economic life of the enslaved can be perceived in multiple ways. On the one hand, slaves were participating in the system that oppressed them in a classic form of hegemonic domination. Through their economic activities, they contributed to local wealth, which in many ways strengthened the grip on power held by slaveholders. Slaves were literally buying into the system. Slaves were also creating important ties to the land that their masters were encouraging, for, as the slaveholders understood, slaves who had a stake in the success of their farms and a connection to where they lived tended to be more compliant.[44] On the other hand, planters were hoping to create an efficient workforce that required a minimal amount of force to extract a maximum amount of labor, but slaves were working for themselves in a way that was undermining the system from within. By actively engaging in productive self-directed activities, slaves were invalidating the notion of the need for coerced labor. They were demonstrating that the land could be productive and profitable without the use of violence and coerced labor. The Africans' choices and actions, expressed through their economic potential, exposed the lie of the slave system and laid bare the avarice that was at its core.

CHAPTER 6

When Everyday Actions Escalate
Resistance, Rebellions, and Cultural Complexity

¡Carajo, queremos libertad! (Shit, we want liberty!)
—Alejo *lucumí*

It is astonishing how long people can live on the surface of a
volcano without realizing its dangers. —Mary Peabody Mann

All slaves exercised agency in both simple and complex ways, but the slaves on the cafetales of the vuelta abajo were exceptional. Agency took many forms, which included personal choices as well as collective actions. The actions taken were sometimes simple and singular and at other times they were complex, with overlapping articulations. They could be passive, nonaggressive, or violent, but they were all forms of resistance. A slave sitting alone in his bohío making a drum or a muñeca was an individual undertaking both a simple deed of creativity and one that was layered with meaning. The result of this endeavor was used in group performance, which was additionally laden with cultural meanings that contested the legitimacy of the slave system. Sometimes these acts of agency were more overtly moves of resistance and insubordination that included violence. Throughout the history of slavery, those in bondage rose up against their oppressors in acts small and large. Violent expressions of resistance offer a unique opportunity to see culture in action through the exercise of practices overlaid with the immediacy of confrontation. An analysis of acts of insubordination located with the cultural and material context of the cafetal also offers additional insight into the construction and functionality of interethnic networks that were vital in transforming individual and group consciousness. When the daily tension between begrudging accommodation and overt resistance ruptured, the lines that delineated shifting cosmologies and the cultural boundaries of proper conduct and past, present, and future identifications were cast in relief.

Overt acts of resistance and rebellions marked the borders of compliance. When slaves revolted, they often were acting in response to a variety of external reasons, which could include poor or abusive treatment, deficient living conditions, or general dissatisfaction with enslavement. More broadly, these actions and reactions can be understood through the intersection of several analytical perspectives. First, the framework of generations of slavery developed by Ira Berlin, writing about enslavement in North America, offers some useful insights. He stated that the slave system went through three distinct phases, which he named the "charter generations," "plantation generations," and "revolutionary generations."[1] Berlin argued that slavery had unique characteristics within each of these periods, from its formational period, with fairly lax legal structures, to its full articulation, with a rigorous social and legal foundation, to the conflicted years at the end of the slave era, which were marked by a general discourse of human liberty, the abolition movements, and an increase in actions by slaves against the system. It was during the years of what Berlin has called the "revolutionary generations" that the American War of Independence, the French Revolution, and the Haitian Revolution occurred. It was also the beginning of the end of the transatlantic slave system, as the British abolition movement achieved a firm foothold at the end of the eighteenth century. The abolitionists made important gains in suppressing the slave trade internationally, with the first treaties outlawing the Atlantic trade in 1808 by Great Britain and the United States, followed by Spain in 1820. Abolitionists were also increasingly active in spreading their message throughout Europe and the Western Hemisphere. Berlin argues that this general climate facilitated or encouraged slaves to agitate for their own freedom. It was in this broad context that the Cuban plantation boom occurred. The model Berlin proposes conforms to North American periodization and therefore might not seem directly applicable to other cases in which slavery followed a different chronology (starting earlier or later, for example). If we set aside the chronological elements and focus on the conceptual framework, we can then see the usefulness of his ideas. In the case of Cuba, the last two stages he proposes happened at a very accelerated pace, with the two unfolding nearly simultaneously.

The exposure to and understanding of enslavement within African societies offers another perspective into the experience of enslaved Africans in Cuba during this period. Slaves arrived in Cuba from African nations in which elites kept slaves. This meant that the newly enslaved who were brought to the island had preexisting knowledge of how a slave system "should" operate. Notions of slavery and the treatment of slaves varied, based on an individual's exposure to systems of slavery. Nevertheless, we can be confident that nearly all new slaves in Cuba had some previous experience in societies with slaves, which imbued them with a general concept of the appropriate or proper way slaves were to be treated and the dynamic of the master/slave relationship. These ideas were also intercut with persistent cosmological ideas about the nature of the universe and the place of humans within the order of things. As discussed in Chapter 4, many Africans shared some basic underlying ideas that produced religious systems with similar notions of how human relationships and the world in which they lived worked or at least ought to work. In this context, I contend that slave concepts of proper codes of conduct—what constituted social and antisocial behavior—informed their decisions to exercise agency passively or aggressively. In other words, enslaved African people and creoles resisted slavery in a variety of ways that were informed by cultural calculations. They were motivated to more active modes when codes of conduct were breached.

From 1790 to 1845 slaves ignited numerous large and small insurrections and rebellions. Acts of resistance were commonplace, as slaves utilized what James Scott has called the "weapons of the weak," by feigning illness, working slowly, or striking out spontaneously against the mayoral or contramayoral.[2] There was also a collection of small-scale incidents of violence containing distinct overtones of collective action based in nascent intra-ethnic networks that referenced deeply held concepts of proper conduct. Four large-scale rebellions occurred during the period. Two of the four rebellions, the 1812 Aponte conspiracy and *La Escalera* (The Ladder) of 1844, were directed at the slave system more broadly, and these actions will not be discussed within this context.[3]

This chapter will explore several examples of slave revolts both large and small that show how slaves were motivated to respond to the limits of their agency with violence. These actions ranged from individual confrontations to those that involved hundreds of people and spanned several plantations. Acts of insubordination were the most visible way that slaves contested systems of control but embedded within slave violence were the same elements of cultural performance that were present in daily life. The chapter will argue for a new understanding of slaves' motivations for revolts. We have often understood slave rebellions as reactions to harsh conditions or as part of the struggle for freedom. These explanations do offer some insight but do not help us to understand other incidents where these types of motives are not evident. The model of struggle and reaction within a violent system does not tell us why some acts of violence against slaves were tolerated while other incidents were grounds for revolt. It tells us nothing of complex incidents where no overt violence had occurred. The examples in this chapter will show that the enslaved often acted in response to or rose up against their oppressors when they felt the social fabric had been breached. When a slaveholder or a mayoral overstepped understood norms or conditions suggested an evil force was at work, as in the case of epidemic disease, then Africans would respond, often collectively. Failing to take seriously the complex motives enslaved Africans acted on impoverishes our understanding to no better than that of their captors. A limited explanatory framework also reduces the African slaves to two-dimensional, less-than-human figures. The incidents that follow redress that imbalance.

In mid-June 1825, the cafetales scattered across the countryside of the valley Guamacaro near Matanzas exploded in rebellion.[4] The revolt that began on the cafetal de Fouquier was the first large slave rebellion of the nineteenth century organized entirely by African-born slaves, and its organization offers an important example of cross-cultural alliances and the role of religion in revolts. Located on the extreme eastern end of the coffee-growing district of western Cuba, it was arguably the bloodiest uprising of slaves in Cuba. The leaders, Pablo *gangá*, Federico *carabalí*, and Lorenzo *lucumí*, plotted for months to strike a blow against their masters and escape their enslavement by fleeing to the plantation. It is notable that the three leaders were of differing backgrounds. In contrast, a significant number of the rebelling slaves were Carabalí and the revolt involved slaves from "eighteen to twenty coffee plantations each one of which had a captain organizing the slave populace."[5] Manuel Barcia points out that this evidence of diversity exposed an idea that slaveholders held—that if they had mixed populations, it would inhibit solidarity among the population and thus reduce the incidence of violent revolt. The diversity of the leadership shows that slaves were able to find common ground, creating interethnic cross-cultural alliances and working together to resist enslavement.

Federico *carabalí* was a religious specialist of considerable power. The slaves reportedly regarded his religious powers as genuine.[6] We do not know the extent of Federico's performance of rituals leading up to the rebellion but he was considered a leader among the slaves. His abilities would have been instrumental in creating the group solidarity that this action demonstrated. The high degree of group cohesion was evident in two ways once the rebellion was underway. First, there were dozens of slaves from a number of plantations involved and they were from several ethnic groups. Second, once fighting commenced, Lorenzo *lucumí* took command of the rebels. The majority of the rebels were Carabalí, and yet they followed the Lucumí Lorenzo into conflict in spite of the great odds against them. They fought bravely, holding their own for several days. In the end, however, they were defeated, as they were outmanned and had inferior weapons. Barcia notes that the slaves' motives were unclear: they were dissatisfied and looked to better their situation through flight, but they sought to punish their oppressors first.[7] While we lack direct evidence, this attitude and the determination and cohesion the group displayed strongly suggests that there had been repeated incidents that the enslaved found intolerable. When it was over, sixteen whites had been killed by the rebelling slaves. Twenty-three slaves were executed and many more received sentences of one hundred lashes. This incident clearly points to the development of networks that crossed ethnic lines and plantation borders. It also suggests the importance of the cafetal environment in the slaves' ability to exercise sufficient agency over their time to organize such a wide-ranging revolt. They were likewise able to use their physical space to plan and achieve cross-cultural understandings through repeated contact between individuals, building the mutual trust required to build a troop of fighters dedicated to a cause. Officials blamed the uprising on "foreign" slaves—creoles from other parts of the Americas—and the "excessively permissive" environment of the cafetales. Both Barcia and García contend that the result of this rebellion was a reexamination of the existing slave code, the *Código Carolino* of 1788, and a rearticulation and clarification of its articles to ensure the peace.[8]

Beatings without reason and the withholding of water by mayorales sparked two uprisings on cafetales in the region. The first occurred on the cafetal El Carmen in 1827, when several slaves plotted and attempted to kill the mayoral, Ramón Viera. The leaders of the slaves were Simón *mina*, Celedonia *mandinga*, and Ventura *congo.* They were thwarted in their plot because of the suspicions of Viera. One thing stands out in this account that is revealed in Simón *mina*'s testimony. According to Simón, the plot was precipitated by what the slaves viewed as an unjust act—the whipping of Nepomuceno *congo.* This final act was consonant with Viera's usual way of interacting with the slaves but was described as particularly egregious on two counts: the whipping was unjustified, and Nepomuceno was young (and thus did not deserve such harsh treatment). The proposed punishment of Viera reflects his habitual inequitable actions against the larger group—Simón *mina* testified that Viera whipped them as often as "water falls from the skies."[9] Viera must have known that the slaves might seek recompense against him; suspecting the plot, he hid in fear for his life.

A similar incident that escalated to a full-scale rebellion happened on the cafetal Juanita, discussed in Chapter 4. On the Juanita, the slaves successfully launched a rebellion with a series of reprisals against plantation authorities that also reached to a neighboring farm. As in the case of El Carmen, the slaves on the Juanita had a complaint against their mayoral, José de la Luz Pino. Slaves testified that de la Luz Pino had withheld water from them, an act that struck at the heart of the social order in which the slaves lived. Water during work in a tropical environment is a most basic need and denying that while at the same time driving the workers to continue their labor went beyond harsh to a level of unreasonable and dangerous. The enslaved felt it within their rights to rid themselves of a person who acted in a harmful and pathological way. Actions such as these were often characterized as wild or savage, but when viewed from within the African framework of understanding social relations, they seem rational and appropriate.

A larger and more complex incident occurred near Banes in 1833 for which more detailed records survive. It offers new insights into African motivations, cooperation, and actions during rebellions. The rebellion that began on the cafetal known as El Salvador was plotted and carried out during an epidemic of cholera morbus that killed hundreds in the region. Banes is southeast of Mariel, west of Havana, and just north of the vuelta abajo, separated from it by a range of steep hills. Hundreds of slaves rose up and killed the overseer of cafetal Salvador in August 1833, beginning a revolt that had many similarities to the 1825 conflict on the cafetal Fouquier. The slave action lasted approximately forty-eight hours and was followed by a lengthy investigation that produced extensive testimony by the slaves, offering not only insight into the events and the motivations of the participants but also additional clues into the nature of life on cafetal Salvador.

Around four o'clock in the afternoon of August 11, 1833, Francisco Santiago Aguirre departed his large coffee plantation, the Salvador, for business in Havana. He left the farm and its 375 slaves in the hands of his trusted employees: the *mayordomo* (plantation manager), Diego Barreiro; the mayoral, Eugenio Damaurrete; the *maestro albañil* (chief mason), Blas Hernandes; and the doctor, Luis José Zepeda. The owner rode to the capital city with a false sense of security, apparently with little thought that a storm might be brewing among his slaves.[10] Two short days after Aguirre departed, on the evening of August 13, the slaves of the cafetal Salvador rose up violently against those left to oversee the farm.

Their action seems to have been sparked by a simple act carried out by the mayoral. According to José Baguero, the doctor's assistant, Damaurrete went down to the batey, the area of the slave quarters, between 8 and 9 o'clock with the intent of closing up the barracón of the bozales. When he attempted to close the door of the building, the slaves, brandishing sticks and rocks, attacked him. He cried out for help, but Baguero, fearing for his own safety, did not aid the mayoral.[11] Joaquín *lucumí*, the contramayoral, led some of the bozales as they attacked Damaurrete furiously. They struck him numerous times on the head and back, beating him until he was dead.[12] Diego Barreiro, the *mayordomo*, reported that around the same time, he was relaxing in his quarters and heard the slaves drumming and singing a loud repeated call in the Lucumí language. The slaves were calling out *hó bé, hó bé*, which he did not understand, but it was a call to come together—a meeting song in the Lucumí language.[13] He went out of the house to see what was happening when a group of indeterminate size approached. Among them was a slave named Alejo, whom Barreiro recognized. He called out to Alejo and asked him what was happening and where he thought he was going. Alejo responded, "Shit, we want liberty!" and continued on his way. Barreiro noted that Alejo held a machete menacingly in his left hand.[14]

Several points emerge from the initial incident. The attack against the mayoral was not an impulsive blow. Two elements reveal preparation. A number of slaves were lying in wait for Damaurrete when he came to close up the barracón. They anticipated that moment of vulnerability and used it to launch their assault. The testimony of Margarita *lucumí* confirms that this was a planned attack. She told of a meeting that had occurred several days earlier in which the Lucumís discussed rebellion. She reported that the question "Who wants to make war?" was raised. A slave called "Labrao" (also known as "Fierabrás") responded by forcefully arguing that they were being abused by the whites and ought to be free. He was persuasive, and plans began to be made.[15] The second important factor was the involvement of Joaquín *lucumí*. His status as contramayoral shows he was considered trustworthy by the slaveholders. As a result, the presence of Joaquín outside of the barracón as Damaurrete approached would not have aroused suspicion. Joaquín stationing himself outside the slave quarters would have reassured Damaurrete and may have led the mayoral to lower his guard. Contramayorales were ladinos (i.e., relatively acculturated), and in leading the bozales, Joaquín bridged a potential gap between the established slave population (of approximately 150) and the new arrivals (numbering nearly 220).

Following the initial flurry of action, Joaquín, Fierabrás, and two other contramayorales, Luís *lucumí* and Alejo *lucumí*, quickly began to organize groups of slaves. Another slave, José *mina*, recounted what he saw of the efforts to organize. In the early evening, José was sitting in the doorway of the kitchen with Nicolas and Francisco Paula when they heard a loud noise coming from the batey. They all turned and could see a large number of bozales assembled in the area between the barracón and the main house, armed with sticks, stones, and machetes. Manuela *lucumí* said that the bozales were singing a war song from their homeland. The four leaders, Fierabrás, Joaquín, Luís, and Alejo, called out *oní oré* and the others responded *o 'fé* in the Lucumí language.[16] This was the call-and-response song summoning people to war. She added that the leaders threatened those who resisted joining the uprising. The group was led by the bozal Fierabrás, whom José described as a very tall Lucumí and the captain of the bozales. Fierabrás called the recently arrived slaves together in front of the main house to rally them and apparently detail a plan. José felt the menacing intent of the crowd as they shouted and brandished their weapons, and he feared for the safety of everyone on the farm.[17]

Fierabrás continued to speak to the bozales, provoking the group into a highly agitated state. As the threat of violence escalated, Blas Hernandes and a young slave removed Baltazara Aguirre, the aged mother of the plantation owner, from the house and carried her away from danger. While they were fleeing, some of the bozales burst into the house and ransacked it. They destroyed the contents of the dwelling, seized the firearms the owner and overseer had stored there, and took everything else that could be used as a weapon.[18] Meanwhile, Joaquín organized the ladino slaves with the intent to proceed to nearby plantations and free the slaves living on those other farms, so that they might "all be free in the vuelta de abajo."[19] José *mina*, either out of loyalty to Aguirre or in fear of the repercussions the revolt might precipitate, fled to the nearby cafetal Sandrino to warn of the rebellion because there were "Christian people there who could hold in check the rebelling negroes."[20] Around the same time, the mayordomo, Diego Barreiro, fled the farm and rode to the town of Guanajay to report the uprising to local officials.[21]

Hundreds of slaves—bozales and ladinos, led by Joaquín, Fierabrás, and Luis *lucumí*—marched to the cafetal Sandrino, seeking to enlist the slaves there in the uprising. Finding few, they took what weapons and provisions they could and marched on. From the Sandrino, they proceeded to the ingenio El Fénix, drumming, blowing cow horns, and singing war songs as they went.[22] Being forewarned of the attack, the owners of both the Sandrino and the Fénix had quickly moved their slaves into the fields and hidden them from the oncoming force. Unable to enlist supporters, the Salvador slaves turned to the destruction of property. They ransacked buildings, took weapons, seized several horses, and set structures on fire, and then set off on the road to Banes. Once they reached Banes, the rebels continued their rampage, setting several houses on fire and attacking the townspeople they encountered, injuring a number and killing at least two. With most residents in hiding, the slaves seized a number of weapons as well as food. According to the testimony of numerous slaves, all the weapons were surrendered to Fierabrás, who redistributed them to those he judged most able to use them, with special attention given to the firearms. The contingent then returned to the cafetal Salvador to regroup.

The rebellion continued throughout the next day and into the following morning, with the slaves of the Salvador attacking other nearby farms and skirmishing with the royal militia, which had arrived on August 14 to suppress the uprising. These encounters were not without cost: many were wounded and some were killed. Among the dead was contramayoral Luis *lucumí*, who, according to descriptions, led slave fighters into conflict dressed in colorful clothes that appeared African in design. José Hernandéz Quintana described seeing Luís on the *camino real*, leading a troop dressed in feathered attire and accompanied by a woman who was carrying a red parasol, shading Luís.[23] This attire and behavior strongly suggests that Luís was acting as an *Oba* or *Oni de Ifé*, a Yoruban (Lucumí) political and spiritual leader.[24]

The high degree of organization in this rebellion was apparent.[25] Out of the seemingly chaotic initial events, the influence of three leaders became apparent; two were ladinos and the other a bozal. Joaquín, Luís, and Fierabrás worked together to coordinate the factions on the farm, leading them in unified action. They directed attacks on a total of six farms and marched a mixed group of fighters, some on horseback and the rest on foot, several kilometers to strike the town of Banes. It is also notable that the group included women who fought alongside the men. The three leaders maintained control over weapons and held together their contingent in the face of the superior force of the militia. A key element in the ability to direct this large number of slaves was the degree of cultural capital available to the group.[26]

The investigation of the uprising revealed two distinct factions that lived on Salvador. The core was the ladino population of approximately 150 people who were, as was typical of many coffee plantations, of various ethnic backgrounds. Significantly, and atypically, the bozal population of approximately 220 people was larger, and nearly all categorized as Lucumí. Cooperation within and between these groups suggests networks of assistance and support fostered by interaction and facilitated through threads of commonality and shared interests and experience. The bozales, through their actions in the field, showed evidence of remnants of past associations from their Oyo homeland. These may have been reinforced through the ordeal of the Middle Passage and further bolstered by their common experiences on the Salvador.[27] The ladino population had time to forge new bonds that did not rely on past connections or behavior but was rooted in locally developed relationships. The leadership of Joaquín and Luis was crucial in forging a working alliance between the two groups as they were both ladinos and of Lucumí origin. They could bridge the gap between the two populations. The depositions revealed that they held important positions of leadership as contramayorales and they used the Lucumí language during the revolt. In addition, and maybe most revealing, was the dress of Luís, the slain contramayoral, who led slaves into skirmishes with the militia dressed as a Lucumí leader.

The costume he wore was not something that could be assembled hastily. Rather, it would have required a great deal of time, preparation, and material. Typically, the main article worn by an Oni de Ifé was a headdress that was distinctively adorned with beads and shells in patterns that represented his town and orisha affiliation. The descriptions of Luís lack detail but mention the use of feathers on his costume.[28] His appearance in regalia reveals the ongoing maintenance of cultural and religious practice on the Salvador. Furthermore, as in other cases, we can glimpse the time and resources available to the slaves who lived and worked on the cafetal. The control of time, to be able to direct the use of this resource, was crucial to the project of cultural expression. We cannot know for certain why Luis chose to wear Lucumí-type garb that day to lead fighters against their oppressors but we can say that there was an underlying assumption that what he wore would be understood as a symbol of strength and power and would have resonance with a cross-section of the warriors.

Further evidence of a surviving and transforming culture can be seen in the words and actions of Joaquín. He displayed a sense of solidarity with other enslaved Africans that transcended ethnic lines and plantation borders when he insisted on following a dangerous course of action to free those on surrounding farms. Joaquín justified this action with his extraordinary statement that all should be "free in the vuelta de abajo."[29] The group followed his lead and by their complicit actions revealed something of their sense of solidarity through a commitment to a goal beyond simple self-interest. A number of elements of this nascent pan-ethnic culture would have been clearly understood by the newly arrived slaves and this shared shard of identity would have been sufficient to fashion a fighting coalition.

The behavior of Joaquín *lucumí* points to what David Geggus, building on the works of Eugene Genovese and Michael Craton, has called the culture of resistance fostered by slave societies.[30] Genovese has argued that cultural constructions, particularly syncretic religious practices, were an important form of resistance, as they were accommodating or adaptive on the one hand but created solidarity against the ruling class on the other.[31] Craton, in his study of slave rebellions in the West Indies, contends that acts of insubordination revealed the tension between accommodation and resistance, and the struggle to shape new identities through emerging culture.[32] Geggus further suggests that cultural solidarity may have been a necessary precondition for uprisings. He agrees there was a culture of resistance but argues that this emerged in conjunction with nascent creole cultures. Before a large-scale or wider rebellion could occur, a large number of the participants had to find some common ground through cultural connections. In other words, some kind of foundation of common interest or cause—what I am calling "cultural capital"—had to accrue prior to action. Manuel Barcia argues that the slave rebellions of the first half of the nineteenth century in Cuba were mainly the consequence of the actions and ideas of enslaved Africans—not, as some have argued, the result of revolutionary ideas circulating during the era.[33] The commonalities of African cultures formed the conceptual base on which new experiences could be built. I concur with Barcia that the evidence points to African organization and conceptual underpinnings throughout the first half of the nineteenth century for slave rebellions. This is contrary to the view held by some that most rebellious actions were fostered by creoles. It is clear that creoles were involved in many actions, but this is a correlation rather than a causal relationship. I contend that these new cultural resources were accrued through alliances and would be drawn on to unite people and to sustain the uprising on the Salvador and elsewhere.[34] I also would add that cultural solidarity can occur, as in the case of the Salvador rebellion, through the intervention of cultural arbiters who had the ability to navigate between native and creole cultural differences. This may help us to understand how the uprising on the cafetal Salvador unfolded, but it does not uncover why the slaves acted when they did.

While cultural solidarity was necessary for wider action and we can often identify the spark or flash point that marked the start of an event, the central issue at stake was often obscured. The motivations to act at a given moment seem to have been a complex mixture of grievances and goals within a framework of agreed-upon responses. It is self-evident to modern observers that slaves would have objected to being in bondage. But to better understand how slaves understood their circumstances, it is important to remember that enslaved Africans acted within an understanding of the world that included slavery as a common institution within the norms of society. Slaves of African origin came from cultures in which slavery existed. They arrived in Cuba with an understanding of slavery based on their own backgrounds that included ideas concerning the parameters of proper relationships, including that of the master and slave.[35] When those norms were approximated in Cuba, as they often were on coffee plantations, day-to-day coexistence was (relatively) peaceful. When owners or their agents crossed the line of acceptable behavior, the system broke down. If a large number of slaves acted, it likely was because of transgressions by owners or their agents of the understood norms of master/slave interactions. The ability to practice culture on coffee plantations created a space in which these norms were cognitively reinforced and valorized. The testimony of the owner of the Salvador, Aguirre, concerning the rebellion on his cafetal, may shed some additional light on the matter.

Upon hearing of the calamity surrounding the uprising, Aguirre immediately returned to the Salvador to find many buildings on the plantation ransacked. His initial reaction was a mix of surprise and consternation at the destruction. He claimed that his slaves were well cared for and perfectly provisioned. They were treated and allowed to convalesce when sick, and had not recently been punished. In response to the epidemic of cholera morbus that had swept through the area, Aguirre had kept his slaves isolated from others, kept a doctor and an assistant on the farm, and reduced work hours to try to ensure the health of his workers.[36] With these public assertions, Aguirre was implicitly appealing to understood norms that reflected the reciprocal nature of the master/slave relationship as he understood them. He was affirming that he had fulfilled his responsibilities to his slaves, and that they owed him obedience and labor in return. Events show the slaves disagreed with his assessment.

A government official, Tomás de Salazar, was dispatched to the cafetal to investigate the cause of the uprising so that order and, more importantly, the confidence of the local slaveholding population might be restored. Salazar began his inquiry, taking testimony from the survivors, free and slave, on August 16.[37] His initial hypothesis was that the slaves had been infiltrated or influenced by outsiders, specifically British abolitionists. This was a common fear at the time, especially in cases when slave actions spilled over to surrounding farms and populations. These fears were rooted in ongoing anxieties about the rebellion that had occurred in the neighboring French colony of Saint Domingue that came to be known as the Haitian Revolution. These fears were further amplified in Cuba by the British movement against the international trade in slaves, ratified by treaty in 1808 and officially supported by the new nation of the United States to Cuba's north. Anxiety among slaveholders on the island continued to grow as English antislavery discourse increased and Madrid and London negotiated a slave trade suppression treaty. The treaty took effect in 1820 and also created a new mixed commission court to oversee compliance with the treaty. This, in effect, placed English abolitionists on Cuban soil. Nevertheless, there was little evidence to support Salazar's initial theory and he soon abandoned it. He next turned his attention to the presence of the bozales and concluded that the rebellion had occurred as a result of the imbalance in the plantation population. About 60 percent of the group were recent arrivals and this, in his view, had resulted in an unstable situation. Salazar reasoned that the large number of unseasoned slaves had become unmanageable and the situation had gotten out of hand. Interestingly, Aguirre was not held responsible in spite of the evidence that the slaves had been acquired from Africa recently, in violation of the standing treaty prohibiting such imports. There is evidence that this would be a pattern with Aguirre, as he was later prosecuted for illegal importation of slaves.[38]

Historian Juan Iduate argued that the uprising may have occurred as a by-product of the cholera morbus epidemic of 1832–1833. He speculated that fear of the disease, from which many thousands across the island died, led to panic on the part of the slaves.[39] The outbreak killed thousands in the area, disproportionately affecting Africans and their descendants, which meant that plantation dotaciones were especially affected by the disease. Cholera struck quickly, killing the afflicted within a few days of first symptoms. It is understandable that people may have feared the spreading disease, but it is unclear why this would prompt a revolt on the part of one group of slaves. Panic does not offer much explanatory insight into this incident, as it fails to account for the planning and organization that was evidenced by the actions of the slaves on the Salvador. Iduate does not offer any other explanation for the rebellion.

It is clear that people were concerned, even afraid, as the disease spread quickly and killed slaves disproportionately. As Kenneth Kiple has noted, this disease was often referred to as the "black man's disease."[40] This concern is reflected in the actions of Governor Mariano Ricafort, which I discussed in Chapter 3. Ricafort paid close attention to the spread of the disease, reporting regularly to Madrid. An examination of the data reveals that slaves were being struck down by the disease at a high rate. The chart in Chapter 3 illustrates the dramatically elevated rate of death among the population of people of color. The figures show that the rise and decline of incidents of cholera morbus was similar in the two population groups, though the impact it had on the enslaved population was much worse. Ricafort solicited cures from the population, and took actions to try to limit its spread. The governor's actions are consistent with apprehension, but there is no evidence of panic among the white population.

Locally, about 2,100 slaves perished in Havana during March and April of 1833. Additionally, in the three jurisdictions of Havana, nearly 3,200 slaves succumbed to the disease in the first nine months of the year.[41] It is likely that the slaves throughout the region were very aware of the spreading disease and death. The only evidence we have of unrest among the enslaved is the revolt on the Salvador. I would suggest that Iduate interpreted African reaction to disease in much the same way as scholars have misunderstood African notions of religious ideas and practices. But, in my view, this conflates later ideas about disease with notions of the primitive that do not do justice to African ideas regarding disease. I am convinced that enslaved Africans understood disease of this type in a particular way that called for specific types of action or remediation. I agree with Iduate that the epidemic affected the slaves' thinking, but not in the way he suggests. One of the leaders of the Salvador rebellion, Joaquín, called for the liberation of nearby slaves; he specifically mentioned freeing those held in the infirmaries, revealing that disease figured into his thinking. Also, the presence of the doctor on the Salvador points to the ongoing and very visible issue of the health of the slaves. I would suggest that Aguirre's slaves were motivated not by blind fear but by their understanding of the epidemic. Their notions of the causes of disease, especially epidemic disease, were shaped by their pasts and rooted in the cultures of west and west central Africa. As discussed in Chapter 4, disease was understood as having a spiritual component and thus would require a variety of responses. Slaves on the Salvador were informed by a way of understanding that also included their concept of reciprocal hierarchical relationships. Reciprocity within relationships is a concept that continues to inform Cuban culture down to the present. These taken together offer insight into possible motivations for a slave uprising in the face of an epidemic outbreak and why they would specifically target the symbols and people in power over them.

Most west African peoples understood disease as a manifestation of either relationships in disarray or of mal-intentioned action.[42] This concept of illness was widespread not only in western Africa but also in much of central Africa. Disease was not thought of as an environmental issue but a part of the dynamic personal and relational universe. Relationships needed to be kept balanced and functioning within established norms or people were adversely affected. Likewise, mal-intentioned or antisocial people who were powerful enough or in powerful positions over people could inflict harm on others. In other words, when leaders transgressed acceptable norms or behaved in antisocial ways, there were visible consequences and sometimes widespread effects, such as an epidemic.[43] Within this cultural universe, a marker of disease that was caused by outside forces was when it struck quickly, such as in the case of a cholera epidemic. The slaves of the Salvador may well have considered the epidemic as proof of the malevolent power of their captors. Furthermore, the steps taken by Aguirre and his agents, such as locking up and isolating the workers from others, may have been understood as further evidence of social evil and intent by those who controlled their movements. Their response could well be considered a pursuit of justice against the transgressors and was justified in their minds. The slave Joaquin's insistence on liberating the sick suggests that the remedy for the ills befalling the slaves was, at least in part, freedom from the hold of their captors, who had antisocial evil powers.

It is my conclusion that the cholera epidemic of the 1830s affected the populations disproportionately. Whites and those of African origin and descent both died in large numbers, but conditions were such that the enslaved died at a higher rate. The white population benefited from better living conditions and less exposure to the disease. How they understood disease and what was happening to them led them to look for treatments and inspired retreat from social interactions and the epidemic. Some may have understood the epidemic as a test from God that had to be endured. This would also elicit endurance in the face of difficulties. Africans did not have this response or the luxury of this sort of action. They read the epidemic as evidence of a social problem with a spiritual dynamic. This called for more direct action against those they deemed responsible—those who engaged the spiritual world in inappropriate ways that brought harm to their subordinates.

Culture was an important element in facilitating rebellion at cafetal Salvador and it may have been the presence of hundreds of new slaves, most with a similar cultural background, that was the critical factor. I would concede that in this case this was an important element, but I would also argue that the ladino culture was crucial, and it was the environment of the coffee plantation that was essential in providing the space in which culture could be reestablished and reimagined. Two more cases demonstrate that the presence of an ethnically homogenous group of bozales was not necessary to facilitate unified action: the uprising in 1835 that began on the cafetal Juanita, discussed earlier, and the 1842 disturbance on the cafetal Perseverancia. Both provide additional insight into the workings of insubordinate slaves on coffee plantations.

In July 1835, Pío *carabalí* of the cafetal Juanita killed Francisco Sánchez and José de la Luz Pino and set some of the farm buildings on fire. He then set out to reunite with Pablo and Gregorio, who were on the cafetal Duarte helping to bag coffee for market. Together, they killed Pablo Rabelo and severely wounded several others.[44] Several of the slaves reported that the mayoral Sánchez was very abusive of the slaves and they wanted to kill him. The Lucumí population of the farm had been meeting regularly with those of the nación on cafetal Duarte and they encouraged the slaves on both farms to do more than just kill the mayoral—to rise up and fight for their freedom and kill all the whites.[45] This was the greatest fear of the slaveholders: an incitement that would be a replication of the Haitian Revolution.

Several important aspects of this uprising reveal the ongoing maintenance of African-based notions of ethnic bonds as well as the possibilities for cross-ethnic action. The initial blow was struck by a Carabalí slave, but the cause was more broadly supported by slaves of diverse backgrounds on both the Juanita and the Duarte farm. Lucumí slaves were responsible for escalating the violence, but there was a faction of Lucumís who took a different approach. When the attack began, eleven Lucumí slaves fled to the nearby hills and hanged themselves, graphically demonstrating the idea that when they died, their souls would return to their homeland.[46] The surviving Lucumís were able to convince their fellow slaves to act together, carrying out a resistance that lasted five days. The interaction between the dotaciones of the two farms demonstrated the ability of slaves on coffee farms not only to see each other but to build relationships that were durable enough to plan and carry out a dangerous and ultimately deadly plan of action.

While some rebellions spilled off the plantation on which they began, involving a wider group of slaves and whites, some were contained either by force or by the nature of the insubordination. In 1842, an outbreak of a smaller scale occurred on the cafetal Perseverancia. The slaves of the cafetal had finished their work for the day and were eating when the sound of an argument filled the air. Basilio *lucumí* was loudly criticizing his wife, Felipa *lucumí*, for her preparation of the evening meal of fufú.[47] Contramayoral Dionisio *gangá* tried to intervene but only made matters worse. The mayordomo, Domingo Gurma, came to check on the disturbance and, seeking to bring things to a quick conclusion, struck down Felipa. Basilio rose to her defense and lashed out. A fight ensued and spilled out of the bohío. Gurma retreated and Basilio and others began to spread the word that the mayordomo had struck Felipa. At this point Andrés *lucumí* and his wife, Rosa *lucumí*, became involved in the widening dispute. They called the dotación together and spoke to them in the Lucumí language, what the mayoral Belén de la Rosa referred to as the work or field language, and Rosa encouraged them to attack the whites and defend their honor.[48] When Gurma returned to the batey with reinforcements, the slaves were waiting. There was a skirmish; Gurma was killed and several others were seriously injured.[49]

This disturbance was more clearly a spontaneous reaction and it was confined to a single plantation. But cultural solidarity was present here, as we can see in the actions of Basilio. When he realized that the mayordomo would return, he called on his fellows to rise to his defense and they responded, both male and female, and across ethnic lines. This incident was also clearly about transgression. The mayordomo had contravened the boundaries of acceptable behavior; he had violated the master/slave relationship on more than one occasion. First, he had whipped Andrés for what some considered normal behavior, and then he had intervened in a marital dispute, which was outside the bounds of his authority in the minds of the slaves. Rosa, the wife of Andrés, felt it was within her rights to seek justice when she proclaimed, "The whites should be killed because they should not castigate my spouse."[50] The slaves were actively trying to enforce boundaries and defend their cultural practices related to gender roles and relations and the use of their language.

The example of the uprising on cafetal Paciencia was not isolated. It was similar to other actions taken by slaves either trying to defend cultural practices or utilizing such activities within the context of revolt. The slaves of the Recompensa, who revolted in 1844, were continuing to exercise the elements of their cultural heritage. They were continuing to speak their language, practicing religious rituals, singing, dancing, and drumming. Within the context of the cultural world they had constructed, they employed religious practices to strike back at their oppressors. The slaves on the cafetal Mercedes also rose to the defense of cultural practice. The dotación revolted because they were not allowed to drum and dance on a religious holiday. These actions, taken together, suggest that the repression of cultural or religious expression, whether or not that was the intention of the authority figure, was sufficient cause in the minds of slaves to rebel.[51] The enslaved on cafetales had more opportunity to practice culture and as a result had more to defend.

It is evident that slavery was a system predicated on violence. Slave traders and slaveholders alike used violence to enslave Africans and bend them to their wills. It is axiomatic that the enslaved would respond with violence against those that held them in bondage. What was not apparent was why slaves rebelled when they did or where the stress points were in the system. Slaveholding elites and those who supported the system worked together to build an economy and a way of life that depended on slavery. They shared values and ideals that embraced a view of the cafetal as a place of beauty and tranquility. This vision included happy slaves living in their bohíos, performing the labor of the farm and living simple, uncluttered, unsophisticated lives. While there was some correspondence between the ideal and reality, there were gaps in its depiction, as in any story: reality is always more complex. Needless to say, this imagined scene did not include rebellious slaves. While slaveholders attempted to construct their idealized world, there were numerous unintended consequences that the slaves were able to exploit. One important element was the time they had under their own control. They used this valuable resource to build networks of social connections and to keep alive their cultures and languages. They built lives in this new place that enabled them to maintain many of their assumptions about the nature of reality and human interactions. When slaveholders' intentions or actions breached the cosmologically rooted assumptions and expectations of the Africans they held in bondage, the enslaved struck back with every means at their disposal.

The large numbers of women on the cafetales also contributed to this unique environment. Their presence created complications and effects that the slaveholding class did not fully understand or anticipate. Women's roles in these accounts of rebellions warrant additional emphasis, for in some cases, they seem almost invisible, while at other times they were more evidently at the center of the revolt. Enslaved women were an crucial element and their larger numbers on cafetales meant that they were more involved in the cultural practices and the preservation of norms on these farms. They were active participants and facilitators and did not conform to the passive ideal of women that the Spanish imagined women to be. The story of women in slave uprisings began on slave ships, where they used their greater access to the ship and crew to plot and expedite revolts.[52] Once in Cuba, they continued to be active agents of change. On the Salvador, women marched and fought right alongside men as they sought to fight back against the evil that brought disease. The incident on the Recompensa uncovered numerous religious objects that had been made by religious specialists on the farm, one of whom was a woman named Petra. On the Perseverancia, the disturbance began with a family argument. This incident could be read as a typical patriarchal story of a man defending his honor and his woman, but there was much more to the uprising than an escalation of male posturing. Family structure was assaulted but it was evident that this was not the first time. And it was a female leader who called for the punishment of death for the mayoral. Often the Spanish minimized the role of women in their investigations, but if close attention is given to the slaves' own words, then it becomes clear that women were always participating and at times taking leadership roles.

Putting aside contemporaneous Spanish gender notions, it seems obvious that women would be involved in all forms of resistance, as they were important in creating the social fabric on which collective actions depended. Women were crucial in creating the private discourses or transcripts that James Scott contends were operating below the surface of control and acted as a counterhegemonic mode of interaction.[53] Rebelling slaves needed networks to draw on in planning and carrying out actions, and these contacts were created and nurtured through cultural practices that women helped sustain.

Coffee plantations provided an essential environment for African agency. Enslaved workers were able to rebuild their lives, and to construct or reimagine their identities and cultures. The process of rebuilding along with redefining individual and collective identifications in the context of the coffee plantation complex involved a balancing act between accommodation and resistance. Slaves' understanding of the master/slave relationship helped them negotiate the tension between these two poles but the slave system in which they were embedded meant they were not in control of all the factors needed to maintain their equilibrium. When owners or their agents transgressed the bounds of proper conduct, the ground on which slaves built their worlds was destabilized. In response, they rose up to try to make the world right again in some limited way. To be sure, they wanted freedom but barring that, they wanted masters to adhere to an acceptable and just code of conduct. For the enslaved, resistance was not futile, but a way for them to impose their sense of justice on an inherently unjust system and its architects.

PART III
Harvest

CONCLUSION

Performing Culture and the Appropriation of Identifications

The hundreds of thousands of Africans and their children who lived and worked on the cafetales of western Cuba during the first half of the nineteenth century endured enslavement and resisted it through various strategies. It has been the aim of this book to restore their story to the historical record in a meaningful way. Their struggle to rebuild their lives and cultures, to adapt to their new environment, and to form new families had profound effects on themselves and on Cuba during their era, but it also affected the future of the island and its peoples. Their experiences and resistance provoked reactions within the slaveholding community and the broader free society that also touched their own lives. Slaveholders responded predictably with attempts to improve control over the population, harsher punishments, and finally the enactment of a new slave code. The free society at large was of two minds. Some supported the status quo while others began to side with abolitionists. These different trajectories created an array of political, social, and cultural reactions. On the part of the enslaved, the most important legacies created through their own actions were the maintenance of cultural traditions and raising of children. All these together would contribute to a distinct historical trajectory that shaped Cuba throughout the nineteenth century.

Slaves on cafetales exercised agency in a variety of ways that challenged the exercise of power projected through planter-defined structure. Slaveholders explicitly sought to mold a compliant, docile workforce and an ordered environment that projected a coherent message of control. The design was focused toward the production of labor. The flaw in the system, from the slaveholders' perspective, was that masters and their agents were unable to control completely the lives of the enslaved. Owners aimed to constrain the entire space that constituted the field of slave action, but they were unable to manage time in a way that left no possibility for the enslaved to act. This was especially true on cafetales. Slaves resisted the control through actions small and large, passive and violent, unintended and planned. In response, slaveholders reacted with increasing violence against the slaves under their control in order to put down uprisings as well as instill fear in the population to forestall further revolts. There are numerous examples of slaveholder violence against the insurgent slaves, such as the case of the Aponte rebellion of 1812. Once the rebels were discovered, they were publicly executed to set an example for others who might consider rebellion.[1] The heads of rebellious executed slaves were displayed following the repression of some uprisings, such as the revolt on the Salvador discussed in Chapter 6.[2] The use of violence continued to escalate until the so-called Escalera rebellion in 1844, in which many slaves were tortured to death to extract confessions and intelligence.[3] This revolt also highlights the increasing anxieties of the slaveholding class during the period, as they imagined vast conspiracies that in their minds resembled the Haitian Revolution.[4]

Slaveholder fears were also expressed in the new slave code promulgated in 1842.[5] The new code reveals the ambivalence within the slaveholding class about the correct approach to managing a large slave population. The new rules continue to emphasize the conversion and instruction of slaves in the Christian religion. The new code also includes an article that mandates teaching slaves to respect members of the slaveholding class. The new rules codified in law what had been customary practices regarding the system of coartación. These rules are clearly designed to instill obedience and passivity among the enslaved while also offering a ray of hope to those who can participate in self-purchase. At the same time, the new code reduced most of the minimal requirements of slaveholders with respect to the material needs of their workers; for example, it lowered clothing and food allotments. This potentially made slavery harsher but there is always the question of enforcement. While it has often been assumed that slave codes were rarely enforced, even selective use of the code would have had a broader impact.[6] On the one hand, we have seen that slaves were participating in coartación in significant numbers.[7] We can observe rising numbers of slave revolts during the period and increasing repression, finding its full expression in 1844.

This era is also when we see more active engagement with the ideas of abolition. Some of the freemen accused of being conspirators in the Escalera rebellion had been arguing for abolition and publicly calling for an end to the system. British abolitionist and consul to Cuba David Turnbull had travelled in Cuba during 1838–1839 and published an account of his travels entitled *Travels in the West: Cuba; With Notices of Porto Rico, and the Slave Trade*. He was a critic of slavery and the slave trade and began to advocate for more vigorous enforcement of the treaty between Great Britain and Spain banning the slave trade. He found support from several prominent Cubans, including José Antonio Saco and Domingo del Monte. Turnbull and del Monte were both implicated in the Escalera conspiracy.[8] But attempts to suppress the ideas of abolition were unsuccessful, as it continued to resurface, finally emerging as a major issue in the Ten Years' War that began in 1868.

For many Cubans, the sugar plantation was emblematic of wealth, hard labor, and struggles with slave populations. It was anything but beautiful; rather, it was the symbol of economic realities. The cafetal, on the other hand, was conceptualized as an idyllic plantation environment of beauty and tranquility.[9] This concept would become firmly embedded in the Cuban consciousness and continue to inform ideas about coffee plantations, and life on them, for generations, through later manuals as well as literature and other cultural productions. The space of the cafetal was often spoken of in feminine terms, as it represented a well-ordered beauty that brought a more civilized way of life to the untamed Cuban countryside.

The increasing numbers of Africans in Cuba, especially near the burgeoning cities of Havana and Matanzas in the west, were concerns, as were shifting notions of race and gender. These anxieties and competing ideas found expression in the emerging Cuban literature of writers such as Cirilo Villaverde and Gertrudis Gómez de Avellaneda. *Cecilia Valdés* and *Sab*, the 1830s novels by Villaverde and Gómez de Avellaneda respectively, weave complicated stories of star-crossed love that challenged ideas of race and gender of the time.[10] While Villaverde set his book in the urban environment of Havana, the work was contextualized by the coffee plantation. The beautiful cafetal stands for the rural plantation experience in the novel. His choice to use a cafetal as the rural setting underscores the importance of coffee during this era in Cuba's development. It also highlights the contradictions Villaverde felt had enmeshed his society. The cafetal stood for an ideal and its population of slaves were a major part of that vision. At the same time, the consequences of fostering that ideal had created challenges to the social order in Cuba. The novel addresses some of the most pressing issues of the day, including emerging notions of Cuban national identity. The story takes place during the period of the plantation boom and tells the story of a beautiful mulatta named Cecilia Valdés and her doomed affair with Leonardo Bamboa, the son of a wealthy planter and trader. As the plot unfolds, the reader learns that Bamboa and Valdés are half-siblings, unbeknownst to them. Bamboa's father and Cecilia's grandmother go to great lengths to hide the identity of Cecilia's father and they try to sabotage the incestuous relationship. Leonardo and Cecilia do enter into an affair, but he tires of her and turns to a "more suitable" match and marries Isabel Ilincheta. Cecilia becomes enraged and seduces another man whom she convinces to kill Leonardo. The story ends tragically, after many twists and turns, and in the process it highlights many of the social tensions of the day. The work has been read as an indictment of slavery and a commentary on race and rightly so. There is an secondary theme of gender and power that warrants scrutiny.

Much of the academic discourse about Cecilia Valdés has centered on the eponymous title character and the so-called racial escape hatch of whitening. Villaverde, though, turns this debate on its head by playing on one of the worst fears of the white population vis-à-vis *blanqueamiento* (whitening), the inability to distinguish true heritage and lineage and who was "really" white. This finds its expression in the incestuous relationship between the "nearly white" Cecilia and her white half-brother Leonardo. Framing the relationship in this way, Villaverde was able to reaffirm the mores of the time while exposing what he viewed as the inherent dangers and futility of the idea of whitening.

Villaverde's novel was part of a larger conversation that was happening among Cuban elites during the 1830s. One of the leading scholars of the day, José Antonio Saco, was arguing that it was becoming increasingly clear that slavery would end in Cuba as well, and that large numbers of Africans and people of African descent were going to become part of the colony and nation. He went on to contend that the only solution to this problem was blanqueamiento, coupled with additional white immigration. In that way Cuba would become, over time, a white island.[11]

This brings me to the puzzle that drew me into trying to make sense of this novel within the prevailing discourse of the day. *Cecilia Valdés* was an antislavery novel that revealed some of the problems within existing thinking about the "slave" problem as well as exposing the corrupt underbelly of Cuban society. And yet the novel was not only hailed as the first great Cuban work of fiction but became understood as both a reflection and shaper of nascent *cubanidad* (Cuban identity). As a result, it has continued to be read and taught in Cuban schools down to the present. To put it another way—why would an antislavery novel, produced in the context of the colony that was the penultimate slave society in the hemisphere, and that was critical in many ways of the culture of its readers, become so universally embraced by that same society?

One possible answer is that in spite of its abolitionist underpinnings, this was not a story that empowered people of color or called for a radical reshaping of the social structure. What Villaverde was advocating was honesty and openness in social relations, which were values that most people could and did support at least tacitly. But, more importantly, he carefully affirmed existing relations of power. This can be seen by taking a closer look at the characters, their relationships, and how power was manifest within and between these relationships.

The development of the character of Cecilia goes through several stages. At the beginning of the text, she is a young girl. Consistent with prevailing stereotypes of mixed people, she is weak and fragile, but also somewhat precocious. She does not yet know the power of her beauty, but as she becomes aware of it, she is depicted as increasingly in control of her life and exercising power over those around her—both male and female. Eventually Leonardo comes into her orbit. He is a symbol of the "natural" power hierarchy—white, male, upper-class elite. And yet the power of Cecilia, the "casi blanca mulata" (nearly white mulatta), brings him to his knees. As their relationship matures, he eventually reasserts control over her and their interactions as well as over his own life. He then begins to shift his attentions to a more "suitable" partner—someone of his own race and class—Isabel.

As the novel unfolds, Cecilia's power is increasingly depicted as problematic and against the natural order of things. Cecilia tries to reassert her power through various manipulations and ultimately her plot against Leonardo. At this stage of her development the author depicts her as petulant and spinning out of control. Cecilia carries out her plot, though she fails to accurately anticipate the consequences and her world comes crashing down around her.

Through the construction of the character of Cecilia as "nearly white," Villaverde explores a world in which whitening was a reality. In some ways, notably Cecilia's desirability, this version of reality seems credible. But as the reader comes to know this character, the author's critique of Saco's view comes into focus. The havoc she creates in her life and in the lives of those around her exposes what Villaverde saw as the naive vision of advocates of assimilation. He also reassured his white readers that they had little to fear from the population of color. He affirms that their systems of order and control were sufficient (if necessary reforms took place) to withstand potential power plays by people of color. In other words, there was no need for a strategy of whitening and in fact such a course could have disastrous consequences. His view, as expressed in the text, is that Cuba could end slavery, bring people of color more directly into their social structure, and, most importantly, remain in control of the entire society. Cecilia challenged power dynamics and the social order in two ways, by crossing the racial boundary and also by acting as a strong woman. Villaverde shows that by the reassertion of male authority, first Leonardo's and then that of the state, order could be restored. By maintaining the gender order, concerns about race could be overcome.

The story of Cecilia is set against the backdrop of the cafetal and its realities during the 1830s. The cafetales of Villaverde's native vuelta abajo were becoming increasingly populated by women and experiencing a rapid creolization by the 1830s. It was here as well as in Havana that women were becoming increasingly visible in ways that challenged and transgressed gender norms. The world of fiction reflected and shaped the reality of women of color. There were deeply ingrained ideas about the roles of women, which included the notion that women needed to be "enclosed."[12] Women of color, through the routines of their daily lives, broke the rules for women. They transgressed the gendered ideas of what women could do and ought to do. This was true for all women of color, including the growing numbers of women on coffee plantations.

It was on the cafetal Angerona that the case of Ursula Lambert unfolded. Lambert was a free woman of color who had met and then worked for Cornelio Souchay in Havana before moving to his cafetal. On the plantation, Lambert managed many of Souchay's affairs, including the house and his accounts. Lambert's skills were impressive and helped turn the farm into a profitable venture. During a period of financial difficulty, Souchay had stopped paying Lambert her wages and she had used other funds and savings to continue paying some other free workers. Souchay, after the farm returned to profitability, created a list of creditors for his lawyer to repay those debts. He listed Lambert among the creditors, in the amount of twenty thousand pesos. A legal fight ensued when the lawyer excluded Lambert, as he could not believe a woman of color could have done the work or had the resources to warrant such a claim. Reminiscent of the fictional Cecilia Valdés, Lambert was rumored to be the mistress of Souchay, although evidence has never been found beyond the suspicions of many. Lambert, for her part, clearly was fearless in challenging the gender expectations of Cuban society, as she took the lawyer to court. Though she failed to win payment of the debt, she did win a pension, to be paid by the farm.[13] Lambert's story highlights the tensions that Villaverde draws out in his novel. She was clearly a powerful woman who violated all the gender norms of Cuban society. Her long alliance with a white planter who lived alone raised questions about their relationship. Mary Peabody Mann included Lambert and the allegations in her novel when she describes "Mariana," the mulatta who runs the plantation of the German immigrant, and the flock of mixed-race children who run through the big house.[14]

Enslaved women were by definition women without honor; therefore, they could be treated in ways that would violate the norms accorded to other women. Their freedom of movement, participation in markets, and manner of dress all violated gender expectations. Their participation in rebellions and other forms of resistance also marked them as different from other women. Their actions created a variety of reactions. On the one hand, it caused a retrenchment and conflation of race and gender. This led to more rigorous attention to the control of white women. Many travelers commented on the dearth of women in Havana and surrounding areas before realizing that they were all kept out of sight. Women of color, though, were always present. They became, as evidenced by *Cecilia Valdés*, objects of desire and in many ways the ideal of beauty and sexuality. Women on coffee farms did some of the most important work of the farm in cleaning, sorting, and grading the beans, and they also worked in planting, picking, and drying. They engaged in all the commercial and cultural activities of men. One could argue that it was women of color who through their actions performed modernity in Cuba.[15] During the 1830s, when the coffee complex had reached a mature stage, the enslaved on cafetales were pushing the boundaries of social and cultural norms even for slaves. Many white Cubans were rethinking ideas of gender and race and how these were complicated by the slave system. There was a realization that they had created a bifurcated view of women based on both race and status, and in Cuba this was intrinsically intertwined with the women on coffee plantations who exposed these contradictions.

In slave communities on cafetales, the effects of physical and cognitive spaces of action and control fostered resistance to the larger system, as they fed the desire for autonomy and ultimately freedom in the enslaved. Small acts of resistance multiplied into larger coordinated actions. Simple acts such as continuing to speak native languages and cook in traditional ways not only maintained some continuity with lives and identifications from African pasts but also subtly challenged fundamental aspects of the plantation system. Enslaved people, by continuing to function in normal ways in an abnormal context, refused to submit to the planter class, which sought to build a totalizing system of control. Religious thought and practice, as discussed in Chapter 4, was a fundamental part of life on the farms, offering hope, ways to cope, and a means to strike back.

Religious practices were transformed over time through contact with other Africans and with Spanish Christians. Core religious concepts continued on, but they gained new dimensions and layers of practice as the oppressed were compelled to celebrate new holidays and recognize new gods. It was the ability to engage in sustained religious practice on the cafetales that enabled translational association between Catholicism and African religious thinking. I am not suggesting that these were synthetic hybrids; rather, they had transculturative properties that ultimately allowed these systems to survive into the twenty-first century. Evidence of this cross-pollination can be seen in the current practice of baptism within the church, which appears as a significant rite within the initiation ritual process of the Regla de Ocha.

The creation of families and the maintenance of cultural traditions was arguably the most important effect of life on the cafetales. The higher numbers of women, the lower levels of physical stress related to working conditions, and the better diet contributed to higher fertility rates and healthier children. This in turn created a more rapidly creolizing population than those found on sugar farms. This emerging generation learned African traditions and carried them forward, reshaping them in an Afro-Cuban culture that would become a foundational element in Cuban life. The ways in which the enslaved lived their lives was also significant. They lived and worked within the constraints of the slave system as semiautonomous individuals and groups. They participated in the accrual of capital in small but significant amounts, and the longer they did this, the more their actual emancipation took shape. This economic activity laid the groundwork for the expansion of free people of color and their integration into the towns of the region, such as Artemisa and Mariel. While more work needs to be done, the evidence suggests that it was former coffee slaves who became the core of the working class in the towns and villages around Havana. Cuban-born Africans were becoming Afro-Cubans at the same time Spaniards were becoming Euro-Cubans.

The hundreds of cafetaleros who established plantations between 1790 and 1845 left few words that referred to Laborie or Boloix. Nevertheless, they left abundant evidence in the way they built their farms, which testifies to the impact of the two authors' ideas and ideals. In conforming to Laborie and Boloix's model, the planters built more than farms; they left a legacy for all Cubans. The birth and growth of a distinct Cuban culture and Cuban identity mirrored that of the rise of the plantation complex on the island. The planters were Spaniards in the process of becoming Cubans and they were also reshaping their identities. One of the most powerful elements that drove them and how they shaped their way of life was their idealized notions of what constituted a good life. Those in power on the island built an economy and a way of living that depended on slavery, and a plantation economy that was the backbone of the economy. They idealized the cafetal as a place of beauty that included happy slaves living in their bohíos, performing the labor of the farm and living simple, uncluttered lives. It is possible that the slaveholders wanted to recreate an adapted vision of the ideal

Spanish life of landholding hidalgos and a peasant class. As the population grew and diversified, as the creole generations became larger, and as the numbers of plantations of all sorts expanded, so did the sense of cubanidad take root in the minds of many inhabitants. This is not to say that there was a fully unified group sense of identification. Rather, during the turbulent times of the early nineteenth century—an era of growth, conflict, disease, and disaster—the people of Cuba came to share a sense of commonality that would continue to develop over the succeeding decades. The agricultural roots of Cuban society strongly influenced cultural development and this nascent sense of Cuban-ness.

During the 1840s, coffee cultivation in the region began to experience stresses that led to new changes that affected individual farms as well as the entire coffee complex. Two hurricanes struck at the heart of the mature coffee plantation complex during the 1840s, which brought a precipitous decline in the fortunes of western coffee growers. Another factor, according to historian Doria González Fernández, was that by the 1840s a number of coffee farmers were losing money as a result of low prices on the world market.[16] There was an increasingly crowded field of competitors on the international scene, notably Brazil, which was capturing a growing share of the US market at the expense of Cuban cafetaleros. These combined pressures pushed many coffee farmers toward other crops or off their farms altogether. Following the second massive hurricane, which struck in 1846, many owners began to consolidate their holdings, and a general decline of the coffee economy followed. Contrary to many accounts, the crop did not disappear from the western end of the island, but over the next several decades the export of coffee declined and most of the crop was consumed by the growing internal market. As outputs declined and officials grew worried, they attempted to reinvigorate the coffee sector. But the damage was done and coffee in the vuelta abajo would never fully recover, as farmers sold out or converted their farms to sugar or other crops that would yield quicker profits. Nevertheless, the legacy of the years of maturity—from the late 1810s to the early 1840s—could not be more profound, as it had a permanent impact on the social, cultural, and economic development of Cuba, and most especially on the trajectory of Afro-Cuban culture and how it would come to influence the broader Cuban culture that was emerging.

APPENDIX A

Demographic Data

According to *Voyages*, the slave trade database, there were 602,463 slaves imported to Cuba between 1776 and 1850. This is a larger number than the documents at the time record, suggesting a need for much more demographic work in locating the enslaved population temporally and geographically. The slave trade database project information suggests that a more thorough survey of the plantation records may reveal a large portion of this population that was hidden during the counts taken across the island and during regional and local assessments.

The data offered here is a small sample to represent the trends that were occurring on the island during the early nineteenth century. The population was expanding steadily over time, but with the exception of 1792, the percentage of women in the population was relatively stable. The 1792 census has been called into question, but I include the information here for comparative purposes. I also include data from three partidos that had significant numbers of cafetales. San Marcos seems to conform to the island-wide numbers, while Puerta de la Güira/ Artemisa and Güines (southeast of the vuelta abajo) show higher numbers of women. It was these sorts of variations that initially caught my attention. As I looked closer at individual plantation records, I began to see how the cafetales had increasing numbers of women while the ingenios had larger numbers of men.

Appendix A. Island Censuses

Census	Number of male adults	Number of female adults	Number listed as slaves	Number listed as bozales	Total	Percentage of females	Ratio of men to women
1774	28,771	15,562			44,333	35 %	1.9
1792	47,424	37,166			84,590	43 %	1.3
1817			199,145	25,976	225,121		
1827	183,290	103,652			286,942	36 %	1.8
1841	281,250	155,245			436,495	36 %	1.8
1841*	207,954	113,320			321,274	35 %	1.8

*The 1841 census figures are taken from only the western (or occidental) region of the island.

Data Source	Number of male adults	Number of female adults	Total	Percentage of females	Ratio of men to women
San Marcos					
1808 padron	1,089	222	1,311	17 %	4.9
1841 census	2,308	1,199	3,507	34 %	1.9
Puerta de la Güira/Artemisa					
1841 census	5,319	3,498	8,817	40 %	1.5
Güines					
1824 padron	278	187	465	40 %	1.5

APPENDIX B

Cafetales

The following are lists of the coffee plantations and owners whose records offered information used in this study. This list is not exhaustive but is intended to provide a reference to the plantations used as source material used in this work.

Cafetal: Owner (Dueño)

Aciento (*sometimes appearing as Asiento*): Ramon Charun
Activo: Carlos Granados
Altagracia: *currently unknown*
Amistad, La: Genaro Montoto
Angerona: Cornelio Souchay, Andrés Souchay (*heir of Cornelio*)
Arabia, La: Felix Lemaur
Arcadia: Francisco Bernardo Stonon
Bagatela: José de Fuertes
Bella Vista: Pedro Boyer and Luis Bourgois
Brillante: *currently unknown*
Bristal: Gregorio González
Bruce-Hal: Honrato Verrier (*administrator*)
Buena Esperanza: Pedro Domech
Calipso: Tereza Merliani, Arnoldo Renato, Conde de Santa María de Loreto
Camarones: *currently unknown*
Campana, La : Felipe Fernandez de Silva , Rita Estremes (*heir of de Silva*)
Carmen, El: *currently unknown*
Casualidad del Prado, La: Juan Ildefonso Alemany , Francisco de Bengochea
Catalina (*also known as Catelina*): Antonio Toscano
Ceiba, La: *currently unknown*
Clementina: Damaso del Campo
Concepción: Josefa Alonso de Tarris
Concordia: Carrera (*first name currently unknown*)
Consistorio: *currently unknown*
Constancia, La: Domingo Armona
Constante Industria: *currently unknown*
Contingencia: Francisca de la Hez
Delicias: Joaquin de Santa Cruz y Cardenas (Conde de Mompox)
Desengaño: Juan Menendez
Diligencia, La: José Lorenzo Orquiage

Dolores: Manuel José Díaz
Dominico, El: Domingo Auget
Eden-Park: Alejandro Deschapeles
Encarnación: José Belén Hernández
Esperanza, La: José Antonio Ramos
Estrella: *currently unknown*
Farina, La: Francisco Baños
Favorito: Martín de Urgarte
Fortuna, La: *currently unknown*
Gabia, La: Dorotea Obando
Gracia Consular: Manuel Abrue y Ger
Gratitud: Tomas Herrera
Industria, La: Phinney (*first name currently unknown; last name may be Finney*)
Java: Patricio Welch , Juan Fouquien, Pedro Soulé de Limendoux
Jesús Nazareno: María de la Luz Valdéz
Jesús Nazareno (*also known as Sierra Morena***):** Teresa Chicano y Asensuria (*possibly a later owner of the above Jesús Nazareno, but the documentation is unclear*)
Josefa: Benito Bermudos
Juan Nepomuzeno: Juan de Arango
Juanita, La (*located in Mariel*)**:** Benito Abreu
Juanita, La (*located in Baynoa*) **:** Juan Garcia y Vigario
Jupiter (*located in the corral of Majana*)**:** Marcos Padron
Jupiter (*near the town of Gabriel*)**:** Juan Francisco del Castillo
Laberinto: Diego Pintado, María de Jesús de Bretos
Limones: Santiago Bellaume
Luisa, La: *currently unknown*
Manuela: Antonio Gonzales del Larrinaga, Joaquin Benítez
Marabillas: Rafael Bertemati
Mariana, La: Herrera (*first name currently unknown*)
Matilde, La: Pedro Calvo
Mercedes, Las: *currently unknown*
Minerva : Joaquin de Santa Cruz y Cardenas (Conde de Mompox), Condesa de Lagunillas (later owner)
Modestia, La: Pedro Chise
Modesto: Modesta Cárdena de Satour
Neptuno: Joaquin de Santa Cruz y Cardenas (Conde de Mompox), Francisco Seca , Juaquin Gomez (*later owner*)
Novedad: José de Fuertes
Nuestra Señora de la Asención: *currently unknown*
Nuestra Señora de las Augustias: José Antonio Rosales
Nuestra Señora del Carmen: Maria de Regla Parez
Nuestra Señora del Rosario: Juan Hernández
Nueva Empresa : Antonio González Larrinaga

Pacencia: Nicolas Bomare (*possibly also known as Morales*)

Paciencia, La (*first known as La Cuca*): Alonso Benigno Muñoz , Maria Trinidad
    de Zayas, Santiago Farnza

Partido: José del Calvo

Paz, La: Mariano Tranco

Pequeña Cabaña: Nataniel Fellowes

Perla, La: Joaquín Español

Perseverancia: José Joaquin Carrera

Petit-Versalles: José Julián Chávez

Pinal, El: Ysabel Carlota Valdés

Placeres: Antonio Robredo

Prisionero: *currently unknown*

Providencia: Andre de Zayas

Recompensa: Covarrubias (*first name currently unknown*)

Recreo, El: Teresa O'Farrill y Herrera , Rafael O'Farrill y Arredondo

Recurso: *currently unknown*

Resolución: Manuel Abreu

Resurrección, La: Joaquín de Herrera , Rosa O'Reilly y Calvo

Reunion: Sr. Conde de la Reunion

Rosa, La: Joaquín de Herrera , Rosa O'Reilly y Calvo

Rosario: Juan Hernández Alvarez

Rosario, El: Francisco Franquiz

Rotunda, La: José M. Seidel, Roberto Blakeley

Salvador: Francisco Aguirre

San Agustín: Agustín Izquierdo

San Antonio de Padua: José Rafael Martin

San Antonio de Paulina: Agustin Martin

San Bernardo: Jose de la Piza

San Enrique: *currently unknown*

San Francisco: Juaquín Garcia

San Francisco or la Liberal: Francisco Bengoechea

San Isidro del Palmar: Jose Ragues , Pedro Sanfelin

San José: Melchor Guitierrez

San Juan de Vuenabista [*sic*]: Ygnacio Carbonel

San Juan Nepomuzeno: Juan de Arango

San Ygnacio: Ventura Tegidor

Santa Ana (*Cayayabos*): Antonio Duarte

Santa Ana de Biajacas (*also known as El Padre*): Presibitero O'Farrill

Santa Clara: *currently unknown*

Santa Lucia: Rosa Montalvo de Díaz Herrera

Santa Ysabel [*sic*]: Dolores Cavillo

Santisima Trinidad: Antonio Gonzáles Larrinaga

Soledad: Eduardo Haüel , Pedro Courtase

Tentativa: Gabriel Limbillo , Nicolas de Mondive

Tisa, La: Joaquín de Alday
Tranquilidad: Juan Bautista Frontis
Ubajai: Antonio García
Unión, La: Marques Huquenu
Uva, La: *currently unknown*
Valiente: Joaquin Ayestarán , Gerónimo Merlhy
Vengador: *currently unknown*
Villa: *currently unknown*
Viertudes [*sic*]**:** Antonio Morejon
Yemen: Oliva (*first name currently unknown*)
Yndustria: Antonio Muñoz
Yolanda, La: Jose María Zeidel

These individuals owned cafetales that were generally known by the name of
the *dueño* (owner) rather than a separate appellation:

Acosta, Manuel Mariano de
Acosta, Rafael de
Aleman, Antonio de
Alfaro, Francisco
Allut, José
André, Musin
Añelo, Camilo
Arambur, Pedro
Arango, Francisco de
Arraigan, Juan de
Asigete, Domingo
Balladares, José
Barreto Nevaran, Dolores
Basques, Nicolas
Benet, Juan Baptista
Benier, Francisco
Bertemeti, Rafael
Blein, Leon
Bowen, Guillermo
Bretos, Domingo
Bussuan, Juan Bautista
Bustamante, José Antonio
Cabañas, Francisco (*the widow of*)
Calvo, Ignacio
Calvo, Luis Jose
Campeche, Nicolas Alv.

Canto Valdespino, José
Cardenas, Agustin de
Carzada, Francisco
Cataloy, José
Charadan, Antonio
Chavitusé, Juan; Rubio, Claudio; Kinós,
    Alexandro (*jointly owned*)
Collazo, Francisco
Conilo, Roberto
Cordova, José de
Crus, José María de la [*sic*]
Cuesta, Francisco María de la
Díaz, Cristobal
Domingo, Bartolomé
Drullón, Pedro
Duarte, Miguel
Ebrano, Marcos
Espingle, Federico
Feliz, Francisco
Fernandez, José María
Fernandez Oñoro, Juan
Ferrete, Juan
Franques, Geronimo
Franquiz, Geronimo
Frontiz, Juan Bautista
Fur, Nicolas

García, Facundo
García, Leonarda
García, Margarita
Garnié, Luvian
Gaticos, Ygnacio
Gonzales, Antonio
Gonzales, Gabriel
Grimien, Francisco
Guiro, Agustin Valdez del
Hallo, Lorenzo
Hernandez, Francisco Gabriel
Herrera, Gregorio
Hobarto, Dorotea
Lafi[t], Juan
Lafice, Juan Bautista
Lamontaña, Pedro
Landa, Juan de and María de la Luz
    Romero
Larquien, Ysidoro
Lay Mescler, Madama de
Ledó, Pedro
Lemán, Felix
Leret, Juan
Leret, Pedro
Llená, Francisco
Loné, Santiago
Maneq, Bernardo (*owned two cafetales*)
Martin, Antonio
Martínez, Diego
Massón, Florimon
Matrés, Ramon
Melendez, Juan
Mengana, Manuel
Meson, Carlos
Molina, Joaquín
Montando, Carlos
Montenegro, Jorge
Montato, Jenaro
Moral, Gregorio del
Noa, Josefa

Olsún, Guillermo
Pedroso, Carlos
Pedroso, Francisco
Pedroso, Pedro Regolado
Peña, Zeferino de la
Pichon, Pedro
Pistolé, Marcos
Pluma, Pablo
Ponton, Calletano
Prence, Andrez
Puentes, Santiago
Puple, Pedro
Quiñones, Manuel
Rasno, Pedro
Reveri, Pedro
Ribo, José
Ricabur, Pedro
Rivera, Deciderio
Rodriguez, Josefa and Francisco Moran
    Rodriguez
Rodriguez, Juan
Rubio y Lezama, Andres and Mariana
    Simoneta
Ruis, José Antonio
Salomón, Juan Bautista
Sanabria, Santiago
Sanchez, Alexandro
Sapoten, Francisco
Sastrá, Manuel Fernandez (*owned two
    cafetal*es)
Torre, José María de la
Torre, Josefa de la
Torres, Juan
Tronco, Maximo
Valdes, FranciscoVerró, Pedro
Vidot, Pedro
Villalobos, José de
Villavicencio, Julian
Youve (Youvea), Jorge

NOTES

INTRODUCTION

Epigraph. Laird W. Bergad et al., *The Cuban Slave Market, 1790–1880* (Cambridge: Cambridge University Press, 1995), 29.

1. Except where otherwise noted, all translations are my own.

CHAPTER 1

Epigraph. P. J. [Pierre-Joseph] Laborie, *The Coffee Planter of Saint Domingo; with an appendix, containing a view of the constitution, government, and state of that colony, previous to the year 1789. To which are added, some hints on the present state of the island, under the British government* (London: T. Cadell and W. Davies, 1798), 14–15.

1. This story is based on a variety of accounts of life on plantations. For example, see Abbot, *Letters*; and Fredrika Bremer, *Cartas desde Cuba*, trans. Matilde Goulard de Westberg (Havana: Fundación Fernando Ortiz, 2002).
2. Pio and Gertrudis were married, but *mandingo* was not their married surname. Rather, it was an ethnic designation given by the slaveholder. I will discuss this issue and the problems related to these ethnic designations later.
3. I will be using the terms *plantation* and *farm* interchangeably for readability. I am aware of the distinction some have drawn between social and economic orders of plantations and haciendas; see, for example, Eric R. Wolf and Sidney W. Mintz, "Haciendas and Plantations in Middle America and the Antilles," *Social and Economic Studies* 6, no. 3 (1957): 380–412. While this is a salient point, especially vis-à-vis my argument that crops matter, my usage nevertheless seems consistent with Spanish custom, in which *plantación* and *finca* are used as synonyms.
4. See, for example, Boubacar Barry, *Senegambia and the Atlantic Slave Trade*, trans. Ayi Kwei Armah (Cambridge: Cambridge University Press, 1998).
5. The limitations of records always hamper these sorts of projects. Pio is not listed in an 1820 census of the farm but does appear in a later 1833 census. Miguel de Quintana, Ylario Loredo, Fran.co de Chappotin, Diego Hasbrook, Juan Llorena, and Fran.co Pedrerro, "Plano a fs. 672 de la 4a pieza. Plano de diez y un cuarto caballerías de tierra que medí en el partido de S. Marcos vínculo de Mey[I] reles y forman el cafetal nombrado La 'Paciencia' que quedó entre los bienes de D. Alonso Benigno Muñoz y hoy corresponde a D. Santiago F. Firmado por Desiderio Herrera. En los autos del concurso de acreedores de Dn. Alonso Benigno Muñoz," 1833 (December 2), Fondo Escribanías de Ortega, Legajo 38,

Número 1, Archivo Nacional de Cuba (hereafter ANC). He was listed as married and appears to be well situated on the farm by that point, so it is reasonable to presume that he had been acquired at least a few years earlier. The acquisition of Pio and Gertrudis during the 1820s, coupled with their African origins, suggests they were part of the burgeoning illegal trade in slaves that continued for several decades in spite of British efforts to halt the practice through both international treaties and force. I make the distinction that Pio was a general laborer because some slaves did have specific skills and jobs, which were noted in the plantation inventory. An example of this distinction is José *mina*, who was listed as "cocinero" (cook) in the 1820 inventory. Manuel Lafita, "Los autos promovidos por D[on] José Silverio O'Halloran como apoderado de Los Colonos del vínculo de Río Grande de Maireles, sobre rebajo de censos," 1820 (January 22), Fondo Escribanías de Varios, Legajo 236, Número 3561, A N C.

6. The *vuelta abajo* or *vueltabajo* is a region primarily known for tobacco cultivation. The territory is almost entirely within the current borders of the province of Pinar del Río and consists of a long narrow strip of land approximately fifteen kilometers wide and about one hundred kilometers long, much of it along the piedmont of the Organos mountains. It begins at the city of Artemisa in the east, near the current provincial border between Artemisa and Pinar del Río. The term *vuelta abajo* appears in documents as two words but also occasionally as a single word. In this work, the two-word spelling will be used with the exception of direct quotations.

7. A *corral* was a territorial division of land used in Cuba during the colonial era. The area of a corral was circular, with a radius of one league.

8. Antonio Núñez Jiménez, *Geografía de Cuba*, 2nd ed. (Havana: Editorial Lex, 1960), 19, 24, 41, 88, 379, 416.

9. The cafetal Paciencia was originally known as "La Cuca." See Cayetano Ponton, "Plano a fs. 672 de la 4a pieza. Plano de diez y un cuarto caballerías de tierra que medí en el partido de S. Marcos vínculo de Mey[I]reles y forman el cafetal nombrado la 'Paciencia' que quedó entre los bienes de D. Alonso Benigno Muñoz y hoy correponde a D. Santiago F. firmado por Desiderio Herrera. En los autos del concurso de acreedores de Dn. Alonso Benigno Muñoz," 1836 (November 12), Fondo Escribanías de Ortega, Legajo 38, Número 1, ANC.

10. Francisco Pérez de la Riva y Pons, *El café: Historia de su cultivo y explotación en Cuba* (Havana: Jesús Montero, 1944), 7. Pérez notes that like other locations, there are competing stories as to the origins of coffee cultivation. He cites José Antonio Saco, who contends that coffee came to Cuba via Puerto Rico in 1768. There is evidence that the Crown was interested in encouraging coffee production in Cuba, as documented by the waiver of duties and extension of privileges to those who undertook to grow coffee beginning in 1768. See appendix 1 in Pérez de la Riva y Pons, *El café*. Also, see Antonio de Bucareli, "Carta de Antonio Bucarely, al marqués de Casa Cagigal, remitiendo testimonio de la Real Cédula del 8 de Junio de este año, por lo que se ha servido el rey, aprobar el proyecto que propuso El Intendente Gral. Miguel De Altarriba, en favor de la siembra del café," 1768 (September 7), Fondo Correspondencia de los Capitanes Generales, Legajo 19, Número 86, ANC.

11. Pérez de la Riva y Pons, *El café*, 8.

12. Ibid., 29.

13. El Yntendente de la Habana, "Remite dos exemplares del censo de población de aquella Ysla: Resumen del censo de población de la isla de Cuba a fin del año de 1841," 1842, Fondo Hacienda de Cuba, Legajo 631, Número 6, Archivo Histórico Nacional (de España) (hereafter AHN). It should be noted that this figure does

not include the growing coffee district in the jurisdiction of Matanzas, east of Havana. This area had seventy-five cafetales by 1817 and over three hundred in 1841. See Laird W. Bergad, *Cuban Rural Society in the Nineteenth Century: The Social and Economic History of Monoculture in Matanzas* (Princeton, NJ: Princeton University Press, 1990), 30, 32.

14. The War of Spanish Succession began in 1701, following the death of the childless Hapsburg king Charles II. Waged between rival families (Hapsburg and Bourbon) with competing claims to the Spanish throne, the war lasted until 1714, ending with an agreement that allowed the Bourbon Philip V to ascend the Spanish throne by renouncing his claim on the French throne.

15. Philip began the changes as the war progressed and then fully realized them at the conclusion of the conflict. The Nueva Planta was a series of decrees that made the provinces of Aragón subject to the laws of Castile. These areas were targeted as they had been the locations that had supported the Hapsburgs during the war. This shows that Philip thought these measures would increase the Crown's level of control over problem areas. This also shows why later reformers sought to use these ideas in the colonies.

16. John Lynch, *Bourbon Spain, 1700–1808* (Oxford: Basil Blackwell, 1989), 62–65.

17. It should be noted that the pace of reform was slowed considerably by the instability of Philip. The state continued to function largely because of the capabilities of the ministers and the strong hand first of Princess des Ursins and later Queen Elizabeth Farnese. In addition, the intendants were opposed by entrenched interests and much of the system was dysfunctional a few short years after its institution. Nevertheless, many elements of the system survived, and some of the men who served as intendants saw the system and their power reestablished under Charles III after 1759. See ibid., 104–6.

18. Juan Balansó, *La corona vacilante* (Barcelona: Plaza y Janés Editores, 1996), 84–85; Lillian Estelle Fisher, *The Intendant System in Spanish America* (Berkeley: University of California Press, 1929), 7–9; and Lynch, *Bourbon Spain*, 164–71. As under the previous monarchy, the push for reform was motivated by an ambitious and powerful adviser to the king. In this instance, it was Ensenada who was the driving force to remake Spanish America. Ensenada had the authority and power to carry out his plans, as he was the head of several ministries, including those of finance, war, the navy, the Indies, and state. He had accumulated so much power that some called him "secretary of everything." This would lead to his downfall at the hands of some disgruntled rivals in 1754.

19. The continued presence of the British at Gibraltar and the loss of Florida acted as thorns that constantly aggravated Spanish leaders and reminded them of the need to be actively on guard against British aggression throughout the empire.

20. Similar to the issue of Gibraltar among Spaniards, the loss of Florida and the presence of immigrants from the former territory reminded Cubans of the need to be vigilant against the British.

21. Following the practice found in the documents of the time, the conde de Ricla will hereafter be referred to as "Ricla."

22. Allan J. Kuethe and Lowell Blaisdell, "The Esquilache Government and the Reforms of Charles III in Cuba," *Jahrbuch für Geschichte von Staat, Wirtschaft und Gesellschaft Lateinamerikas* 19 (1982): 129–30.

23. Ibid., 131.

24. Ibid., 132.

25. Ibid., 132–33. Kuethe and Blaisdell make a strong case that the minister of the Indies at that time, Arriaga, had little input on the reform process during this period. He had been tarred with the failures of the Seven Years' War and the real

power lay with Esquilache. Ricla and O'Reilly kept the lines of communication open with Arriaga but followed the direction of Esquilache, as they understood that he had the ear of the king.

26. Ibid., 134. The other ports were Santo Domingo, Puerto Rico, Margarita, and Trinidad.

27. Ibid., 135.

28. Miguel de Altarriba, "Inclinación a fomentar esta planta como el fruto se habilitase a comercio con libertad de derechos," 1767, Fondo Reales Ordenes, Legajo 6, Número 37, ANC; Antonio de Bucareli, "Carta." Bucareli, writing to the Crown in support of Altarriba, also thanked the king for his efforts to stimulate coffee production on the island and for considering an extension of the current waiver.

29. H. E. Friedlaender, *Historia económica de Cuba* (Havana: Jesús Montero, 1944), 83.

30. Leví Marrero, *Cuba: Economía y sociedad azúcar, ilustración y conciencia (1763–1868)* (Madrid: Editorial Playor, 1985), 12:109.

31. Friedlaender, *Historia económica de Cuba*, 81–82. While earlier dates are claimed by various sources, this cafetal appears to be the first farm that produced a substantial crop and was an ongoing working plantation.

32. Charles III, "Reglamento de comercio libre de España a Indias," in *Documentos para La Historia de Cuba*, ed. Hortensia Pichardo Viñals (Havana: Editorial Pueblo y Educación, 2000), 165.

33. Ibid., 166–67.

34. Charles IV, "Libertad de comercio de esclavos," in Pichardo Viñals, *Documentos.*

35. These figures are complied from Kenneth F. Kiple, *Blacks in Colonial Cuba, 1774–1899* (Gainesville: University Presses of Florida, 1976). The population figures for the enslaved of Cuba are currently undergoing reassessment as a result of the work of David Eltis and the Trans-Atlantic Slave Trade Database project. The revised figures show importation of no slaves between 1776 and 1780 but numbers steadily increasing to a total of 56,289 slaves between 1780 and 1800. There were an additional 39,932 slaves imported between 1800 and 1805 for a total of 96,221 slaves for the period. This, of course, doesn't take into account births and deaths, but it does represent a net increase over earlier census data. The increase is also evident in the number of voyages landing in Cuba. There were, on average, four ships landing per year prior to liberalization of the trade. That number began to increase rapidly, with twenty ships landing in 1791. See Emory University, *Voyages: The Trans-Atlantic Slave Trade Database, slavevoyages.org* (accessed July 3, 2009).

36. See, for example, Roland T. Ely, *Cuando reinaba su majestad el azúcar* (Buenos Aires: Editorial Sudamericana, 1963), 87–95; and Hugh Thomas, *Cuba; or, The Pursuit of Freedom*, updated ed. (New York: Da Capo Press, 1998), 68–71. In these classic works, the authors discuss the process of reform, relating its benefits and motivations exclusively within the context of the sugar industry. For examples of similar treatment in more recent monographs and general texts, see Allan J. Kuethe, *Cuba, 1753–1815: Crown, Military, and Society* (Knoxville: University of Tennessee Press, 1986), 131–34; and Geoff Simons, *Cuba from Conquistador to Castro* (New York: St. Martin's Press, 1996), 112–14.

37. Charles IV, "Real Cédula concediendo livertad para el Comercio de Negros, con Las Islas De Cuba, Santo Domingo, Puerto Rico, y Provincia de Caracas, á Españoles, y estrangeros, baxo las Reglas que se expresan," in *Documentos para La Historia Argentino*, ed. Ricardo Levene (Buenos Aires: Compañía Sud-Americana de Billetes de Banco, 1915), 397.

38. Coffee planters continued to receive support from the Crown throughout the early period of development. In 1796, the king extended for a further ten years the reduction of the *diezmos* and allowed for the free marketing of coffee in European ports. The only stipulation on sales of coffee in Europe was that vessels transporting coffee from Cuba to foreign ports had to dock in Spain prior to their return to Cuba. See El Rey [Charles IV], "Expediente instruido con el objeto de fomentar en esta isla el plantío, cultivo y beneficio del café," 1796 (November 22), Fondo Real Consulado y Junta de Fomento, Legajo 92, Número 3929, ANC.

39. The Sociedad Económica de Amigos del País (The Economic Society of Friends of the Country) will hereafter be referred to as the "Sociedad Económica." Stuart McCook has argued that there was a rising interest in scientific approaches to agriculture during the period under consideration here that can be attributed to the political and economic reforms directed from the Bourbon regime in Spain. Increased pressure to produce as well as fewer restraints from the government meant that planters and local officials alike sought out ways to expand agricultural production and revenues. While botanical gardens and research expeditions were organized, these efforts did little to promulgate knowledge of coffee cultivation in Cuba. McCook also argues that scientific agriculture was an important element in the construction of the nation, as it was a way to define geographic space and some of the characteristics that were considered intrinsic to the nation. See McCook, *States of Nature: Science, Agriculture, and Environment in the Spanish Caribbean, 1760–1940* (Austin: University of Texas Press, 2002), 1–16 and 77–82.

40. Lorenzo de Quintana and Antonio del Valle Hernández, "Expediente instruido con el objeto de fomentar en esta isla el plantío, cultivo y beneficio del café," 1796 (April 27), Fondo Real Consulado y Junta de Fomento, Legajo 92, Número 3929, ANC. In fact, there was such interest in coffee that there was authorization in this same letter for loans to establish two plantations that could serve as experimental farms to instruct growers or potential planters: "Dos cafetales mejor cultivados y mas propios para servir de escuela á los cultivadores de este ramo."

41. Pablo Boloix, "Expediente instruido con el objeto de fomentar en esta isla el plantío, cultivo y beneficio del café," 1797 (March 22), Fondo Real Consulado y Junta de Fomento, Legajo 92, Número 3929, ANC. Coffee plants require several years of growth—a minimum of three years, with an average of five years—before producing a crop. I will discuss this aspect of plantation management in more detail later. It should be noted that Boloix did not mention the physical size of the farms he visited. The smaller dimensions of cafetales was an important factor in the cost to establish a farm, so it is a notable omission.

42. Ibid. "Está muy bien delineado, pero la distancia que tienen los cafetos de 2 1/2 var.s uno de otro es á mi parecer muy corta: tiene un paño de tierra baxa aunque no muy grande donde no se producen muy bien: noté tambien buena porcion maltratados y otros muertos de resultas del temporal del años prox.o pasado."

43. Tranquilino Sandalio de Noda estimated the cost of establishing a cafetal ca. 1820 as 80,000 pesos, while Ramón de la Sagra figuró that an ingenio ca. 1831 required a starting investment of approximately 170,000 pesos. Noda, "Memoria sobre el café," in *Memorias de la Sociedad Económica de Amigos del País* (Havana: Oficina del Gobierno y de la Real Sociedad Patriótica por SM, 1820); and Sagra, *Historia económica, política y estadística de la isla de Cuba; ó, Sea de sus progresos en la población, la agricultura, el comercio y las rentas* (Havana: Arazoza y Soler, 1831). Both are cited in Doria González Fernández, "Acerca del mercado cafetalero cubano durante la primera mitad del siglo XIX,"

Revista de la Biblioteca Nacional José Martí 31, no. 2 (May–August 1989): 151–76.

44. This is a general ratio used, but a close analysis of the available data reveals a ratio that was very close to 1.8:1. See, for example, Robert L. Paquette, *Sugar Is Made with Blood: The Conspiracy of La Escalera and the Conflict between Empires over Slavery in Cuba* (Middletown, CT: Wesleyan University Press, 1988); and Manuel Moreno Fraginals, *El Ingenio: Complejo económico social cubano del azúcar*, 3 vols. (Havana: Editorial de Ciencias Sociales, 1978).

45. José María O'Halloran, "Correspondencia de los capitanes de los partidos de San Marcos, Sibarimar, Batabanó, Pozas, Consolación del Sur, Cayajabo, Mariel y San Pedro, con el Capitán General de Cuba, Marqués de Someruelos," 1808 (August 10), Fondo Cuba, Legajo 1682, Archivo General de Indias (hereafter AGI). The aggregation of population among the types of farms complicates analysis, but it is possible to draw some conclusions that will be confirmed by the later inquiry into the structure of populations on individual cafetales. In addition, it should be noted that many sitios in coffee districts were in fact small cafetales that fell below the threshold set by officials for the farms to be counted as cafetales. See Comisión de Estadísticas, *Cuadro estadístico de la siempre fiel isla de Cuba correspondiente al año 1827* (Havana: Arazoza y Soler, 1829) following 58, note on table 4. *Sitios de labor* typically refer to small, unspecified types of farms. *Portreros* refer to farms with food crops and livestock.

46. The counts listed in the padrones are broken down into age groups, with delineations of ages 1 to 7, 7 to 16, 16 to 25, 25 to 40, 40 to 50, and 50 and above. Comparing the padrones to plantation inventories indicates that around age 16, a slave was considered to be working age and was listed as "de campo," corresponding to the age divisions represented in the census records.

47. There were two padrones of San Marcos in 1808; they recorded differing slave counts for August and September, with higher totals in the earlier count. The number of males varied by 151, while the female total was identical. It is unclear what accounted for the variance. The earlier count offers an age breakdown of the male population while the female numbers were aggregated by status and race. The padron from September presents age, race, and sex categories for males and females. See José María O'Halloran, "Correspondencia"; and Comisión de Estadísticas, *Cuadro estadístico*.

48. José María O'Halloran, "Correspondencia."

49. Laborie, *Coffee Planter.*

50. Some accounts of Laborie's story report that he produced the book while still living in Saint Domingue during the revolutionary period in an area occupied by the British.

51. There existed a long tradition of agricultural manuals in Europe and the Americas, stretching back to at least the eighth century. See Ibn Bas.s.a-1 et al., eds., *Libro de Agricultura* (Seville: Sevilla Equipo 28, 1995). The *Kita-h al-fila-b.a*, a work from Islamic Spain, was translated from the Arabic into Spanish and published in Spain in 1802 as *Libro de Agricultura* by J. A. Banqueri. Also, see James Grainger et al., *The Sugar-Cane! A Poem, in Four Books, with Notes* (London: R. and J. Dodsley, 1764); McCook, *States of Nature;* María Teresa Oliveros de Castro and Julio Jordana de Pozas, *La agricultura de los reinos españoles en tiempo de los Reyes Católicos* (Madrid: Ministerio de Agricultura Instituto Nacional de Investigaciones Agronómicas, 1968); and Margaret W. Rossiter, *The Emergence of Agricultural Science: Justus Liebig and the Americans, 1840–1880* (New Haven: Yale University Press, 1975). This tradition was continued in Cuba mainly through the work of the Sociedad Económica. In

its role as advocate, the group conducted inquiries, commissioned studies, and published results. Examples of this include the study mentioned earlier that was conducted by Pablo Boloix and the work by Juan Montalvo and Boloix published in 1818 in *Memorias de la Real Sociedad Económia de Amigos del País.* As an intermediary, the Sociedad Económica also published letters and works of advice on coffee growing, which sparked debate among growers. In 1816, the group published an anonymous work that advocated a return to methods used in Arabia.

52. According to Pablo Boloix, Laborie wrote his treatise on coffee production in 1788, during the height of coffee farming in the French colony of Saint Domingue. It was a work of considerable merit that was soon translated into English and proved to be influential in Jamaica. This was followed by its translation into Spanish and publication in Cuba in 1809. Excerpts of the translated text were circulated as early as 1809 but the final version was not available for sale to the public until 1820. See Pablo Boloix, "Prospecto a la obra sobre el cultivo y beneficio del café." 1809 (April 28), Fondo Asuntos Políticos, Legajo 297, Número 56, ANC; and J. [Pierre-Joseph] Laborie, *Cultivo del cafeto; ó, Árbol que produce el café, y modo de beneficiar este fruto*, trans. Pablo Boloix (Havana: Arazoza y Soler, 1820).

53. Francisco Pérez de la Riva wrote that the first technical manual published in Cuba was written by Florencio Basile, a French colonist, in 1801. This work may have been influential, but it appeared four years after the report by Boloix, which lends further support to the theory that the development of Cuban coffee commenced prior to the Haitian Revolution and the influx of French planters that followed. See Pérez de la Riva y Pons, *El café*, 149–50.

54. Laborie, *Coffee Planter*, 5.

55. Ibid., 5–9.

56. Ibid., 10.

57. There were shifting ideas and debates concerning the best methods for growing and processing coffee. Issues included the best spacing of plants, how to prevent erosion, the use of shade, and the amount of time newly picked fruit should be left in water to soften. Francisco Pérez de la Riva traces these arguments in chapter 3 of *El café* (149–67). An anonymous author proposed to the Sociedad Económica in 1832 that shade was not needed and that other methods currently in use could yield greater harvests while utilizing fewer workers. In spite of the appeal of the writer's arguments, the body rejected the manuscript as lacking "assurance." Ibid., 158. There is also some question over which trees were used for shade. In many cases, fruit trees are thought to have been the chief form of shade for the rows of coffee plants. Writing about the devastation wrought by the great hurricanes of 1844 and 1846, Louis A. Pérez notes that "no less devastating for the coffee growers was the destruction of the dense foliage that protected the maturing coffee plants. Shade trees were shattered and splintered, others were uprooted." Pérez, *Winds of Change: Hurricanes and the Transformation of Nineteenth-Century Cuba* (Chapel Hill: University of North Carolina Press, 2001), 86. The evidence suggests that the chief form of shade for coffee bushes was plantain trees, which were planted between the rows of coffee, and that the paths dividing the fields were lined with fruit trees. This method provided a double layer of shade but also allowed direct sunlight for a limited amount of time each day, an element that was important to the healthy growth of the coffee bushes and their fruit. Moreover, it should be noted that the presence of fruit trees continued to be one of the chief observations by travelers throughout the period, even after the two great storms of the 1840s. See, for example, Bremer, *Cartas*

desde Cuba; and Richard Henry Dana, Jr., "A Trip to Cuba," *Atlantic Monthly* 4, no. 22 (1859): 184–94.

58. Laborie, *Coffee Planter*, 122.

59. See, for example, Abbot, *Letters*, 136; and Bremer, *Cartas desde Cuba*, 114

60. While there is clear evidence of women owning coffee farms, as of yet no documented cases of women establishing new cafetales have emerged.

61. Laborie, *Cultivo del cafeto*, 9.

62. Laborie, *Coffee Planter*, 61–62, 152. This would translate to approximately one hundred thousand coffee plants, as he states that the average yield can be assumed to be one pound per plant or slightly more.

63. Laborie, *Cultivo del cafeto*, 10–11.

64. Laborie recommended a variety of other crops to feed the slaves, including squash, melons, yams, sweet potatoes, spinach, legumes, cucumbers, rice, and especially plantains. He also suggests planting some tobacco for the use of the slaves. See ibid., 17–19.

65. Ibid., 16.

66. Ibid., 16, 18.

67. Ibid., 17.

68. Laborie does state explicitly that building housing for slaves upon the establishment of a new plantation and not letting them sleep outside will develop in them a connection to the new farm and the land, making them less likely to flee and also easier to manage. His implication is that these other elements are all related. See ibid., 10–18.

69. John G. Wurdemann, *Notes on Cuba Containing an Account of Its Discovery and Early History: A Description of the Face of the Country, Its Population, Resources, and Wealth; Its Institutions, and the Manners and Customs of Its Inhabitants; With Directions to Travellers Visiting the Island* (Boston: J. Munroe, 1844), 139.

70. The novel *Cecilia Valdés* continues to be available to the public. The story was also transformed and performed as a zarzuela (a Spanish lyrical dramatic form), and a film version was made in Cuba and shown in theaters and on television. It has been taught in general literature courses in Cuban secondary schools as recently as 2002. Private communication with Gladys García, Havana, May 11, 2002. Cirilo Villaverde, *Cecilia Valdés; ó, La Loma del Ángel* (Havana: Editorial Letras Cubanas, 2001).

71. Laborie, *Coffee Planter,* 61–62.

72. A few farms did not have mill houses, but these were very small farms and few in number.

73. The processes and labor involved in the production of coffee will be explored in the next chapter. In fact, disputes over access to water broke out from time to time between neighboring cafetaleros. See "Plano demostrativo de las nivelaciones practicadas en los cafetales la Amistad, Calipso y la Minerva para ver las vestientes del terreros. firmado Man.1 Ant.o de Madina. En los remidos por de Conde de Santa Maria de Loreto y D. Ygnacio de Herrera con Jorge Montenago [unsure of last name]," 1816, Fondo Escribanías de Gobierno, Legajo 113, Número 26, ANC. The collection of documents in this file trace the disputes over water between the owners of the cafetales Amistad, Calipso, and Minerva. The problem began when the Conde de Santa María de Loreto, owner of the Amistad, began to divert water into cisterns and thus reduced the natural water flow to the other farms below his. Eventually the two complaints were resolved.

74. The grater mill was also sometimes referred to in the singular (*molino de quitar la cereza*).

75. Laborie, *Coffee Planter*, 73.
76. Domingo Macías and Jorge G. Jouve, "Testamentaria de José Rubio Campos," 1834 (November 4), Fondo Escribanías de Galletti, Legajo 976, Número 1, ANC.
77. Antonio de Morejón et al., "Plano a fs. 1129, 4a pieza. Plano que manifiesta el terreno que ocupa el cafetal tituraldo la Campana de la propiedad de los herederos de la sra. D. Rita Estremes, en el partido de S. Marcos. firmado José Govín. se encuentra en la testamentaria de Rita Estremes," 1832 (May 3), Fondo Escribanías de Salinas, Legajo 238, Número 3752, 8, ANC.
78. There were many types of broken and ground stone types of construction materials that were referred to as *mampostería*. Some were very rough and irregular, while others were pounded to a finer consistency. The documents used in this account referred to mampostería pounded to a very fine consistency
79. Laborie, *Cultivo del cafeto*, 9.
80. Ibid., 20–21.
81. Desiderio Herrera, "Plano a fs. 672 de la 4a pieza. Plano de diez y un cuarto caballerías de tierra que medí en el partido de S. Marcos vínculo de Mey[I]reles y forman el cafetal nombrado la 'Paciencia' que quedó entre los bienes de D. Alonso Benigno Muñoz y hoy correponde a D. Santiago F. firmado por Desiderio Herrera. En los autos del concurso de acreedores de Dn. Alonso Benigno Muñoz," 1839 (September 30), Fondo Escribanías de Ortega, Legajo 38, Número 1, ANC. As noted earlier, the cafetal was built prior to 1813 and was known first as "La Cuca." See Cayetano Ponton, "Plano a fs. 672."
82. In some cases, these buildings went up simultaneously. Sometimes a planter house was roughly constructed as a core building that was later expanded as time and money allowed.
83. Ramiro Guerra Sánchez, *Mudos testigos: Crónica del ex-cafetal Jesús Nazareno* (Havana: Editorial Lex, 1948), 52–53; and Domingo Macías and Jorge G. Jouve, "Testamentaria de José Rubio Campos." The core construction was of hardwood covered with several layers of a plaster made of lime and crushed rocks. This was usually referred to as *mampostería* and would be difficult for the average observer to differentiate from a stone building similarly plastered. The main house of the Jesús Nazareno also was built in this manner.
84. Pedro del Peña, "Los autos promovidos por D[on] José Silverio O'Halloran como apoderado de los colonos del vinculo de Rio Grande de Maireles, sobre rebajo de censos," 1819 (September 13) and 1820 (January 29), Fondo Escribanías de Varios, Legajo 236, Número 3561, 758v–764, ANC.
85. Domingo Macías and Jorge G. Jouve, "Testamentaria de José Rubio Campos."
86. Abbot, *Letters*, 140.
87. Ibid., 142.
88. Guerra Sánchez, *Mudos testigos*, 51. The "batey" refers to the area of the farm on which the slave quarters were located.
89. Ibid., 52–53; Miguel de Quintana et al., "Plano a fs. 672."
90. Rafael O'Farrill y Herrera, "Autos relativos a testamentaría de la sra. Teresa O'Farrill Y Herrera. Adjunto tasación extrajudicial que hace Rafael O'Farrill y Arredondo de las dotaciones de esclavos, animales y enseres de los ingenios San Ignacio y Sta. Teresa, cafetal el Recreo y otros. Testamentaría de la señora D.a Teresa O'Farrill y Herrera, esposa del señor Teniente Coronel D[on] Ygnacio Herrera y Pedroso," 1824 (August 30), Fondo Donativos y Remisiones, Legajo 327, Número 3, ANC.
91. Zeferin de la Peña and Cristoval de Fagle, "Los autos promovidos por D[on] José Silverio O'Halloran como apoderado de los colonos del vinculo de Rio Grande

de Maireles, sobre rebajo de censos," 1820 (January 20), Fondo Escribanías de Varios, Legajo 236, Número 3561, 654–56, ANC.

92. Oficina del Gobierno Constitucional, "Tasación y venta del cafetal Valiente en el partido de Güines, y de la estancia del refugio de Regla, con todos sus edificios," 1821, Folleto C. 216 Número 9, Biblioteca Nacional José Martí, 3; and Zeferin de la Peña and Cristoval de Fagle, "Los autos promovidos." An example of an intermediate-size structure could be seen on the cafetal Casa de Campana, owned by Rita Estremes. The casa de mayoral was about 650 square feet. Antonio de Morejón et al., "Plano a fs. 1129."

93. Zeferin de la Peña and Cristoval de Fagle, "Los autos promovidos."

94. Laborie makes this very point when he contends that it is more efficient to train a slave or slaves to make shingles than to hire an outside craftsman. See Laborie, *Coffee Planter*, 69.

95. Michel Foucault, *Discipline and Punish: The Birth of the Prison*, trans. Alan Sheridan, 2nd ed. (New York: Vintage, 1995), 143–45.

96. Antonio de Morejón et al., "Plano a fs. 1129."

97. Flooring in the most expensive houses was tile, but this was rare, as was the use of wood flooring. Most common was the use of a finely ground, deeply layered, and polished mampostería.

98. Mary Peabody Mann, *Juanita: A Romance of Real Life in Cuba Fifty Years Ago* (Charlottesville: University Press of Virginia, 2000; first published 1887 [Boston: D. Lothrop]), 73. Mann set her novel on a cafetal of the vuelta abajo and, according to editor Patricia Ard, based the work and its detailed descriptions of the area on her observations during a visit to the region from December 1833 to April 1835.

99. Abbot, *Letters*, 142–43.

100. Ibid., 55, 142.

CHAPTER 2

1. Bergad et al., *Cuban Slave Market*, 29.

2. Ibid., 28.

3. See Ortiz, *Contrapunteo cubano del tabaco y el azúcar* (Havana: Editorial de Ciencias Sociales, 1991); and Pérez de la Riva y Pons, *El café*.

4. This view of tobacco farmers was overturned by Charlotte Cosner in her dissertation, in which she convincingly argues that there was great diversity among tobacco farmers and that many used slaves in the production of the crop. See Cosner, "Rich and Poor, White and Black, Free and Slave: The Social History of Cuba's Tobacco Farmers, 1763–1817" (Florida International University, 2008).

5. Pérez, *Winds of Change*, 47–52.

6. William Whatley Pierson, Jr., "Francisco de Arango y Parreño," *Hispanic American Historical Review* 16, no. 4 (1936): 456–66.

7. In this context, *discursos* (lit., speeches) were addresses in the form of essays.

8. Francisco de Arango y Parreño, "Problemas de la economía cubana en el siglo XVIII," in Pichardo Viñals, *Documentos*, 185. Arango consistently argues throughout the piece for the development of coffee, tobacco, indigo, and cotton as companions to sugar.

9. Francisco de Arango y Parreño, "Informe al Real Consulado de la Habana, en el expediente para formar las instrucciones y proponer á la persona que se encargue de la comisión de pasar a Jamaica a examinar el estado de adelanto en que se

halla esa isla con respecto al cultivo y elaboración de los frutos coloniales," in *Obras* (Havana: Howson y Heinen, 1888), 508–11.

10. In much of the historiography of plantation agriculture in Cuba, Arango y Parreño has been characterized as an advocate of sugar and a member of the sugar oligarchy. The works of Vera Kutzinski and Robert Paquette are representative of this trend. See Kutzinski, *Sugar's Secrets: Race and the Erotics of Cuban Nationalism* (Charlottesville: University of Virginia Press: 1993), 209–10n5; and Paquette, *Sugar Is Made with Blood*, 83–85. As I have argued, when the body of Arango's work is examined, it is evident that he was an advocate of agricultural expansion and diversity. He consistently promoted alternatives to sugar, including traditional products such as tobacco, and the adoption of new crops (at least new to Cuba), including but not limited to coffee, indigo, and cotton. As his writings and travels reveal, he intuitively understood the dangers of over-reliance on a single export crop. Also, see Boloix, "Prospecto."

11. Pierre Pluchon, *Toussaint Louverture de l'esclavage au pouvoir* (Paris: l'Ecole; Port au Prince: Editions Caraïbes, 1979), 275.

12. See appendix B, table B-2, in Robert I. Rotberg with Christopher K. Clague, *Haiti: The Politics of Squalor* (Boston: Houghton Mifflin, 1971), 387–88.

13. David Nicholls, *Haiti in Caribbean Context: Ethnicity, Economy and Revolt* (New York: St. Martin's Press, 1985), 92–93. The author argues that the new leaders of Haiti tried to maintain plantation production, with some success, following the ouster of the French.

14. One way it is clear that the Haitian Revolution helped coffee development in Cuba was through the immigration of a number of coffee planters to the island. They brought agricultural expertise and were able to demonstrate the success of the plant. They may well have augmented the efforts of others to expand coffee cultivation. The presence of French immigrants was relatively short, as they were expelled from Cuba following Napoleon's invasion of Spain in 1808. Many relocated to Louisiana and some planters maintained ties to Cuba, as Rebecca Scott has shown. See Scott, *Degrees of Freedom: Louisiana and Cuba after Slavery* (Cambridge, MA: Belknap Press of Harvard University Press, 2008).

15. Ortiz, *Contrapunteo Cubano.*

16. Ibid., 56. Also, see Cosner, "Rich and Poor." Cosner shows that slaves made up a larger contingent of the labor force in tobacco agriculture than has previously been known, further calling into question Ortiz's thesis.

17. As mentioned earlier, there were nearly as many slaves on coffee farms as on sugar farms, and coffee was also the second most valuable export crop. See Bergad et al., *Cuban Slave Market;* Doria González Fernández, "La economía cafetalera en Cuba, 1790–1860," *Arbor* 139, nos. 547–48 (1991): 161–79; and Leví Marrero, *Cuba: Economía y sociedad azúcar, ilustración y conciencia (1763–1868)* Vol. 12 (Madrid: Editorial Playor, 1985).

18. Oscar Zanetti Lecuona and Alejandro García Alvarez, *Sugar and Railroads: A Cuban History, 1837–1959* (Chapel Hill: University of North Carolina Press, 1998), 105–6. Zanetti specifically names the Herrera, O'Reilly, and Calvo families as three of the dozen or so families that made up the core group.

19. Rafael O'Farrill y Herrera, "Autos relativos."

20. Manuel O'Reilly y Calvo, "Expediente manuscrito que contiene las cuentas de la administración de los bienes que quedarón, por fallecimiento de Joaquín de Herrera, y Rosa de O'Reilly y Calvo, en la zafra de 1833, incluyendo datos sovre [*sic*] ingresos y erogaciones del ingenio 'Santa Teresa de Jesús' y los cafetales, 'la Rosa' y 'la Resurrección,' venta de azúcar, café y gastos familiares y cobro de

impuestos de tierras demolindas [*sic*] en la hacienda 'Jaiguan,'" 1834 (January 13), Fondo Donativos y Remisiones, Legajo 630, Número 7, ANC.

21. See "Los autos promovidos por D[on] José Silverio O'Halloran como apoderado de los colonos del vinculo de Rio Grande de Maireles, sobre rebajo de censos," 1817, Fondo Escribanías de Varios, Legajo 236, ANC; "Plano a fs. 846. Plano del cafetal del Teniente Coronel D.n Pedro Calvo compuesto de catorce caballerias de tierra mas un tercio de otra. firmado Jose Ma. Oliva, Cristobal de Gallegos. pertenece a la hacienda San Marcos. Se encuetra su los seguidos por José Selverio O'Halloran, como apoderado de los colonos del vinculo de Rio Grande de Meireles sobre refajo de censo," 1820, Fondo Escribanías de Varios, Legajo 236, ANC; Fernando Ortiz, "Felix Varela, amigo del país," *Revista Bimestre Cubana* 6, no. 6 (1911): 479; and Antonio de la Torre and Juan Acradexicras, "Documento referende al sobre de 16 negros, quince varones bosales y una hembra, el 25 de julio del coriente año en el cafetal de D. Ignacio Calvo cituado [*sic*] en las inmediaciones de Arco de Canasi sospechando puedo ser el author D. José de Jesús Josanillo," 1824 (September 23), Fondo Gobierno General, Legajo 460, ANC.

22. Zanetti Lecuona and García Alvarez, *Sugar and Railroads*, 426n6.

23. Ibid., 106–7.

24. See ibid., chapter 6.

25. "Expediente sobre la sublevación de la negrada de Cafetal de D.n Francisco Aguirre," 1833, Fondo Gobierno Superior Civil, Legajo 936, ANC.

26. Cirulio, "Se propone la adquisición de mujeres de raza negra en paises donde existe la esclavitud para conseguir, por medio de la reproducción maternal, que no disminuya la mano de obra dedicada a la agricultura," 1855 (July 1), Fondo Cuba Gobierno, Legajo 3549, Número 4, AHN.

27. See Andrés Souchay and Rafael Díaz, "Testamentaria del Teniente Coronel D[on] Andrés Souchay," 1841 (July 22), Fondo Escribanías de Guerra, Legajo 781, Número 12111, 51–53, ANC; Mann, *Juanita,* 71–75; Manuel Isidro Méndez, *Bibliografía del Cafetal Angerona*, folleto ed. (Havana: n.p., 1952), 57.

28. Ibid., 51.

29. Marrero, *Cuba*, 9:199. This does not include Spaniards or Canary Islanders, whose numbers also increased.

30. Marrero, *Cuba*, 13:73.

31. See Abbot, *Letters;* Richard Henry Dana, Jr., *To Cuba and Back* (Carbondale: Southern Illinois University Press, 1966); Joseph John Gurney and Henry Clay, *Familiar Letters to Henry Clay of Kentucky, Describing a Winter in the West Indi*es (New York: Press of Mahlon Day, 1840); William Henry Hurlbert, *Gan-Eden; or, Pictures of Cuba* (Boston: John P. Jewett, 1854); Robert Jameson, *Letters from the Havana, during the Year 1820: Containing an Account of the Present State of the Island of Cuba, and Observations on the Slave Tra*de (London: John Miller, 1821); W. M. L. Jay [Julia Louisa M. Woodruff], *My Winter in Cuba* (New York: E.P. Dutton, 1871); Mann, *Juanita;* and Karen Robert, ed., *New Year in Cuba: Mary Gardner Lowell's Travel Diary, 1831–1832* (Boston: Massachusetts Historical Society; Northeastern University Press, 2003). Mann's novel is a useful source, as it is a narrativized account of her visit to Cuba that is closer to a travel account than to fiction.

32. By the 1850s, there were also several US firms operating mines and refineries across the island. See Basil Rauch, *American Interest in Cuba: 1848–1855* (New York: Columbia University Press, 1948), 195–96.

33. The connections of the Brooks family, which stretched back to 1820s Havana as well as to Boston and England, are representative of the growing international ties

of outsiders in Cuba. See David C. Carlson, "In the Fist of Earlier Revolutions: Postemancipation Social Control and State Formation in Guantánamo, Cuba, 1868–1902" (PhD diss., University of North Carolina, 2007).

34. See chapter 7, "Economic Considerations," in Rauch, *American Interest*, 181–209.

35. Many farms had a portrero for the production of food that was for the slaves of the farm and also supplemented the income of the planter as a cash crop that could be exported or sold to other farms or in nearby markets. The use of provision grounds for slaves will be discussed later.

36. This is not to say that this shift was absolute. Rather, it was calibrated to the labor needs of the farm. Often, planters began to acquire more females when their farms reached a stable, productive period. If a planter wanted to expand his or her farm, it was necessary to have enough men to open new fields—that is, to cut down trees and break the land for plowing. If the intention was to increase production, then new processing capabilities, especially in the form of drying platforms and storage facilities, had to be constructed as well. This was a typical approach, but there were exceptions that I will discuss later. The general trend, though, was that as a plantation matured, the number of women on the farm increased and its population became more balanced.

37. If an owner considered his plantation to be a long-term investment for not only himself but also his heirs, then it was important, and understood, that new fields had to be brought under cultivation every few years. This was to ensure continual harvests even when older fields began to decline after twenty or thirty years.

38. Gregory Dicum and Nina Luttinger, *The Coffee Book: Anatomy of an Industry from Crop to the Last Drop* (New York: New Press, 1999).

39. It should be noted, though, that harvests could and did vary from year to year, depending on conditions related to weather as well as the quality of care the plants received. Complaints about levels of harvests can be seen in letters from creditors. See, for example, Diego de la Barrera, "Ildefonso Ruiz del Río," 1809 (January 19), Fondo Ultramar, Legajo 152, Número 3, AGI.

40. Alejandro Dumont et al., *Memoria sobre el cultivo del café en la Isla de Cuba*, folleto ed. (Sampaloc, Philippines: Por la Real Sociedad Económica de Filipinas en la Imprenta de Sampaloc, 1827); and Laborie, *Coffee Planter*, 115.

41. The *barreta* method was so named from the use of iron bars as implements to cut holes into the earth.

42. Dumont et al., *Memoria*, 9–11.

43. The spacing of the plants was determined by the lay of the land, soil conditions, and anticipated exposure. On properties where windy conditions prevailed, for instance, managers would direct slaves to prune the coffee bushes in such a way as to limit their height to protect them from damaging winds. The plants responded to this by growing wider. Planters anticipating this need instructed workers to spread the young plants farther apart during the transplantation stage.

44. Laborie, *Coffee Planter*, 113, 16–17.

45. Ibid., 117–18.

46. Mann, *Juanita*, 69.

47. Laborie, *Coffee Planter*. The work required stamina and was hard on the body but did not demand as much strength as plowing or felling trees, for example.

48. Oficina del Gobierno Constitucional, "Tasación y venta."

49. Belén de la Rosa, "Criminal contra varios esclavos de la dotación del cafetal Perseverancia, acusados de haverse [*sic*] amotinado contra el mayoral y otros dependientes blancos de dicha finca. Complicados: Andrés Lucumí, Rosa Lucumí, Eulogio Lucumí, Luciano Lucumí, Lucas Lucumí, Cleto Lucumí, Basilio Lucumí, Felipa Lucumí, Lorenzo Colorado, Emeterio, Genaro Lucumí, Agapito

Lucumí, Canuto Lucumí, Víctor Lucumí, Lucio Lucumí, Facundo Lucumí, Lopio Lucumí, Amá Lucumí, Florentino Lucumí, Lorenzo Prieto, Francisco Carabalí, y Vincente Mandinga. Fiscal El Teniente Coronel D. Felipe Arango, Secretario El Teniente D. Antonio Cas . . . ," 1842 (September 19), Fondo Comisión Militar, Legajo 27, Número 3, ANC.

50.   Ramón Charun, "Plano de fs. 76. Plano de los Cafetales Acierto y Laborinto ubicados en el corral y partido de San Marcos, el 1º de Ramón Charun y el 2º de Diego Pintado y consortes. firmado José Ma Oliva. Se encuentra en diligencias criminales practicadas a consecuencia de las faltas cometidas por Jorge Castillo, mayoral del Cafetal Laberinto propiedad de Diego Pintado a Ramón Charun, propietario del Cafetal Aciento," 1838 (February 15), Fondo Escribanías de Varios, Legajo 174, Número 2362, ANC.

51.   Laborie, *Coffee Planter*, 130.

52.   Juan Tomás de Jaurepir and J. Manuel López, "Hojas manuscritas sobre el cultivo de café y algodón. Adjunto copia mecanografiadas sobre el mismo escrito titulado 'Café en la Habana,'" 1803 (September 19), Fondo Donativos y Remisiones, Legajo 603, Número 4, ANC. This manuscript also describes the process of removing superfluous growth from coffee bushes and the necessity of the task.

53.   These special machetes appear in many of the plantation inventories I surveyed. See, for example, Pedro Soroa, "Cuaderno (3 pz) mandado forma intestad de D. Pedro Hecheverría para tratar del remate del cafetal San Francisco la Liberal," 1833 (November 22), Fondo Escribanías de Cotés, Legajo 161, Número 1, ANC.

54.   Laborie, *Coffee Planter*, 127.

55.   Ibid., 151. Laborie noted that the task was defined as filling one barrel with ripe cherries. This usually required picking two baskets' worth, but it clearly depended on the size of the basket used. Baskets regularly show up in plantation inventories. There were ninety-seven listed in the contents of cafetal Valiente, for instance. Oficina del Gobierno Constitucional, "Tasación y venta."

56.   Laborie, *Coffee Planter*, 151.

57.   Dumont et al., *Memoria sobre el cultivo del café*, 15.

58.   Laborie, *Coffee Planter*, 150.

59.   Boloix, "Expediente instruido"; and Dumont et al., *Memoria sobre el cultivo del café,* 16. In the second account, Dumont echoes the earlier advice offered by Boloix.

60.   Some commentators such as Laborie claimed that the cherries could be soaked for up to forty-eight hours, but most emphasized that twenty-four hours was optimal; more time than that could result in loss or degradation of the final product.

61.   Laborie, *Coffee Planter.*

62.   Abbot, *Letters,* 51–52; and Laborie, *Coffee Planter*, 45–47. Laborie knew that beans dried "in cherry" were a greater weight than those cleaned and dried out of their covering and conceded that this could be a persuasive argument for the approach. He nevertheless contended that beans processed out of their coverings were of a superior quality and that there was a risk of spoilage—what he called "must"—that could overtake beans dried "in cherry." In addition, he mentions that working with the fruit in this manner required larger and thicker drying platforms, and that the raking created more wear on the platforms, requiring additional maintenance. This meant that whatever increased revenues were derived from the additional weight would likely be offset by other related expenses. I think that this along with the evidence mentioned earlier shows that planters were weighing their options and carefully considering proper methods to maintain their farms as well as maximize profits. This is significant because it also can be seen in how they shaped their workforces over time.

63. Abbot, *Letters,* 51. Abbot reported the grades as "good," "inferior," and "bad." Pedro Soroa, "Cuaderno." The inventory lists six "mesas de escoger café" (tables for sorting coffee).

64. Abbot, *Letters,* 140; and Mann, *Juanita,* 72. M. Isidro Méndez cites the descriptions of Abbot and Cirilo Villaverde, which correspond to what Mann describes in her fictionalized account. See Méndez, "Tres tipos de cafetales en San Marcos de Artemisa," *Revista Bimestre Cubana,* 59 (1947).

65. [Illegible], "Plano a fs. 1129, 4a pieza. Plano que manifiesta el terreno que ocupa el Cafetal titulado la Campana de la propiedad de los herederos de la Sra. D. Rita Estremes, en el partido de S. Marcos. firmado José Govín. se encuentra en la testamentaria de Rita Estremes," 1835 (July 2), Fondo Escribanías de Salinas, Legajo 238, Número 3752, ANC. This inventory from the cafetal Campana reports both a carpenter and a mason, both of whom were slaves. Antonio M. de la Torre y Cárdenas, "Expediente sobre la sublevación de los negros del Cafetal Tentativa, partido de la Puerta de la Güira," 1827 (January 8), Fondo Real Consulado y Junta de Fomento, Legajo 150, Número 7436, ANC. Torre y Cárdenas reported that as a result of a rebellion on the cafetal Tentativa, several people were killed, including the carpenter and mason from the nearby cafetal Manuela, noting that neither man was a slave.

66. Abbot, *Letters*, 54.

67. Dana, "Trip to Cuba"; and Robert, *New Year in Cuba,* for example.

68. In the census of 1774, there were 27,691 slaves in the western region of Cuba, and of that number, there were 9,011 females. The count of 1817 reported 121,569 slaves living in the west, of which 38,450 were females. See Alexander von Humboldt, *The Island of Cuba: A Political Essay* (Princeton, NJ: Markus Wiener, 2001), 129. The census of 1827 showed a total of 197,415 slaves in the western department, which included 143,690 in the partidos heavily farmed in coffee, revealing the diversity of the agricultural growth that was occurring. The zones extensively planted in coffee included Havana and its outlying partidos, Santiago and its ten partidos, and San Antonio and its two nearby villages. These held 937 cafetales and 272 ingenios and trapiches. See Comisión de Estadísticas, *Cuadro estadístico de la siempre fiel Isla de Cuba correspondiente al año 1827* (Havana: Arazoza y Soler, 1829).

69. The effects were uneven and thus created some uncertainty and instability. There was an increased buildup of Spanish troops on the island and changes in regulations regarding imports and exports. By 1827, there was a notable increase in investments in the island economy, and exports began to rise. See, for example, Nadia Fernández de Pinedo Echevarría, *Comercio exterior y fiscalidad: Cuba (1794–1860)* (Bilbao, Spain: Servicio Editorial de la Universidad del País Vasco, 2002), 178–82.

70. Comisión de Estadísticas, *Cuadro estadístico.*

71. Ibid.

72. Ibid., table following 59.

73. Lafita, "Los autos promovidos."

74. The person or persons who categorized the slaves for this inventory counted girls as young as seven years old and boys as young as four as "de campo," meaning they could work in the fields. This presumably was an acknowledgment of the work done on cafetales. As mentioned previously, much of the work on coffee farms was less physically demanding, and jobs such as picking coffee cherries, as the unprocessed fruit was called, could be done by children. This issue will be addressed more fully in Chapter 4.

75. Miguel de Quintana et al., "Plano a fs. 672."

76. Manuel de Abreu, "Correspondencia de los capitanes de los partidos de San Marcos, Sibarimar, Batabanó, Pozas, Consolación del Sur, Cayajabo, Mariel y San Pedro, con el Capitán General de Cuba, Marqués de Someruelos," 1810 (June 19), Fondo Cuba, Legajo 1682, AGI. In a letter dated June 19, Abreu informed the Marqués de Someruelos about the death of a runaway slave belonging to Fernández de Silva, owner of the cafetal Campana. Antonio de Morejón et al., "Plano a fs. 1129." This is an 1832 inventory of the Campana, occasioned by the death of the widow of Fernández de Silva, Rita Estremes. The later inventory shows the property as consisting of eight caballerías of arable land, with one additional caballería of mountainous land, plus the one and one-half caballerías of land for a portrero.

77. Antonio de Morejón et al., "Plano a fs. 1129"; and [illegible], "Plano a fs. 1129."

78. José Pablo Hernández, "Correspondencia de los capitanes de los partidos de San Marcos, Sibarimar, Batabanó, Pozas, Consolación del Sur, Cayajabo, Mariel y San Pedro, con el Capitán General de Cuba, Marqués de Someruelos," 1808 (September 12), Fondo Cuba, Legajo 1682, AGI.

79. Ibid.

80. Pedro Soroa, "Cuaderno." These figures are derived from the inventory conducted in accord with the testament of Bengoechea.

81. Pedro Hechevarría requested the inventory to set the value for sale. See Francisco Boucourt et al., "Cuaderno (3 pz) mandado forma intestad de D[on] Pedro Hecheverría para tratar del remate del cafetal San Francisco la Liberal," 1841 (June 5), Fondo Escribanías de Cotés, Legajo 161, Número 1, ANC.

82. These numbers are based on the percentage of the population under the age of one year.

83. Francisco Boucourt et al., "Cuaderno"; and Pedro Soroa, "Cuaderno."

84. The 2.1 percent rate of reproduction is based on the census of 1861, the first census to include data for children under the age of one year. According to Kiple, he and others have used this figure because earlier island-wide data is unavailable. See Kiple, *Blacks in Colonial Cuba*, 53n31.

85. Domingo Macías and Jorge G. Jouve, "Testamentaria de José Rubio Campos."

86. *Trapiches* were smaller sugar farms with the older type of cane press equipment.

87. Comisión de Estadísticas, *Cuadro estadístico,* 55.

88. Marrero, *Cuba,* 11:118.

89. Each of the three led a statistical category in 1846. Alquízar had the highest number of cafetales at 63; Güira de Melena had the largest average size of dotación at 78 slaves per cafetal; Artemisa had the largest slave population on cafetales, with 3,200 slaves working on coffee farms. See ibid., 123.

90. Joaquín Santa Cruz y Cárdenas, "Expedientes de tabacos, azúcar y otros frutos, y remesas de dinero," 1808 (July 1), Fondo Santo Domingo, Legajo 2018, Número 36–44, AGI; and Pedro Vidal Rodríguez, "Plano a fs. 913, 4a pieza. Plano del cafetal 'Novedad,' situado en el partido de Alquízar que quedó por bienes de José de Fuertes y rematado por Lorenzo Pérez y Julián Villoch. firmado: José María Oliva. Se encuentra en incidente testamentaria de José de Fuertes formado para tratar del remate de los cafetales titulados 'Bagatela' y 'Novedad,'" 1831 (March 13), Fondo Escribanías de Hacienda, Legajo 215, Número 9094, ANC. The latter reference is an 1831 advertisement of the sale of the two cafetales following the death of Fuertes.

91. Antonio Gutiérrez, "Plano a fs. 913, 4a pieza. Plano del cafetal 'Novedad,' situado en el partido de Alquízar que quedó por bienes de José de Fuertes y rematado por Lorenzo Pérez y Julián Villoch. firmado: José María Oliva. Se

encuentra en incidente testamentaria de José de Fuertes formado para tratar del remate de los cafetales titulados 'Bagatela' y 'Novedad.'" 1831 (June 21), Fondo Escribanías de Hacienda, Legajo 215, Número 9094, ANC.

92.   All the figures for the cafetales Bagatela and Novedad are derived from Antonio Ximénez y Olivera and Juan Francisco Morejón, "Plano a fs. 913, 4a pieza. Plano del cafetal 'Novedad,' situado en el partido de Alquízar que quedó por bienes de José de Fuertes y rematado por Lorenzo Pérez y Julián Villoch. firmado: José María Oliva. Se encuentra en incidente testamentaria de José de Fuertes formado para tratar del remate de los cafetales titulados 'Bagatela' y 'Novedad,'" 1835 (July 21), Fondo Escribanías de Hacienda, Legajo 215, Número 9094, ANC.

PART II

1.   See, for example, Manuel Barcia Paz, *Seeds of Insurrection: Domination and Resistance on Western Cuban Plantations, 1808–1848* (Baton Rouge: Louisiana State University Press, 2008); and Matt D. Childs, *The 1812 Aponte Rebellion in Cuba and the Struggle against Atlantic Slavery* (Chapel Hill: University of North Carolina Press, 2006).

2.   A notable exception is Paquette, *Sugar Is Made with Blood.* Chapter 6 will engage with aspects of Paquette's argument, as it is somewhat problematic when considered in light of evidence from the cafetales.

CHAPTER 3

Epigraph. Abbot, *Letters*, 51.

1.   The idea that each type of plant had specific needs inherent to that plant was widely held at the time. That coffee required certain types of care is attested to by the uniformity of the manuals written to instruct farmers on the care of coffee bushes. Compare Dumont et al., *Memoria sobre el cultivo del café*, with Laborie, *Coffee Planter.* Embedded within those notions was the implicit understanding that there was some variability or adaptability of the plant, but there is little evidence that farmers thought they could reshape plants to suit their own needs. Planters understood the needs or demands of the plant in particular ways that suggest they realized that the plant could be adapted with some success to varying soils and climates. Thus, planters had a hand in shaping the needs of the plant they cultivated, rather than being strictly bound by its biology. See Barbara Hahn, "Making Tobacco Bright: Institutions, Information, and Industrialization in the Creation of an Agricultural Commodity, 1617–1937," *Enterprise and Society* 8, no. 4 (2007): 790, for a similar case in the development of tobacco in North America.

2.   "Task labor" was a system under which the master or overseer assigned each worker a specific job or task for the day. Once completed, the obligations of the slave were fulfilled for that day. Under the gang labor system, slaves were worked under the direct oversight of the overseer or a driver for the entire day or a fixed number of hours. The way these systems applied to labor on cafetales will be discussed later.

3.   Mme. Calderón de la Barca, *Life in Mexico during a Residence of Two Years in That Country*, reprint of 1843 ed. (Mexico: Ediciones Tolteca, 1952), 9; and Mann, *Juanita,* 39. In her novel, Mann described in great detail the bohíos of the plantation her protagonist visited. This description resulted from the personal experience of the author on the cafetal La Recompensa, located in the vuelta abajo.

4. Edwin Farnsworth Atkins, *Sixty Years in Cuba: Reminiscences of Edwin F. Atkins* (Cambridge: Riverside Press, 1926), 96.

5. Belén de la Rosa, "Criminal contra varios esclavos."

6. *Vegas* (lit. field or plain) was used in Cuba to designate tobacco farms.

7. Bremer, *Cartas desde Cuba*, 125–26.

8. See, for example, Henry Koster, *Travels in Brazil by Henry Koster in the Years from 1809 to 1815* (Philadelphia: M. Carey & Son, 1817).

9. See Manuel Gonzales Barredo, "Criminal en averiguación del movimiento contra los blancos que se proyectabe en el cafetal titulado Recompensa, en el partido de Batabanó por parte de su dotación, exitados por el negro Federico Gangá esclavo de D. Felipe Candal," 1844 (May 6), Fondo Comisión Militar, Legajo 32, Número 1, ANC; Carlos *congo*, "Criminal contra varios esclavos de la dotación del cafetal Perseverancia, acusados de haverse [*sic*] amotinado contra el mayoral y otros dependientes blancos de dicha finca. Complicados: Andrés Lucumí, Rosa Lucumí, Eulogio Lucumí, Luciano Lucumí, Lucas Lucumí, Cleto Lucumí, Basilio Lucumí, Felipa Lucumí, Lorenzo Colorado, Emeterio, Genaro Lucumí, Agapito Lucumí, Canuto Lucumí, Víctor Lucumí, Lucio Lucumí, Facundo Lucumí, Lopio Lucumí, Amá Lucumí, Florentino Lucumí, Lorenzo Prieto, Francisco Carabalí, y Vincente Mandinga. Fiscal El Teniente Coronel D. Felipe Arango, Secretario El Teniente D. Antonio Cas . . . ," 1842 (September 20), Fondo Comisión Militar, Legajo 27, Número 3, ANC; José Baquero, "Comisión Militar. Criminal contra los autores y complices principales de la sublevación de negros del Cafetal Salvador de D. Francisco Santiago de Aguirre ubicado en Banes ocurrida la noche del 13 de agosto por cuyo delito se jusgan á Pedro el carretero; Gonzalo Mandinga; Eusebio Gangá; Luis idem; Pascual Lucumí; Bernualdo id.; Antonio Lucumí; Agustín id.; Atilano id.; Juan id.; Hermenegildo id.; Juez Fiscal: El Capitán de Ynfantería D.n Tomás de Salazar; Secretario: El Teniente graduado D.n Lorenzo Baltanas," 1833 (August 16), Fondo Miscelánea de Expedientes, Legajo 540, Número B, ANC; Fernando *congo*, "Expediente sobre la fuga de 14 negros del Cafetal 'Catalina' de D.n Antonio Toscano," 1828 (July 10), Fondo Gobierno Superior Civil, Legajo 936, Número 33025, ANC; Pablo *lucumí*, "Comisión Militar. Autos criminales contra los negros de la dotación del cafetal titulado 'La Juanita,' Habana 1835," 1835 (July 17), Fondo Miscelánea de Expedientes, Legajo 86, Número D, 7, ANC; and Oficina del Gobierno Constitucional, "Tasación y venta."

10. See Bremer, *Cartas desde Cuba;* Barca, *Life in Mexico;* Robert, *New Year in Cuba;* and Mann, *Juanita.*

11. Juan Pérez de la Riva, *El barracón y otros ensayos* (Havana: Editorial de Ciencias Sociales, 1975), 21–22. Pérez de la Riva contends that the Cuban origins of the barracón can be traced to an 1831 work by Honorato Bernard de Chateausalins entitled *El vademécum de los hacendados cubanos; ó, Guía práctica para curar la mayor parte de las enfermedades* (Philadelphia: J. Van Cort, 1848).

12. See Pérez de la Riva, *El barracón.*

13. Méndez, *Bibliografía del cafetal Angerona*, 58.

14. Francisco de Santiago Aguirre, "Comisión Militar. Criminal contra los autores y complices principales de la sublevación de negros del Cafetal Salvador de D. Francisco Santiago de Aguirre ubicado en Banes ocurrida la noche del 13 de agosto por cuyo delito se jusgan á Pedro el carretero; Gonzalo Mandinga; Eusebio Gangá; Luis idem; Pascual Lucumí; Bernualdo id.; Antonio Lucumí; Agustín id.; Atilano id.; Juan id.; Hermenegildo id.; Juez Fiscal: El Capitán de Ynfantería D.n

Tomás de Salazar; Secretario: El Teniente graduado D.n Lorenzo Baltanas," 1833 (August 16), Fondo Miscelánea de Expedientes, Legajo 540, Número B, ANC.

15. James A. Delle, *An Archaeology of Social Space: Analyzing Coffee Plantations in Jamaica's Blue Mountains* (New York: Plenum Press, 1998); and B. W. Higman, *Jamaica Surveyed: Plantation Maps and Plans of the Eighteenth and Nineteenth Centuries* (Barbados: University of the West Indies Press, 2001). Theresa Singleton also offers some insight into spatial control on coffee plantations in Cuba. Singleton used the approach of Henri Lefebvre to describe a dialectical relationship between slaveholders and the enslaved on plantations. She argues that this relationship develops through the use and manipulation of the plantation's spatial organization. I will argue that the relationship was often dialogical. See Singleton, "Slavery and Spatial Dialectics on Cuban Coffee Plantations," *World Archaeology* 33, no. 1 (2001): 98–114.

16. Delle, *Archaeology of Social Space*, 156.

17. For the full story, see "Plano de fs. 76. Plano de los Cafetales Acierto y Laborinto ubicados en el corral y partido de San Marcos, el 1º de Ramon Charun y el 2º de Diego Pintado y consortes. firmado José Ma Oliva. se encuentra en dilgs criminales practicadas a consecuencia de las faltas cometidas por Jorge Castillo, mayoral del Cafetal Laberinto propiedad de Diego Pintado a Ramon Charun, propietario del Cafetal Acierto," 1838, Fondo Escribanías de Varios, Legajo 174, Número 2362, ANC. The danger that could have occurred was during the confrontation on the Laborinto. Each group of slaves was armed in some manner and the mayorales also had brought dogs along for protection.

18. Andrew Parker and Eve Kosofsky Sedgwick, eds., *Performativity and Performance* (New York: Routledge, 1995), 1.

19. See ibid. Their argument is in the context of the 1993 congressional hearings on the "don't ask, don't tell" policy adopted by the US military toward homosexuals. They convincingly show that people generally consider speech and action coequal and as expressions of identity. Though this is a substantially different context, I am convinced that this argument can be applied across time and cultures successfully. For a greater contextualization of Parker and Sedgwick's argument, see J. L. Austin, *How to Do Things with Words*, 2nd ed. (Oxford: Clarendon Press, 1975); Jacques Derrida, "Signature Event Context," in *Margins of Philosophy* (Chicago: University of Chicago Press, 1982); Jean-François Lyotard, *The Postmodern Condition: A Report on Knowledge*, trans. Geoff Bennington and Brian Massumi (Minneapolis: University of Minnesota Press, 1984); and Paul de Man, *Allegories of Reading: Figural Language in Rousseau, Nietzsche, Rilke, and Proust* (New Haven: Yale University Press, 1979). Also useful may be Victor W. Turner, *The Anthropology of Performance* (New York: PAJ Publications, 1986); Dennis Tedlock and Bruce Mannheim, eds., *The Dialogical Emergence of Culture* (Urbana: University of Illinois Press, 1995); Judith Butler, *Bodies That Matter: On the Discursive Limits of "Sex"* (New York: Routledge, 1993); and Paul Connerton, *How Societies Remember* (New York: Cambridge University Press, 1989). More specifically regarding this phenomenon in the slave context, see Sidney W. Mintz, *Sweetness and Power: The Place of Sugar in Modern History* (New York: Penguin, 1986); Sidney W. Mintz and Richard Price, *The Birth of African-American Culture: An Anthropological Perspective* (Boston: Beacon Press, 1992); and Gwendolyn Midlo Hall, *Africans in Colonial Louisiana: The Development of Afro-Creole Culture in the Eighteenth Century* (Baton Rouge: Louisiana State University Press, 1992).

20. This account is from a series of documents in Julio de la Naya et al., "Auto de proceder—[Office of the Brigadier] Gobernador de Matanzas," 1861 (October 18–November 7), Fondo Cimarrones, Legajo 16, Número 30, Archivo Historico Provincial de Matanzas (hereafter APHM).

21. Homi K. Bhabha, *The Location of Culture* (London: Routledge, 1994), 83.

22. I have argued elsewhere that the mobilization of African-derived religious practice was used both as a strategy of resistance and as an expression of identification for newly arrived slaves in the Caribbean. It is also clear from the historical record that owners and their agents often accused slaves of engaging in "magic" to explain resistance and understood it as a category to understand African practices. Slaves also seemed to use the discourse of the masters in order to frame other comments or to play on the fears of those over them. See William C. Van Norman, Jr., "The Process of Cultural Change among Cuban Bozales during the Nineteenth Century," *Americas* 62, no. 1 (2005).

23. Julio de la Naya et al., "Auto de proceder."

24. Delle, *Archaeology of Social Space*, 157–59.

25. Foucault, *Discipline and Punish*, 200–201.

26. Singleton, "Slavery and Spatial Dialectics."

27. Control of the enslaved workers was the purpose behind this piece of advice offered by Laborie. He wrote that the chief reason to locate the buildings away from the center of the farm was if there was a public road that divided the property. He advised in such a case to move as much of the operational structures of the farm as far from the road as possible so as to isolate the slaves from this potential threat. See Laborie, *Coffee Planter*, 12.

28. Bremer, *Cartas desde Cuba*, 125.

29. Ramiro Guerra Sánchez, *Mudos testigos*, 51. I will return to the issue of religious practice in Chapter 4.

30. Mann, *Juanita*, 75.

31. See Singleton, "Slavery and Spatial Dialectics."

32. Laborie, *Coffee Planter*, 38.

33. Kenneth F. Kiple and Virginia Himmelsteib King, *Another Dimension to the Black Diaspora: Diet, Disease, and Racism* (Cambridge: Cambridge University Press, 1981), 67.

34. It should be noted that David Sartorius and Rebecca J. Scott have both shown that the use of provision grounds on sugar cane farms continued throughout the period of nineteenth-century slavery in Cuba. See Sartorius, "Slavery, Conucos, and the Local Economy: Ingenio Santa Rosalia, Cienfuegos, Cuba, 1860–1886" (MA thesis, University of North Carolina, 1997); and Scott, *Slave Emancipation in Cuba: The Transition to Free Labor, 1860–1899* (Princeton: Princeton University Press, 1985). While their findings complicate the overall picture and challenge certain premises of Kiple, and by extension Manuel Moreno Fraginals, their conclusions show that Cuban plantation owners of all sorts balanced economic issues with concerns about slave control.

35. José García de Arboleya, "Cafetales and Vegas in Cuba," in *Haciendas and Plantations in Latin American History*, ed. Robert G. Keith (New York: Holmes and Meier Publishers, 1977), 153.

36. Rafael O'Farrill y Herrera, "Autos relativos"; and Jorge Dias Rodrigues, "Plano a fs. 672 de la 4a pieza. Plano de diez y un cuarto caballerías de tierra que medí en el partido de S. Marcos vínculo de Mey[i]reles y forman el cafetal nombrado la 'Paciencia' que quedó entre los bienes de D. Alonso Benigno Muñoz y hoy correponde a D. Santiago F. Firmado por Desiderio Herrera. En los autos del

concurso de acreedores de Dn. Alonso Benigno Muñoz," 1833 (September 25), Fondo Escribanías de Ortega, Legajo 38, Número 1, ANC.

37. [Illegible], "Plano a fs. 1129." The inventory of the Campana, for instance, lists among its 10 1/2 caballerías of land 1 1/2 caballerías as a portrero.

38. The O'Farrill y Herrera and Herrera y Pedroso families owned several ingenios and cafetales, including the cafetal Recreo and the ingenios San Ignacío and Santa Teresa.

39. Bremer, *Cartas desde Cuba*, 125.

40. Ibid., 117–24.

41. Manuel O'Reilly y Calvo, "Expediente manuscrito."

42. Kiple and King, *Another Dimension*, 68–69.

43. Kiple draws on a 1977 article by Moreno Fraginals for his data on Cuba which, in spite of some table headings that indicate the totals are from coffee and sugar plantations, appears to be drawn from information from sugar plantations. Moreno Fraginals argues for the primacy of sugar and draws his evidence concerning the diet and the height of slaves from the period of the 1840s to 1869, citing a study published by Henri Dumont in 1869 as most important. The evidence he offers, then, is skewed to the period when coffee was already in decline. In addition, his closest analysis is based on a sample consisting of 1,635 slaves from 1855 to 1859. See Moreno Fraginals, "Africa in Cuba: A Quantitative Analysis of the African Population in the Island of Cuba," *Annals of the New York Academy of Sciences*, 292 (1977), especially 198 (table 9).

44. Jorge Le-Roy y Cassá, *Estadística demográfica en Cuba: Trabajo presentado al intercambio sanitario de la Liga de las Naciones celebrado en La Habana del 1° al 10 de Marzo de 1925* (Havana: El "Siglo XX," 1925).

45. Mann, *Juanita*, 57.

46. Le-Roy y Cassá, *Estadística demográfica en Cuba.*

47. World Health Organization, "Cholera: Fact Sheet N° 107," *www.who.int* (accessed September 2012).

48. M. L. Lizárraga-Partida et al., "Association of Vibrio Cholerae with Plankton in Coastal Areas of Mexico," *Environmental Microbiology* 11, no. 1 (2009): 201–8.

49. See Bremer, *Cartas desde Cuba*, 57. Bremer offers some insights into contemporary thinking on the connection between hurricanes and epidemics. For recent scholarship, see Sherry Johnson, "El Niño and Environmental Crisis: Reinterpreting American Rebellions in the 1790s" (paper presented at the Allen Morris Conference on the History of Florida and the Atlantic World, Florida State University, Tallahassee, FL, 2004). Johnson argues that not only was there an immediate and short-term impact from the passing storms, but there were longer-term effects as a result of the el Niño effect that comes on the heels of an active hurricane season. For a fuller discussion of the broader effects of hurricanes on the Cuban people and economy, see Sherry Johnson, *Climate and Catastrophe in Cuba and the Atlantic World in the Age of Revolution* (Chapel Hill: University of North Carolina Press, 2011); and Pérez, *Winds of Change*, 199.

50. Mariano Ricafort, "Aparición de los primeros casos de cólera en el barrio de San Lázaro, de La Habana," 1833 (March 4), Fondo Correspondencia de Cuba, Legajo 6374, Número 21, 1, AHN.

51. Ramón de la Sagra, "Envía relación de personas muertas en La Habana a causa del cólera," 1833 (May 31), Fondo Correspondencia de Cuba, Legajo 6374, Número 27, 7, AHN.

52. Mariano Ricafort and Ramón de la Sagra, "Informa sobre el estado de la epidemia, que en La Habana ha disminuido notablemente, pues según el último

parte del Protomedicato, sólo se había producido una defunción diaria en la semana anterior. En toda la isla decrece la mortalidad, como puede ver por la relación que adjunta que comprende desde el 25 de febrero al 30 de septiembre. Anuncia remisión de impresos. Da cuenta de los festejos que se habían celebrado con motivo de la jura de la princesa Isabel Luisa," 1833 (October 30), Fondo Correspondencia de Cuba y Puerto Rico, Legajo 6374, Número 44, 1 and 2, AHN.

53.   Manuel Lafita, "Los autos promovidos." The figures cited earlier were derived through a comparison of the two inventories.

54.   Simon Vicente de Hevia, "Al haber cesado la epidemia de cólera en Europa y América se habian levantado la medidas preventivas," 1833 (February 2), Fondo Correspondencia de Cuba, Legajo 6374, Número 19, AHN.

55.   Sebastian Fornes y Guma, "Medicina empleada para luchar contra el cólera," 1833 (September 2), Fondo Correspondencia de Cuba, Legajo 6374, Número 38, AHN. *Vino de malaga* (lit., Malaga wine) is a sweet, dark wine.

56.   The *real* was the basic monetary unit. There were eight reales in a peso.

57.   Manuel O'Reilly y Calvo, "Expediente manuscrito." A *médico accidental* was someone practicing medicine who came to the profession by chance or inadvertently.

58.   Kenneth F. Kiple, *The Caribbean Slave: A Biological History* (New York: Cambridge University Press, 1984), 146–48.

59.   Ibid., 147–48.

60.   "The power, the violence, the sordid interest, the insatiable desire for riches triumphs over all." See José Leopoldo Yarini Klupffel, "Cólera en el ingenio," *Wikiversity, en.wikiversity.org* (last modified September 10, 2008).

61.   Ibid. Also see Adrián López Denis, "Sugar in the Times of Cholera," *Wikiversity, en.wikiversity.org* (last modified October 27, 2009).

CHAPTER 4

Epigraph. Jameson, *Letters from the Havana*, 20.

1.   See Frederick Solt et al., "Economic Inequality, Relative Power, and Religiosity," *Social Science Quarterly* 92, no. 2 (2011): 447–65.

2.   A number of historians of Africa and the African diaspora argue that to understand the diaspora on its own terms, it is critical to begin with Africa and the origins of the diasporic community. See, for example, John K. Thornton, *Africa and Africans in the Making of the Atlantic World, 1400–1680*, (Cambridge: Cambridge University Press, 1992); Paul E. Lovejoy, *Transformations in Slavery: A History of Slavery in Africa* (New York: Cambridge University Press, 1983); Colin A. Palmer, "From Africa to the Americas: Ethnicity in the Early Black Communities," *Journal of World History* 6, no. 2 (Fall 1995): 223–36; and James H. Sweet, *Recreating Africa: Culture, Kinship, and Religion in the African-Portuguese World, 1441–1770* (Chapel Hill: University of North Carolina Press, 2003).

3.   Thornton, *Africa and Africans*, 184–92.

4.   These categories are assigned commercial categories that were understood as designations of nación that we would understand today as ethnicity. But these were categories traders typically assigned based on ports of debarkation and adopted by slaveholders. This does shed some light on African connections, but it will be necessary to carefully unpack those ties across the Atlantic. At the same

time, as we will see, African people in Cuba adopted these markers and defined them for themselves. This move on the part of subordinated people reveals much, and for that reason, the markers have some salience in this analytical context.

5.   See Suzanne Miers and Igor Kopytoff, "African 'Slavery' as an Institution of Marginality," in *Slavery in Africa: Historical and Anthropological Perspectives*, ed. Miers and Kopytoff (Madison: University of Wisconsin Press, 1977), for their explanation of how a broad cross-section of African peoples have used ritual to understand and define their worlds. Victor Turner and Maurice Bloch have shown how peoples of west central Africa have used ritual to resolve a variety of seemingly nonreligious conflicts. See Turner, "Social Dramas and Stories about Them," in *On Narrative*, ed. W. J. T. Mitchell (Chicago: University of Chicago Press, 1981); and Bloch, *Prey into Hunter: The Politics of Religious Experience* (Cambridge: Cambridge University Press, 1992). For Yoruban ideas concerning ritual, see James Lorand Matory, *Sex and the Empire That Is No More: Gender and the Politics of Metaphor in Oyo Yoruba Religion* (Minneapolis: University of Minnesota Press, 1994), 295.

6.   See Sweet, *Recreating Africa*, 106. Sweet draws on the work of Robin Horton, in which Horton critiques the works of Victor Turner, E. E. Evans-Pritchard, John Mbiti, E. Bolaji Idowu, and others, each of whom created a distorted view of African religious practices as a result of their own religious concepts, which influenced their thinking. See Horton, *Patterns of Thought in Africa and the West: Essays on Magic, Religion, and Science* (Cambridge: Cambridge University Press, 1993), especially chapter 6.

7.   This applies both to this specific case as well as other cases in west Africa, including that of the Yoruban people, which I take up in this chapter. I contend that it is crucial to understand African and diasporic religious practice and thinking on its own terms. Anything less distorts the meaning and intentionality of its practitioners and undermines our ability to search for motives and explanations for actions taken by enslaved Africans in Cuba.

8.   I am drawing heavily on Sweet, *Recreating Africa*, 107–8, for this section.

9.   Sweet is an exemplary case of a scholar who has advanced his thinking on African religious concepts significantly but does not fully extricate Western concepts from his work. For example, Sweet makes a very good case, as noted previously, about the universal high god concept in earlier scholarship being problematic in the central African context. But he also differentiates between the sacred and secular, also Western concepts, when he writes that "religious beliefs and everyday secular activities were intimately connected" (107). The Durkheim/Lévy-Brühl debate over the sacred and profane split (which involves the distinction between emphasis of the sacred over the profane in "primitive" societies and the shift to greater emphasis on the profane in so-called modern societies as connected to either an evolutionary process or a replacement process as societies move from the primitive to the modern) is a false debate. I do agree that there are societies that see the world in terms of the sacred and the profane, but I am convinced that these are tied to particular cosmological visions as well as other sociological factors. The presence of a sacred/profane conceptual framework in societies is rooted in religious systems with a remote high god figure or a deep fissure between the spiritual and visible planes. Sociologically, this is more likely to be found when there is a greater inequality in the group as well as lack of dialogical orientation in the culture. It is a Western perspective to see societies and cultures as moving along an evolutionary scale rooted in Enlightenment thought as well as nineteenth-century notions of progress, e.g.,

positivism. See Horton, *Patterns of Thought*, 75–82; and Tedlock and Mannheim, *Dialogical Emergence*, 2–5.

10.　Sweet, *Recreating Africa*, 119. Sweet notes that "across Africa, one of the diviner's primary roles was to determine the cause of social fissure in society."

11.　See Mary Elizabeth Perry, *Gender and Disorder in Early Modern Seville* (Princeton, NJ: Princeton University Press, 1990), 31.

12.　The Inquisition in Spain was founded initially to oversee conversions by Jews and Moors that had been compelled by the crown during the reconquest of territory by Christians. Church courts and investigations were used by the Inquisition and expanded to include searching out and punishing other forms of heresy over time.

13.　See, for example, Fernando Ortiz, *Hampa afro-cubana: Los negros esclavos; Estudio sociológico y de derecho público* (Havana: Revista Bimestre Cubana, 1916). Rómulo Lachatañeré comments on this problematic usage by Ortiz in his early work. See Lachatañeré, *El sistema religioso de los afrocubanos* (Havana: Editorial de Ciencias Sociales, 1992), 196–204.

14.　See Jorge Castellanos and Isabel Castellano*s*, *Cultura afrocubana: Las religiones y las lenguas*, (Miami: Ediciones Universal, 1992), 140; see also 140n1.

15.　George Brandon, *Santería from Africa to the New World: The Dead Sell Memories* (Bloomington: Indiana University Press, 1993), 11.

16.　Possession rituals will be taken up later, but see Matory, *Sex and the Empire*, 4–8.

17.　See, for example, ibid.; Brandon, *Santería*; Jacob K. Olupona and Terry Rey, eds., *Orisa Devotion as World Religion: The Globalization of Yoruba Religious Culture* (Madison: University of Wisconsin Press, 2008); Joseph M. Murphy and Mei-Mei Sanford, ed., *Oṣun across the Waters: A Yoruba Goddess in Africa and the Americas* (Bloomington: Indiana University Press, 2001); and James Lorand Matory, *Black Atlantic Religion: Tradition, Transnationalism, and Matriarchy in the Afro-Brazilian Candomblé* (Princeton, NJ: Princeton University Press, 2005).

18.　Jacob K. Olupona, "The Study of Yoruba Religious Tradition in Historical Perspective," *Numen* 40 (1993): 245.

19.　Jacob K. Olupona, "The Spirituality of Matter: Religion and Environment in Yoruba Tradition, Nigeria," *Dialogue and Alliance* 9, no. 2 (1995): 70. Olupona inadvertently affirms Sweet's and Horton's arguments when he uses the term "sacred" to begin his argument to reframe the understanding of Yoruban people to the natural environment. As I have argued earlier, many African peoples, including the Yorubans, have a wholly different cosmological view.

20.　Ibid., 70. To quote Mbiti, "The physical and spiritual are but two dimensions of one and the same universe. These dimensions dovetail into each other to the extent that at certain times and places one is apparently more real than, but not exclusive of, the other." John Mbiti, *African Religions and Philosophy* (London: Heinemann, 1969), 57.

21.　The problem with Olupona's analysis is his insistence on the category of the sacred to describe an increasing range of spaces, places, and features or objects. "Sacred" is a binary category, requiring some spaces to be reserved for its oppositional category of the "mundane" or "profane." As Olupona rightly points out, nearly anywhere or anything could be "sacred," thus rendering the distinction meaningless. If we shift our thinking away from this notion, it is easier to see how rich and meaningful the Yorubans' landscapes were. See Olupona, "Spirituality of Matter," 72–75.

22.　See Bruce Mannheim and Dennis Tedlock, "Introduction," in Tedlock and Mannheim, *Dialogical Emergence*.

23.　Matory, *Sex and the Empire*, 4–5. The idea of "mounting" is a complex part of the story that will be taken up in the discussion of gender.

24. Brandon, *Santería*, 14.

25. Godwin S. Sogolo, "The Concept of Cause in African Thought," in *The African Philosophy Reader*, ed. P. H. Coetzee and A. P. J. Roux (New York: Routledge, 1998), 183.

26. The example of some clear physical accidents are the exception to this model.

27. Sogolo, "Concept," 181–83.

28. See ibid.

29. See Sharla M. Fett, *Working Cures: Healing, Health, and Power on Southern Slave Plantations* (Chapel Hill: University of North Carolina Press, 2002); Mbiti, *African Religions and Philosophy*; and Horton, *Patterns of Thought*.

30. This view goes back to the days of slaveholding and is reflected in the account of Stanislas Foäche (1737–1806) and the instructions he sent to the manager of his plantation at Jean-Rabel, Saint Domingue, concerning the treatment of new slaves. He warned of the dangers present in the extreme malleability of "new negroes" and said they should be treated with a great deal of care to avoid "damaging" them. Gabriel Debien, *Plantations et esclaves a Saint-Domingue: La Sucrerie Foäche a Jean-Rabel et ses esclaves] (1770–1893)* (Dakar: Imprimerie Protat Frères, 1962) 67:46–53. See also Frank Tannenbaum, *Slave and Citizen: The Negro in the Americas* (New York: Vintage, 1946).

31. Anthropologists have been on the leading edge of the debate over African cultural survivals, with Sidney Mintz and Richard Price being among the most influential in the latter decades of the twentieth century. See Mintz and Price, *Birth of African-American Culture*. Their work draws on and advances older works, reaching back to those of Melville Herskovits and Fernando Ortiz. See, for example, Herskovits, *The Myth of the Negro Past* (New York: Harper, 1941); and Ortiz, *La africanía de la música folklórica de Cuba* (Havana: Ministerio de Educación, Dirección de Cultura, 1950). See also Richard Price and Sally Price, *The Root of Roots; or, How Afro-American Anthropology Got Its Start* (Chicago: Prickly Paradigm Press, 2003). They argue that there were cultural survivals—threads of culture that remained intact—but that there was also relatively rapid creolization, and as a result, new African American cultures emerged. Other scholars took up their challenge for further research and began to argue more vigorously for broader African survivals among slave populations.

32. See Sweet, *Recreating Africa*, especially chapter 6. For similar views on African cultural survivals, see also Gwendolyn Midlo Hall, *Slavery and African Ethnicities in the Americas: Restoring the Links* (Chapel Hill: University of North Carolina Press, 2005); Linda M. Heywood, ed., *Central Africans and Cultural Transformations in the American Diaspora* (Cambridge: Cambridge University Press, 2002); Paul E. Lovejoy, "The African Diaspora: Revisionist Interpretations of Ethnicity, Culture and Religion under Slavery," *Studies in the World History of Slavery, Abolition and Emancipation* 2, no. 1 (1997): 1–23; and John K. Thornton, "African Dimensions of the Stono Rebellion," *American Historical Review* 96, no. 4 (1991): 1101–13.

33. See Baron L. Pineda, *Shipwrecked Identities: Navigating Race on Nicaragua's Mosquito Coast* (New Brunswick, NJ: Rutgers University Press, 2006).

34. Jameson, *Letters from the Havana*, 20–21.

35. *Santería* is a popular term that is more widely known outside of Cuba for the religious practices known as the *Regla de Ocha*. This term also is used occasionally to include the *Regla de Ifá*, the divination practices of Babalawos, as it is part of the larger orisha complex. See Brandon, *Santería*, 140–42. The list of African-derived religious practices noted here is not comprehensive. Those

mentioned here are related to the practices of the regions of Africa mentioned in this chapter. For more on the longer-term implications of Yoruban religious thought in Cuba, see Stephan Palmié, *Wizards and Scientists: Explorations in Afro-Cuban Modernity and Tradition* (Durham, NC: Duke University Press, 2002). For more on Palo Monte, see Todd Ramón Ochoa, *Society of the Dead: Quita Manaquita and Palo Praise in Cuba* (Berkeley: University of California, 2010).

36. Abbot, *Letters*, 139.
37. Manuel Gonzales Barredo, "Criminal en averiguación."
38. Federico *gangá*, "Criminal en averiguación del movimiento contra los blancos que se proyectabe en el cafetal titulado Recompensa, en el partido de Batabanó por parte de su dotación, exitados por el negro Federico Gangá esclavo de D. Felipe Candal," 1844 (May 6), Fondo Comisión Militar, Legajo 32, Número 1, 16v–17, ANC.
39. Onofre *criollo*, "Criminal en averiguación del movimiento contra los blancos que se proyectabe en el cafetal titulado Recompensa, en el partido de Batabanó por parte de su dotación, exitados por el negro Federico Gangá esclavo de D. Felipe Candal," 1844 (May 6), Fondo Comisión Militar, Legajo 32, Número 1, 18v–19, ANC. Onofre, when questioned, responded that he did not understand the meaning of the words, but that others had chanted or sung along with Federico, suggesting that they understood the meaning. Onofre, a creole, was less likely to have a working knowledge of an African language—or, he may have been deflecting culpability, along the lines of what I argued in the previous chapter about slaves and testimony.
40. Antonio González Larrinaga et al., "Plano á fajas 85. Plano topográfico del cafetal nombrado Santísima Trinidad ubicado en el partido de la Güira y de la propiedad el Sr. Coronel de Caballería D. Antonio González Larrinaga el que he formado por disposición del Ecmo. Sor. Procer, Governador, y Capn. General de esta Isla. Cristobal de Gallegos, Agremensor. En los seguidos por el mismo González Larrinaga," 1836 (March 16), Fondo Escribanías de Galletti, Legajo 24, Número 9, 36v, ANC.
41. Rituals directed against another person often or usually involved the specialist using things that the targeted person had handled and things the specialist had collected surreptitiously, such as a piece of clothing worn by the person, hair clippings, or other "leavings." See Eugenio Matibag, *Afro-Cuban Religious Experience: Cultural Reflections in Narrative* (Gainesville: University Press of Florida, 1996), 154–72. For a broader overview of Afro-Cuban religious practices, see Lachatañeré, *El sistema religioso*.
42. Mariano Paradas, "Comunicación a Antonio García Oña, Gobernador de Matanzas, sobre ranchería contra una partida de cimarrones apostados en los barracones del cafetal Santa Ana de Biajacas, del presbítero O'Farrill, a los que se les incorporaron negros de esa finca," 1837 (December 25), Fondo Cimarrones, Legajo 12, Número 50, AHPM.
43. The designation of *carabalí* denoted an ethnic identity understood by Cuban planters. This designation was derived from the knowledge that a slave had been shipped from the port of Calabar, which was located on the eastern side of the Niger delta, the homeland of the Igbo people. It is also possible that Damián was of a different ethnicity, as he may have been brought down the river from somewhere inland. Nevertheless, he was almost certainly of a different origin than the slaves considered Lucumí or Gangá.
44. See Fernando Ortiz, *Los bailes y el teatro de los negros en el folklore de Cuba*, 2nd ed. (Havana: Editorial Letras Cubanas, 1985), 267–72.

45. Matibag, *Afro-Cuban Religious Experience*, 15.

46. Juan Pérez de la Riva, *Cuadro sinóptico de la esclavitud en Cuba (Suplemento de la Revista Actas del Folklore)* (Havana: Tipografía Ponciano, 1961). The information is taken from a non-numbered chart.

47. Jameson, *Letters from the Havana*, 21–22.

48. Guerra Sánchez, *Mudos testigos*, 30.

49. See María Teresa Vélez, *Drumming for the Gods: The Life and Times of Felipe García Villamil, Santero, Palero, and Abakuá* (Philadelphia: Temple University Press, 2000), 50–51, 97–98.

50. Bremer, *Cartas desde Cuba*, 42.

51. Juan Alcozer, "Comisión Militar. Autos criminales contra los negros de la dotación del cafetal titulado 'La Juanita,' Habana 1835," 1835 (July 24), Fondo Miscelánea de Expedientes, Legajo 86, Número D, 3–4, ANC.

52. For a complete list of casualties, see Juan Mondesy, "Comisión Militar. Autos criminales contra los negros de la dotación del cafetal titulado 'La Juanita,' Habana 1835," 1835 (November 13), Fondo Miscelánea de Expedientes, Legajo 86, Número D, 164–66, ANC.

53. The slaves involved included Marcelino *lucumí*, Ricardo *lucumí*, Serapio *lucumí*, Sacarias *lucumí*, Domingo *lucumí*, José Esperansa *lucumí*, Cresencio *lucumí*, Silvestre *lucumí*, Julio *lucumí*, Clemente *lucumí*, Simon *lucumí*, Pablo *lucumí*, Marcos *lucumí*, Canuto *lucumí*, Gonsalo *lucumí*, and Polomino *lucumí*. See Pio García, "Comisión Militar. Autos criminales contra los negros de la dotación del cafetal titulado 'La Juanita,' Habana 1835," 1835 (July 18), Fondo Miscelánea de Expedientes, Legajo 86, Número D, 130v–132, ANC.

54. Pablo *lucumí*, "Comisión Militar. Autos criminales contra los negros de la dotación del cafetal titulado 'La Juanita,' Habana 1835," 1835 (July 17), Fondo Miscelánea de Expedientes, Legajo 86, Número D, 7, ANC.

55. There were analogs to the Cuban cabildo de nación in other contexts, such as the *candombe* in Buenos Aires and the *candomblé* in Brazil. For more on the cabildos de nación, see Philip A. Howard, *Changing History: Afro-Cuban Cabildos and Societies of Color in the Nineteenth Century* (Baton Rouge: Louisiana State University Press, 1998); and Matt D. Childs, "'The Defects of Being a Black Creole': The Degrees of African Identity in the Cuban Cabildos De Nación, 1790–1820," in *Slaves, Subjects, and Subversives: Blacks in Colonial Latin America*, ed. Jane G. Landers and Barry M. Robinson (Albuquerque: University of New Mexico Press, 2006).

56. Miguel (esclavo de Miguel Duarte), "Comisión Militar. Autos criminales contra los negros de la dotación del cafetal titulado 'La Juanita,' Habana 1835," 1835 (July 21), Fondo Miscelánea de Expedientes, Legajo 86, Número D, 36v–37v, ANC.

57. Nicolas *lucumí*, "Comisión Militar. Autos criminales contra los negros de la dotación del cafetal titulado 'La Juanita,' Habana 1835," 1835 (August 1), Fondo Miscelánea de Expedientes, Legajo 86, Número D, 93v–95v, ANC.

58. Juan García, "Comisión Militar. Autos criminales contra los negros de la dotación del cafetal titulado 'La Juanita,' Habana 1835," 1835, Fondo Miscelánea de Expedientes, Legajo 86, Número D, ANC.

59. Trinidad *lucumí*, "Comisión Militar. Autos criminales contra los negros de la dotación del cafetal titulado 'La Juanita,' Habana 1835," 1835 (August 2), Fondo Miscelánea de Expedientes, Legajo 86, Número D, 96v–97v, ANC.

60. This was happening much earlier and more quickly than it did in the slave population located on sugar cane farms.

61. For a discussion on performativity, see the introductory essay by Parker and Sedgwick in *Performativity and Performance.*
62. John Charles Chasteen, *National Rhythms, African Roots: The Deep History of Latin American Popular Dance* (Albuquerque: University of New Mexico Press, 2004), 106–13.
63. Matory, *Sex and the Empire.*
64. Brandon, *Santería.*
65. Bremer, *Cartas desde Cuba*, 66.

CHAPTER 5

Epigraph. Abbot, *Letters*, 136.

1. There is scant mention of conucos in much of the existing literature on slavery in Cuba. Earlier works focused on planters and their world and therefore did not devote attention to slave life. Francisco Pérez de la Riva, for example, extensively documents cafetal economy and planter culture. Within his chapters on life and labor on the cafetal, he does discuss slave housing, work, and fiestas, but does not detail how or what the slaves were fed. See chapters 2 and 3 of Pérez de la Riva y Pons, *El café*, 117–73. More recently, scholars have explored slave life more closely. Manuel Moreno Fraginals briefly mentions conucos, though he suggests that they were not widely used on ingenios until after 1860 as a result of changing ideas about slave treatment. See Moreno Fraginals, *El Ingenio: Complejo económico social cubano del azúcar* (Havana: Editorial de Ciencias Sociales, 1978), 2:89-90.
2. See Scott, *Slave Emancipation*, 16–17. Scott insists that we should be careful not to overstate the case, but she also notes that this clearly was a factor in slave life. Her study focuses on the transition to freedom after 1860. The period she looks at was dominated by sugar farms and therefore the conditions under which slaves lived and labored was distinct from the earlier period and context of this study.
3. See, for example, Moreno Fraginals, *El Ingenio*; Pérez de la Riva y Pons, *El café*; Zanetti Lecuona and García Alvarez, *Sugar and Railroads*; and González Fernández, "Acerca del mercado cafetalero cubano."
4. Dana, "Trip to Cuba," 188.
5. Hurlbert, *Gan-Eden*, 145-47.
6. Abbot, *Letters*, 140, 142.
7. Guerra Sánchez, *Mudos testigos*, 60, 74.
8. Alfonso W. Quiroz, "The Scientist and the Patrician: Reformism in Cuba" (paper presented at Alexander von Humboldt: From the Americas to the Cosmos, New York, 2004), 115n11; and Santa Cruz y Cárdenas, "Expedientes de tabacos."
9. Diego de la Barrera, "Ildefonso Ruiz del Río."
10. González Fernández, "Acerca del mercado cafetalero cubano," 154–57.
11. See Pérez, *Winds of Change.*
12. Guerra Sánchez, *Mudos testigos*, 65, 79.
13. Laborie, *Coffee Planter*, 35–39.
14. One *cordel* equaled 414 square meters and 324 square cordeles equaled one caballería.
15. Domingo Macías and Jorge G. Jouve, "Testamentaria de José Rubio Campos."
16. [Illegible], "Plano a fs. 1129."
17. "Yerba de guinea para las bestias y conucos para los negros." Ximénez y Olivera and Morejón, "Plano a fs. 913."
18. [Illegible], "Plano a fs. 1129."

19. Miguel de Quintana et al., "Plano a fs. 672."
20. Lafita, "Los autos promovidos"; Miguel de Quintana et al., "Plano a fs. 672."
21. Anastasio Carrillo de Arango, "Plano a fs. 672 de la 4a pieza. Plano de diez y un cuarto caballerías de tierra que medí en el partido de S. Marcos vínculo de Mey[i]reles y forman el cafetal nombrado la 'Paciencia' que quedó entre los bienes de D. Alonso Benigno Muñoz y hoy correponde a D. Santiago F. Firmado por Desiderio Herrera. En los autos del concurso de acreedores de Dn. Alonso Benigno Muñoz," 1834 (September 30), Fondo Escribanías de Ortega, Legajo 38, Número 1, ANC.
22. Manuel O'Reilly y Calvo, "Expediente manuscrito."
23. Gloria García, *Conspiraciones y revueltas: La actividad política de los negros en Cuba, 1790–1845* (Santiago de Cuba: Editorial Oriente, 2003), 91. García notes that although the conduct of mayorales was the subject of numerous regulations, the enforcement of these rules was lax. The presence of legal codes is more suggestive of what was happening through their identification of what were considered problems. In other words, the codes reflected ideals that were unmet and the issues they highlighted were representative of actual behaviors.
24. Abbot, *Letters*, 57.
25. Ibid., 136.
26. L. José Agustín Govantes et al., "Plano a fs. 672 de la 4a pieza. Plano de diez y un cuarto caballerías de tierra que medí en el partido de S. Marcos vínculo de Mey[i]reles y forman el cafetal nombrado la 'Paciencia' que quedó entre los bienes de D. Alonso Benigno Muñoz y hoy corresponde a D. Santiago F. Firmado por Desiderio Herrera. En los autos del concurso de acreedores de Dn. Alonso Benigno Muñoz," 1834 (September 23), Fondo Escribanías de Ortega, Legajo 38, Número 1, ANC.
27. Rafael O'Farrill y Herrera, "Autos relativos."
28. See Natalia Bolívar Aróstegui and Carmen González Díaz de Villegas, *Mitos y leyendas de la comida afrocubana* (San Juan, Puerto Rico: Editorial Plaza Mayor, 2000).
29. See, for example, Lydia Cabrera, *Cuentos negros de Cuba* (Madrid: Ediciones CR, 1972), 71–75.
30. "El café es un consuelo y una necesidad que Dios le dió [*sic*] a los pobres . . . sin café la vida no sirve . . . [y] en las ofrendas que se tributan a los muertos, jamás falta la taza de café que siempre apetecieron." Lydia Cabrera, *El Monte, Igbo Finda Ewe Orisha, Vititi Nfinda* (Madrid: Ediciones CR, 1954), 348.
31. Bolívar Aróstegui and González Díaz de Villegas, *Mitos y leyendas*, 29.
32. *Brujo*, Spanish for "witch (doctor)," was the term used by whites to refer to slaves who performed African-based religious rituals. I use the term "ritual specialist" because it more accurately conveys the actions in which slaves were engaged.
33. Federico *gangá*, "Criminal en averiguación del movimiento contra los blancos que se proyectabe en el cafetal titulado Recompensa, en el partido de Batabanó por parte de su dotación, exitados por el negro Federico Gangá esclavo de D. Felipe Candal," 1844 (May 6), Fondo Comisión Militar, Legajo 32, Número 1, 16v–17, ANC.
34. Abbot, *Letters*, 141 (emphasis in the original).
35. Scott, *Slave Emancipation*, 110. Scott is arguing in this case about the use of plantation stores during the latter half of the nineteenth century, but her point applies to the earlier period, when the system was evolving rather than fully formed.
36. See, for example, Manuel Gonzales Barred, "Criminal en averiguación del movimiento contra los blancos que se proyectabe en el cafetal titulado

Recompensa, en el partido de Batabanó por parte de su dotación, exitados por el negro Federico Gangá esclavo de D. Felipe Candal," 1844 (May 6), Fondo Comisión Militar, Legajo 32, Número 1, ANC.

37. Abbot, *Letters*, 141.
38. Ibid., 149–50.
39. This discussion is drawn from Alejandro de la Fuente, "Slaves and the Creation of Legal Rights in Cuba: Coartación and Papel," *Hispanic American Historical Review* 84, no. 3 (2007): 659–92. It is important to note that while the system was not fixed in law, it had become firmly established in legal practice by the nineteen century. It was formally incorporated into law in 1842 under the Reglamento de Esclavos. Also, see Gloria García Rodriguez, *La esclavitud desde la esclavitud: La visión de los sievos* (Mexico City: Centro de Investigación Científica, 1996); and Alejandro de la Fuente, "Slave Law and Claims-Making in Cuba: The Tannenbaum Debate Revisited," *Law and History Review* 22, no. 2 (2004): 339–69.
40. L. José Agustín Govantes et al., "Plano a fs. 672."
41. Hurlbert, *Gan-Eden*, 189–90.
42. Manuel O'Reilly y Calvo, "Expediente manuscrito." This reference is from the combined accounts of the cafetales Rosa and Resurrección. Rafael *gangá* from the dotación of the Resurrección is listed as paying five hundred pesos on December 15, 1832, for his freedom ("por su libertad").
43. "El Yntendente de la Habana, remite dos exemplares." According to the two censuses, the population of free people grew from 106,494 to 152,838.
44. Moreno Fraginals explicitly contends that slaveholders thought allowing slaves to grow their own food could minimize violent incidents on their farms. Owners instructed slave provision grounds to be located near the commercial fields and also close by slave housing, thereby connecting slave well-being more explicitly to the land and the general state of the farm. This was thought to reduce the likelihood of slaves sabotaging the main crop by setting it on fire, as it would endanger their own "property." Scott confirms these views in her work. See Moreno Fraginals, *El Ingenio*, 89; and Scott, *Slave Emancipation*, 15–16.

CHAPTER 6

Epigraphs. Alejo lucumí quoted in Diego Barreiro, "Comisión Militar. Criminal contra los autores y complices principales de la sublevación de negros del Cafetal Salvador de D. Francisco Santiago de Aguirre ubicado en Banes ocurrida la noche del 13 de agosto por cuyo delito se jusgan á Pedro el carretero; Gonzalo Mandinga; Eusebio Gangá; Luis idem; Pascual Lucumí; Bernualdo id.; Antonio Lucumí; Agustín id; Atilano id.; Juan id; Hermenegildo id.; Juez Fiscal: El Capitán de Ynfantería D.n Tomás de Salazar; Secretario: El Teniente graduado D.n Lorenzo Baltanas," 1833 (August 16), Fondo Miscelánea de Expedientes, Legajo 540, Número B, 12–14, ANC. Mann, *Juanita*, 52.

1. Ira Berlin, *Many Thousands Gone: The First Two Centuries of Slavery in North America* (Cambridge: Belknap Press of Harvard University Press, 1998).
2. James C. Scott, *Weapons of the Weak* (New Haven: Yale University Press, 1985); and James C. Scott, *Domination and the Arts of Resistance: Hidden Transcripts* (New Haven: Yale University Press, 1990), especially 4–5. Scott shows how subordinate groups use a variety of subtle tactics to resist powerful dominant groups. He also argues that there are numerous discourses in play, including private discourses or transcripts that are hidden from the dominant group. These act as counter-hegemonic modes of interaction.

3. The 1812 Aponte conspiracy, centered in Havana, involved free blacks and slaves. This attempt at rebellion was inspired by the ideas enshrined in the Haitian Revolution and the discourse of the Rights of Man and Citizen. This conspiracy is only tangentially related to the arc of plantation-based rebellions that would occur in the coming decades. For a fuller discussion of the Aponte conspiracy, see Childs, *1812 Aponte Rebellion*. Also see García, *Conspiraciones y revueltas*, 66–74. The rebellion known as "La Escalera" was understood to be a revolt against the plantation complex that was inspired by abolitionists and free blacks. It has generally been understood as a sugar cane plantation–based rebellion, but a closer look at the accused reveals that a significant number of the slaves alleged to have been involved lived on cafetales. The best work on the affair is Paquette, *Sugar Is Made with Blood*.

4. This section owes a debt to the works of Manuel Barcia and Gloria García. Each has written descriptions and analyses of the 1825 rebellion. See Barcia Paz, *Seeds of Insurrection*, 34–35; and García, *Conspiraciones y revueltas*. Also see Barcia Paz, "La rebelión de esclavos de 1825 en Guamacaro" (MA thesis, Universidad de Habana, 2000).

5. García, *Conspiraciones y revueltas* 84. Also see Barcia Paz, *Seeds of Insurrection*, 35.

6. Barcia Paz, *Seeds of Insurrection*, 35.

7. Ibid.

8. Ibid.; and García, *Conspiraciones y revueltas*, 83–92.

9. Simón *mina*, "Criminal contra los esclavos insubordinados del cafetal El Carmen. Güira de Melena, Octubre-Noviembre 1827," 1827 (October), Fondo Miscelánea de Expedientes, Legajo 570, Número F, ANC.

10. Francisco de Santiago Aguirre, "Comisión Militar."

11. José Baquero, "Comisión Militar."

12. Ibid. As we have seen, names such as *lucumí* were names owners gave to their slaves that they understood as correlating with African origins. They used these names in a way similar to family names and also used them to inform buying and management decisions, as they attributed traits to so-called tribal origins. It should be noted that the slaves of the cafetal Salvador continued to use their African names rather than their assigned Spanish names.

13. *Ho bé* (lit., "knife") can also be translated as a call to war. Personal conversation with Professor Lisa Lindsay, University of North Carolina, Chapel Hill, November 5, 2003.

14. Diego Barreiro, "Comisión Militar."

15. Margarita *lucumí*, "Comisión Militar. Criminal contra los autores y complices principales de la sublevación de negros del Cafetal Salvador de D. Francisco Santiago de Aguirre ubicado en Banes ocurrida la noche del 13 de agosto por cuyo delito se jusgan á Pedro el carretero; Gonzalo Mandinga; Eusebio Gangá; Luis idem; Pascual Lucumí; Bernualdo id.; Antonio Lucumí; Agustín id; Atilano id.; Juan id.; Hermenegildo id.; Juez Fiscal: El Capitán de Ynfantería D.n Tomás de Salazar; Secretario: El Teniente graduado D.n Lorenzo Baltanas," 1833 (August 17), Fondo Miscelánea de Expedientes, Legajo 540, Número B, ANC.

16. Manuela *lucumí*, "Comisión Militar. Criminal contra los autores y complices principales de la sublevación de negros del Cafetal Salvador de D. Francisco Santiago de Aguirre ubicado en Banes ocurrida la noche del 13 de agosto por cuyo delito se jusgan á Pedro el carretero; Gonzalo Mandinga; Eusebio Gangá; Luis idem; Pascual Lucumí; Bernualdo id.; Antonio Lucumí; Agustín id; Atilano id.; Juan id.; Hermenegildo id.; Juez Fiscal: El Capitán de Ynfantería D.n Tomás de Salazar; Secretario: El Teniente graduado D.n Lorenzo Baltanas," 1833

(August 19), Fondo Miscelánea de Expedientes, Legajo 540, Número B, 58-59, ANC.

17. José *mina*, "Comisión Militar. Criminal contra los autores y complices principales de la sublevación de negros del Cafetal Salvador de D. Francisco Santiago de Aguirre ubicado en Banes ocurrida la noche del 13 de agosto por cuyo delito se jusgan á Pedro el carretero; Gonzalo Mandinga; Eusebio Gangá; Luis idem; Pascual Lucumí; Bernualdo id.; Antonio Lucumí; Agustín id; Atilano id.; Juan id.; Hermenegildo id.; Juez Fiscal: El Capitán de Ynfantería D.n Tomás de Salazar; Secretario: El Teniente graduado D.n Lorenzo Baltanas," 1833 (August 17), Fondo Miscelánea de Expedientes, Legajo 540, Número B, 24–25, ANC.

18. Diego Barreiro, "Comisión Militar."

19. Margarita *lucumí*, "Comisión Militar." The wife of Joaquín, Margarita *lucumí*, a domestic slave, was quoting her husband.

20. José *mina*, "Comisión Militar."

21. Diego Barreiro, "Comisión Militar."

22. Manuela *lucumí*, "Comisión Militar."

23. The *camino real* (lit., royal road) was the central road to an area.

24. José Hernández Quintana, "Comisión Militar. Criminal contra los autores y complices principales de la sublevación de negros del Cafetal Salvador de D. Francisco Santiago de Aguirre ubicado en Banes ocurrida la noche del 13 de agosto por cuyo delito se jusgan á Pedro el carretero; Gonzalo Mandinga; Eusebio Gangá; Luis idem; Pascual Lucumí; Bernualdo id.; Antonio Lucumí; Agustín id; Atilano id.; Juan id.; Hermenegildo id.; Juez Fiscal: El Capitán de Ynfantería D.n Tomás de Salazar; Secretario: El Teniente graduado D.n Lorenzo Baltanas," 1833 (August 21), Fondo Miscelánea de Expedientes, Legajo 540, Número B, ANC. There were also reports that Luís had taken some women's clothes from the main house and used them as part of his attire.

25. Manuela *lucumí*, "Comisión Militar." Manuela confirms the leadership of Fierabrás, stating that he was at the head of the group that marched to Banes and that the group was highly integrated, including ladinos and bozales, and men and women.

26. Juan Iduate wrote an article on the rebellion on the Salvador mapping out the actions of the slaves and the logistics of the rebellion. See Iduate, "Noticias sobre sublevaciones y conspiraciones de esclavos: Cafetal Salvador, 1833," *Revista de la Biblioteca Nacional José Martí* 24, no. 1–2 (1982): 117–52.

27. Manuela *lucumí*, "Comisión Militar." The testimony of Manuela, which was representative of the bozales, reveals that many of the group still only spoke Lucumí, as they had to use another slave as a translator during the proceedings.

28. José Hernández Quintana, "Comisión Militar."

29. Manuela *lucumí*, "Comisión Militar."

30. Geggus has also cited the work of Julius S. Scott III and his idea of a "culture of expectation." Scott, "The Common Wind: Currents of Afro-American Communication in the Era of the Haitian Revolution" (PhD diss., Duke University, 1986), 122, 158, cited in David Geggus, "Slavery, War, and Revolution in the Greater Caribbean," in *A Turbulent Time: The French Revolution and the Greater Caribbean*, ed. David Barry Gaspar and David Patrick Geggus (Bloomington: Indiana University Press, 1997).

31. Eugene D. Genovese, *Roll, Jordan, Roll: The World the Slaves Made* (New York: Vintage, 1976), 597–98.

32. Michael Craton, "The Passion to Exist: Slave Rebellions in the British West Indies, 1629–1832," *Journal of Caribbean History* 13 (1980), 2, 28–29. Also,

see Michael Craton, *Testing the Chains: Resistance to Slavery in the British West Indies* (Ithaca, NY: Cornell University Press, 1982).

33. Barcia Paz, *Seeds of Insurrection*, 47. Barcia goes on to say that the rebellions that did have revolutionary content and aimed to overthrow the existing system were based in urban contexts and led by free men. Examples of these types are the Aponte rebellion of 1812 and La Escalera of 1844 in Havana and Matanzas respectively. See Childs, *1812 Aponte Rebellion*; and Paquette, *Sugar Is Made with Blood*.

34. David Geggus, *Slave Resistance Studies and the Saint Domingue Slave Revolt: Some Preliminary Considerations* (Miami: Latin American and Caribbean Center, Florida International University, 1983). Geggus also develops his ideas further in "Slave Resistance in the Spanish Caribbean," in *A Turbulent Time*. In the later piece, Geggus looks primarily at the spread of ideas of freedom as a result of the Haitian Revolution.

35. See chapter 6 in Patrick Manning, *Slavery and African Life: Occidental, Oriental, and African Slave Trades* (Cambridge, UK: Cambridge University Press, 1990), 110–25; Miers and Kopytoff, "African 'Slavery' as an Institution of Marginality."

36. Francisco de Santiago Aguirre, "Comisión Militar."

37. Ibid.

38. Cirulio, "Se propone."

39. Iduate, "Noticias."

40. Kenneth F. Kiple, *The Caribbean Slave: A Biological History* (New York: Cambridge University Press, 1984), 147–48.

41. José Antonio Saco, "Carta sobre el cólera morbo asiático." In *Colección de papeles científicos, históricos, politicos y de otros ramos sobre la Isla de Cuba* (Havana: Dirección General de Cultura, Ministerio de Educación, 1857). The three jurisdictions referred to were Madruga, Pipián, and Nueva Paz.

42. As discussed in Chapter 4, this concept of illness was widespread not only in western Africa but also in much of central Africa. Disease was not thought of as solely an environmental issue but a part of the dynamic personal and relational universe. Relationships needed to be kept balanced and functioning within established norms, or people were affected. Likewise, mal-intentioned or antisocial people who were powerful enough could inflict harm on others. See Chapter 4, and also Evan M. Zuesse, *Ritual Cosmos: The Sanctification of Life in African Religions* (Athens: Ohio University Press, 1979), 44, 88, 101; Benjamin C. Ray, *African Religions: Symbol, Ritual, and Community* (Englewood Cliffs, NJ: Prentice-Hall, 1976), especially 150–52. Sharla Fett and Theophus Smith show these that concepts were carried over to the Americas in Fett, *Working Cures: Healing, Health, and Power on Southern Slave Plantations*, and Smith, *Conjuring Culture: Biblical Formations of Black America* (New York: Oxford University Press, 1995).

43. A. J. H. Latham, "Witchcraft Accusations and Economic Tension in Pre-Colonial Old Calabar," *Journal of African History* 13, no. 2 (1972): 249–60 (see especially 250). Also, see Victor W. Turner, *The Drums of Affliction: A Study of Religious Processes among the Ndembu of Zambia* (Bath, UK: Oxford University Press, 1968), 14–15.

44. Francisco Letamendí, "Comisión Militar. Autos criminales contra los negros de la dotación del cafetal titulado 'La Juanita,' Habana 1835," 1835 (October 16), Fondo Miscelánea de Expedientes, Legajo 86, Número D, ANC.

45. Pablo *lucumí*, "Comisión Militar."

46. Fredrika Bremer, *The Homes of the New World: Impressions of the New World*,

trans. Mary Howitt (New York: Harper, 1853), 331; and Juan García, "Comisión Militar."

47.   Dionisio *gangá*, "Criminal contra varios esclavos de la dotación del cafetal Perseverancia, acusados de haverse [*sic*] amotinado contra el mayoral y otros dependientes blancos de dicha finca. Complicados: Andrés Lucumí, Rosa Lucumí, Eulogio Lucumí, Luciano Lucumí, Lucas Lucumí, Cleto Lucumí, Basilio Lucumí, Felipa Lucumí, Lorenzo Colorado, Emeterio, Genaro Lucumí, Agapito Lucumí, Canuto Lucumí, Víctor Lucumí, Lucio Lucumí, Facundo Lucumí, Lopio Lucumí, Amá Lucumí, Florentino Lucumí, Lorenzo Prieto, Francisco Carabalí, y Vincente Mandinga. Fiscal El Teniente Coronel D. Felipe Arango, Secretario El Teniente D. Antonio Cas," 1842 (September 19), Fondo Comisión Militar, Legajo 27, Número 3, ANC. Dionisio mentions that she was preparing *fufú*, a dish common to many parts of western Africa, made with flour ground from manioc or potatoes. In Cuba, during this period, it was made from *plátanos* (plantains).

48.   Ibid.; and Belén de la Rosa, "Criminal contra varios esclavos." Dionisio did not quote Andrés or Rosa but reported that Andrés had been whipped two or three days earlier for speaking with the slaves in the field in Lucumí and he resented it and refused to speak Spanish. Rosa called for the punishment of the whites in defense of her husband, Andrés.

49.   Belén de la Rosa, "Criminal contra varios esclavos." This account is based on the testimony of the mayoral.

50.   Domingo Gusmán, "Criminal contra varios esclavos de la dotación del cafetal Perseverancia, acusados de haverse [*sic*] amotinado contra el mayoral y otros dependientes blancos de dicha finca. Complicados: Andrés Lucumí, Rosa Lucumí, Eulogio Lucumí, Luciano Lucumí, Lucas Lucumí, Cleto Lucumí, Basilio Lucumí, Felipa Lucumí, Lorenzo Colorado, Emeterio, Genaro Lucumí, Agapito Lucumí, Canuto Lucumí, Víctor Lucumí, Lucio Lucumí, Facundo Lucumí, Lopio Lucumí, Amá Lucumí, Florentino Lucumí, Lorenzo Prieto, Francisco Carabalí, y Vincente Mandinga. Fiscal El Teniente Coronel D. Felipe Arango, Secretario El Teniente D. Antonio Cas," 1842 (September 19), Fondo Comisión Militar, Legajo 27, Número 3, ANC.

51.   [Unsigned], "Expediente sobre la presentación al capitán de Guanajay de la dotación del Cafetal 'Las Mercedes' quejándose de falta de alimento," 1850 (January 9), Fondo Gobierno Superior Civil, Legajo 946, Número 33375, ANC.

52.   See Eric Robert Taylor, *If We Must Die: Shipboard Insurrections in the Era of the Atlantic Slave Trade; Antislavery, Abolition, and the Atlantic World* (Baton Rouge: Louisiana State University Press, 2006).

53.   See Chapter 1, note 2.

CONCLUSION

1.   Childs, *1812 Aponte Rebellion*, 189.

2.   See Iduate, "Noticias."

3.   See Paquette, *Sugar Is Made with Blood*, especially chapter 8. Also see de la Fuente, "Slave Law and Claims-Making," 364.

4.   Ada Ferrer, "Cuba en la sombra de Haití: Noticias, sociedad y esclavitud." In *El rumor de Haití en Cuba: Temor, raza y rebeldía, 1789–1844*, ed. María Dolores González-Ripoll et al. (Madrid: Consejo Superior de Investigaciones Científicas, 2004).

5.   Paquette, *Sugar Is Made with Blood*, 267–72.

6.   See de la Fuente, "Slaves and the Creation of Legal Rights."

7.   At least thirteen percent of the slave sales on the island between 1790 and 1880

were coartados according to Bergad et al., *Cuban Slave Market*, 668. De la Fuente cites Bergad et al., *Cuban Slave Market*, 123.

8. See David Turnbull, *Travels in the West: Cuba; With Notices of Porto Rico, and the Slave Trade* (London,: Longman Orne Brown Green and Longmans, 1840); Paquette, *Sugar Is Made with Blood*, chapter 3.

9. The ideal of the farm was enlarged to include the coffee region of the vuelta abajo, which came to be viewed as the garden region of the island. See Cirilo Villaverde, *Excursión a Vueltabajo* (Havana: Consejo Nacional de Cultura, Ministerio de Educación, 1961).

10. Villaverde wrote the original manuscript of *Cecilia Valdés* during the 1830s and it was in circulation in Havana and Matanzas by 1839. The author later returned to the text, revising and extending it for publication in 1879. The later version included a new section with additional material—notably, an account of a trip to an ingenio, as well as some more pointed critiques of the slave system in Cuba. This later version is the one with which most recent readers are familiar. See Cirilo Villaverde, *Cecilia Valdés; ó, La Loma del Ángel* (Havana: Imprenta Literaria, 1839; Havana: Editorial Excelsior, 1879).

11. See José Antonio Saco, *Historia de la esclavitud de la raza africana en el Nuevo Mundo y en especial en los países Américo-Hispanos*, 4 vols. (Havana: Cultural SA, 1938; first published 1875–1879).

12. See Perry, *Gender and Disorder*.

13. Luz Mena, "Stretching the Limits of Gendered Spaces: Black and Mulatto Women in 1830s Havana," *Cuban Studies* (2005): 93–95.

14. Mann, *Juanita*, 71–75.

15. See Luz Mena, "Stretching the Limits."

16. González Fernández, "Acerca del mercado cafetalero cubano."

BIBLIOGRAPHY

ARCHIVAL SOURCES

Havana, Cuba
    Archivo Nacional de Cuba
        Comisión Militar
        Correspondencia de los Capitanes Generales
        Donativos y Remisiones
        Escribanías
        Gobierno General
        Gobierno Superior Civil
        Miscelánea de Expedientes
        Real Consulado y Junta de Fomento
        Reales Cédulas y Ordenes

Matanzas, Cuba
    Archivo Histórico Provincial de Matanzas
        Cimmarones

Madrid, Spain
    Archivo Histórico Nacional
        Correspondencia de Cuba
        Correspondencia de Cuba y Puerto Rico
        Cuba Gobierno
        Hacienda de Cuba
        Ultramar

Seville, Spain
    Archivo General de Indias
        Contratación
        Cuba
        Santo Domingo

PRINTED PRIMARY SOURCES

Abbot, Abiel. *Letters Written in the Interior of Cuba, between the Mountains of Arcana, to the East, and of Cusco, to the West, in the Months of February, March, April, and May, 1828.* Boston: Bowles and Dearborn, 1829.

Arango y Parreño, Francisco de. "Informe al Real Consulado de la Habana, en el expediente para formar las instrucciones y proponer á la persona que se encargue de la comisión de pasar á Jamaica á examinar el estado de adelanto en que se halla esa isla con respecto al cultivo y elaboración de los frutos coloniales." In *Obras,* 507–32. Havana: Howson y Heinen, 1888.

———. "Problemas de la economía cubana en el siglo XVIII." In Pichardo Viñals, 172–204.

Atkins, Edwin Farnsworth. *Sixty Years in Cuba: Reminiscences of Edwin F. Atkins.* Cambridge, MA: Riverside Press, 1926.

Barca, Mme. Calderón de la. *Life in Mexico during a Residence of Two Years in That Country.* Edited by Camille Destillieres Comas. Reprint of 1843 ed. Mexico: Ediciones Tolteca, 1952.

Bremer, Fredrika. *Cartas desde Cuba.* Translated by Matilde Goulard de Westberg. Havana: Fundación Fernando Ortiz, 2002

———. *The Homes of the New World: Impressions of the New World.* Translated by Mary Howitt. New York: Harper, 1853

Charles III. "Reglamento de comercio libre de España a Indias." In Pichardo Viñals, 165–67.

Charles IV. "Libertad de comercio de esclavos." In Pichardo Viñals, 168–71.

———. "Real Cédula concediendo livertad para el Comercio de Negros, con las Islas de Cuba, Santo Domingo, Puerto Rico, y Provincia de Caracas, á Españoles, y estrangeros, baxo las Reglas que se expresan." In *Documentos para La Historia Argentino,* edited by Ricardo Levene, 394–99. Buenos Aires: Compañía Sud-Americana de Billetes de Banco, 1915.

Chateausalins, Honorato Bernard de. *El vademécum de los hacendados cubanos; ó, Guía práctica para curar la mayor parte de las enfermedades.* Philadelphia: J. Van Cort, 1848.

Dana, Richard Henry, Jr. *To Cuba and Back.* Edited and with a new introduction by C. Henry Gardiner. Carbondale: Southern Illinois University Press, 1966.

———. "A Trip to Cuba." *Atlantic Monthly* 4, no. 22 (August 1859): 184–94.

Debien, Gabriel, ed. *Plantations et esclaves a Saint-Domingue: La Sucrerie Foäche a Jean-Rabel et ses esclaves (1770–1893).* Vol. 67, *Notes d'histoire coloniale.* Dakar: Imprimerie Protat Frères, 1962.

Dumont, Alejandro, José M. Velázquez, and Alberto Parreño. *Memoria sobre el cultivo del café en la Isla de Cuba.* Folleto ed. Sampaloc, Philippines: Por la Real Sociedad Económica de Filipinas en la Imprenta de Sampaloc, 1827.

Estadísticas, Comisión de. *Cuadro estadístico de la siempre fiel Isla de Cuba correspondiente al año 1827.* Havana: Arazoza y Soler, 1829.

Grainger, James, William Beauclerk, R. Dodsley, and J. Dodsley. *The Sugar-Cane! A Poem, in Four Books, with Notes.* London: R. and J. Dodsley, 1764.

Gurney, Joseph John, and Henry Clay. *Familiar Letters to Henry Clay of Kentucky, Describing a Winter in the West Indies.* New York: Press of Mahlon Day, 1840.

Humboldt, Alexander von. *The Island of Cuba: A Political Essay.* Princeton, NJ: Markus Wiener, 2001. First published Paris: J. Renouard, 1827.

Hurlbert, William Henry. *Gan-Eden; or, Pictures of Cuba.* Boston: John P. Jewett, 1854.

Jameson, Robert. *Letters from the Havana, during the Year 1820; Containing an Account of the Present State of the Island of Cuba, and Observations on the Slave Trade.* London: John Miller, 1821.

Jay, W. M. L. [Julia Louisa M. Woodruff]. *My Winter in Cuba.* New York: E.P. Dutton, 1871.

Koster, Henry. *Travels in Brazil by Henry Koster in the Years from 1809 to 1815.* Philadelphia: M. Carey and Son, 1817.

Laborie, P. J. [Pierre-Joseph].*The Coffee Planter of Saint Domingo; with an appendix, containing a view of the constitution, government, and state of that colony,* previous to the year 1789. To which are added, some hints on the present state of the island, under the British government. London: T. Cadell and W. Davies, 1798.

———. *Cultivo del cafeto; ó, Árbol que produce el cafe, y modo de beneficiar este fruto*. Translated by Pablo Boloix. Havana: Arazoza y Soler 1820.

Mann, Mary Peabody. *Juanita: A Romance of Real Life in Cuba Fifty Years Ago.* Edited by Patricia M. Ard. Charlottesville: University Press of Virginia, 2000. First published 1887 (Boston: D. Lothrop).

Noda, Tranquilino Sandalio de. "Memoria sobre el café." In *Memorias de la Sociedad Económica de Amigos del País,* 121–52. Havana: Oficina del Gobierno y de la Real Sociedad Patriótica por SM, 1820.

Oficina del Gobierno Constitucional. *Tasación y venta del Cafetal Valiente en el partido de Güines, y de la estancia del refugio de Regla, con todos sus edificios.* Havana: Oficina del Gobierno Constitucional, 1821.

Pichardo Viñals, Hortensia, ed. *Documentos para La Historia De Cuba.* Havana: Editorial Pueblo y Educación, 2000.

Saco, José Antonio. "Carta sobre el cólera morbo asiático." In *Colección de papeles científicos, históricos, politicos y de otros ramos sobre la Isla de Cuba,* 260–97. Havana: Dirección General de Cultura, Ministerio de Educación, 1960–1963, First published 1857.

———. *Historia de la esclavitud de la raza africana en el Nuevo Mundo y en especial en los países Américo-Hispanos.* 4 vols. Havana: Cultural SA, 1938–1940. First published 1875–1879.

Sagra, Ramón de la. *Historia económica, política y estadística de la isla de Cuba; ó, Sea de sus progresos en la población, la agricultura, el comercio y las rentas.* Havana: Arazoza y Soler 1831.

Turnbull, David. *Travels in the West: Cuba; With Notices of Porto Rico, and the Slave Trade.* London: Longman Orne Brown Green and Longmans, 1840.

Villaverde, Cirilo. *Cecilia Valdés; ó, La Loma del Ángel.* Havana: Imprenta Literaria, 1839.

———. *Cecilia Valdés; ó, La Loma del Ángel.* Havana: Editorial Excelsior, 1879.

———. *Cecilia Valdés; ó, La Loma del Ángel.* Havana: Editorial Letras Cubanas, 2001.

———. *Excursión a Vueltabajo.* Biblioteca Basica de Cultura Cubana. Havana: Consejo Nacional de Cultura, Ministerio de Educación, 1961.

Wurdemann, John G. *Notes on Cuba Containing an Account of Its Discovery and Early History: A Description of the Face of the Country, Its Population, Resources, and Wealth; Its Institutions, and the Manners and Customs of Its Inhabitants; With Directions to Travellers Visiting the Island.* Boston: J. Munroe, 1844.

SECONDARY SOURCES

Austin, J. L. *How to Do Things with Words.* 2nd ed. Oxford: Clarendon Press, 1975. First published 1962.

Balansó, Juan. *La Corona Vacilante.* Barcelona: Plaza y Janés Editores, 1996.

Barcia Paz, Manuel. "La rebelión de esclavos de 1825 en Guamacaro." MA thesis, Universidad de Habana, 2000.

———. *Seeds of Insurrection: Domination and Resistance on Western Cuban Plantations, 1808–1848.* Baton Rouge: Louisiana State University Press, 2008.

Barry, Boubacar. *Senegambia and the Atlantic Slave Trade.* Translated by Ayi Kwei Armah. Cambridge: Cambridge University Press, 1998.

Bas.s.a-1, Ibn, José María Millás Vallicrosa, Expiración García Sánchez, J. Esteban Hernández Bermejo, and Muhammad Aziman, eds. *Libro de Agricultura.* Facsimile

and preliminary study by Expiración García Sánchez. Edited by J. Esteban
   Hernández Bermejo. Seville: Sevilla Equipo 28, 1995.

Bergad, Laird W. *Cuban Rural Society in the Nineteenth Century: The Social and
   Economic History of Monoculture in Matanzas.* Princeton, NJ: Princeton
   University Press, 1990.

Bergad, Laird W., Fe Iglesias García, and María del Carmen Barcia. *The Cuban Slave
   Market, 1790–1880.* Cambridge: Cambridge University Press, 1995.

Berlin, Ira. *Many Thousands Gone: The First Two Centuries of Slavery in North
   America.* Cambridge, MA: Belknap Press of Harvard University Press, 1998.

Bhabha, Homi K. *The Location of Culture.* London: Routledge, 1994.

Bloch, Maurice. *Prey into Hunter: The Politics of Religious Experience.* Cambridge:
   Cambridge University Press, 1992.

Bolívar Aróstegui, Natalia, and Carmen González Díaz de Villegas. *Mitos y leyendas de
   La Comida Afrocubana.* San Juan, Puerto Rico: Editorial Plaza Mayor, 2000.

Brandon, George. *Santería from Africa to the New World: The Dead Sell Memories.*
   Bloomington: Indiana University Press, 1993.

Butler, Judith. *Bodies That Matter: On the Discursive Limits of "Sex."* New York:
   Routledge, 1993.

Cabrera, Lydia. *Cuentos negros de Cuba.* Madrid: Ediciones CR, 1972.

———. *El Monte, Igbo Finda Ewe Orisha, Vititi Nfinda.* Madrid: Ediciones CR, 1954.

Carlson, David C. "In the Fist of Earlier Revolutions: Postemancipation Social Control
   and State Formation in Guantánamo, Cuba, 1868–1902." PhD diss., University of
   North Carolina, 2007.

Castellanos, Jorge, and Isabel Castellanos. *Cultura Afrocubana: Las religiones y las
   lenguas.* Colección Ébano Y Canela, vol. 3. Miami: Ediciones Universal, 1992.

Chasteen, John Charles. *National Rhythms, African Roots: The Deep History of Latin
   American Popular Dance.* Albuquerque: University of New Mexico Press, 2004.

Childs, Matt D. "'The Defects of Being a Black Creole': The Degrees of African
   Identity in the Cuban Cabildos de Nación, 1790–1820." In *Slaves, Subjects, and
   Subversives: Blacks in Colonial Latin America,* edited by Jane G. Landers and
   Barry M. Robinson, 209–45. Albuquerque: University of New Mexico Press, 2006.

———. *The 1812 Aponte Rebellion in Cuba and the Struggle against Atlantic Slavery.*
   Chapel Hill: University of North Carolina Press, 2006.

Connerton, Paul. *How Societies Remember.* New York: Cambridge University Press,
   1989.

Cosner, Charlotte A. "Rich and Poor, White and Black, Free and Slave: The Social
   History of Cuba's Tobacco Farmers, 1763–1817." PhD diss., Florida International
   University, 2008.

Craton, Michael. "The Passion to Exist: Slave Rebellions in the British West Indies,
   1629–1832." *Journal of Caribbean History* 13 (Spring 1980): 1–20.

———. *Testing the Chains: Resistance to Slavery in the British West Indies.* Ithaca, NY:
   Cornell University Press, 1982.

Delle, James A. *An Archaeology of Social Space: Analyzing Coffee Plantations in
   Jamaica's Blue Mountains.* New York: Plenum Press, 1998.

de Man, Paul. *Allegories of Reading: Figural Language in Rousseau, Nietzsche, Rilke,
   and Proust.* New Haven: Yale University Press, 1979.

Derrida, Jacques. "Signature Event Context." In *Margins of Philosophy.* Chicago:
   University of Chicago Press, 1982.

Dicum, Gregory, and Nina Luttinger. *The Coffee Book: Anatomy of an Industry from
   Crop to the Last Drop.* New York: New Press, 1999.

Ely, Roland T. *Cuando reinaba su majestad el azúcar.* Buenos Aires: Editorial
   Sudamericana, 1963.

Emory University. *Voyages: The Trans-Atlantic Slave Trade Database.slavevoyages.org* (accessed July 3, 2009).

Fernández de Pinedo Echevarría, Nadia. *Comercio exterior y fiscalidad: Cuba (1794–1860).* Bilbao, Spain: Servicio Editorial de la Universidad del País Vasco, Euskal Herriko Unibertsitateko Argitalpen Zerbitzua, 2002.

Ferrer, Ada. "Cuba en la sombra de Haití: Noticias, sociedad y esclavitud." In *El rumor de Haití en Cuba: Temor, raza y rebeldía, 1789–1844,* edited by María Dolores González-Ripoll, Consuelo Naranjo, Ada Ferrer, Gloria García, and Josef Opatrný, 179–231. Madrid: Consejo Superior de Investigaciones Científicas, 2004.

Fett, Sharla M. *Working Cures: Healing, Health, and Power on Southern Slave Plantations.* Chapel Hill: University of North Carolina Press, 2002.

Fisher, Lillian Estelle. *The Intendant System in Spanish America.* Berkeley: University of California Press, 1929.

Foucault, Michel. *Discipline and Punish: The Birth of the Prison.* Translated by Alan Sheridan. 2nd ed. New York: Vintage, 1995.

Friedlaender, H. E. *Historia económica de Cuba.* Havana: Jesús Montero, 1944.

Fuente, Alejandro de la. "Slave Law and Claims-Making in Cuba: The Tannenbaum Debate Revisited." *Law and History Review* 22, no. 2 (2004): 339–69.

———. "Slaves and the Creation of Legal Rights in Cuba: *Coartación* and *Papel.*" *Hispanic American Historical Review* 84, no. 3 (2007): 659–92.

García de Arboleya, José. "Cafetales and Vegas in Cuba." In *Haciendas and Plantations in Latin American History,* edited by Robert G. Keith, 153–57. New York: Holmes and Meier Publishers, 1977.

García Rodriguez, Gloria. *Conspiraciones y revueltas: La actividad política de los negros en Cuba, 1790–1845.* Santiago de Cuba: Editorial Oriente, 2003.

———. *La esclavitud desde la esclavitud: La visión de los sievos.* Mexico City: Centro de Investigación Científica, 1996.

Gaspar, David Barry, and David Patrick Geggus, eds. *A Turbulent Time: The French Revolution and the Greater Caribbean.* Bloomington: Indiana University Press, 1997

Geggus, David. "Slave Resistance in the Spanish Caribbean." In Gaspar and Geggus, 131–55.

———. *Slave Resistance Studies and the Saint Domingue Slave Revolt: Some Preliminary Considerations.* Edited by Lowell W. Gudmundson. Occasional Papers Series, vol. 4. Miami: Latin American and Caribbean Center, Florida International University, 1983.

———. "Slavery, War, and Revolution in the Greater Caribbean." In Gaspar and Geggus, 1–50.

Genovese, Eugene D. *Roll, Jordan, Roll: The World the Slaves Made.* New York: Vintage, 1976.

González Fernández, Doria. "Acerca del mercado cafetalero cubano durante la primera mitad del siglo XIX." *Revista de la Biblioteca Nacional José Martí* 31, no. 2 (May–August 1989): 151–76.

———. "La economía cafetalera en Cuba, 1790–1860." *Arbor* 139, nos. 547–48 (1991): 161–79.

Guerra Sánchez, Ramiro. *Mudos testigos: Crónica del ex-cafetal Jesús Nazareno.* Havana: Editorial Lex, 1948.

Hahn, Barbara. "Making Tobacco Bright: Institutions, Information, and Industrialization in the Creation of an Agricultural Commodity, 1617–1937." *Enterprise and Society* 8, no. 4 (2007): 790–98.

Hall, Gwendolyn Midlo. *Africans in Colonial Louisiana: The Development of Afro-*

Creole Culture in the Eighteenth Century. Baton Rouge: Louisiana State University Press, 1992.

———. *Slavery and African Ethnicities in the Americas: Restoring the Links.* Chapel Hill: University of North Carolina Press, 2005.

Herskovits, Melville J. *The Myth of the Negro Past.* New York: Harper, 1941.

Heywood, Linda M., ed. *Central Africans and Cultural Transformations in the American Diaspora.* Cambridge: Cambridge University Press, 2002.

Higman, B. W. *Jamaica Surveyed: Plantation Maps and Plans of the Eighteenth and Nineteenth Centuries.* Barbados: University of the West Indies Press, 2001.

Horton, Robin. *Patterns of Thought in Africa and the West: Essays on Magic, Religion, and Science.* Cambridge: Cambridge University Press, 1993.

Howard, Philip A. *Changing History: Afro-Cuban Cabildos and Societies of Color in the Nineteenth Century.* Baton Rouge: Louisiana State University Press, 1998.

Johnson, Sherry. *Climate and Catastrophe in Cuba and the Atlantic World in the Age of Revolution.* Chapel Hill: University of North Carolina Press, 2011.

———. "El Niño and Environmental Crisis: Reinterpreting American Rebellions in the 1790s." Paper presented at the Allen Morris Conference on the History of Florida and the Atlantic World, Florida State University, Tallahassee, FL, 2004.

Kiple, Kenneth F. *Blacks in Colonial Cuba, 1774–1899.* Gainesville: University Presses of Florida, 1976.

———. *The Caribbean Slave: A Biological History.* Studies in Environment and History. New York: Cambridge University Press, 1984.

Kiple, Kenneth F., and Virginia Himmelsteib King. *Another Dimension to the Black Diaspora: Diet, Disease, and Racism.* Cambridge: Cambridge University Press, 1981.

Kuethe, Allan J. *Cuba, 1753–1815: Crown, Military, and Society.* Knoxville: University of Tennessee Press, 1986.

Kuethe, Allan J., and Lowell Blaisdell. "The Esquilache Government and the Reforms of Charles III in Cuba." *Jahrbuch für Geschichte von Staat, Wirtschaft und Gesellschaft Lateinamerikas* 19 (1982): 117–36.

Kutzinski, Vera M. *Sugar's Secrets: Race and the Erotics of Cuban Nationalism.* Charlottesville: University of Virginia Press, 1993.

Lachatañeré, Rómulo. *El sistema religioso de los afrocubanos.* Colección Echú Bi. Havana: Editorial de Ciencias Sociales, 1992.

Latham, A. J. H. "Witchcraft Accusations and Economic Tension in Pre-Colonial Old Calabar." *Journal of African History* 13, no. 2 (1972): 249–60.

Le-Roy y Cassá, Jorge. *Estadística demográfica en Cuba: Trabajo presentado al Intercambio Sanitario de la Liga de las Naciones Celebrado en la Habana del 1° al 10 de marzo de 1925.* Havana: El "Siglo XX," 1925.

Lizárraga-Partida, M. L., E. Mendez-Gómez, A. M. Rivas-Montaño, E. Vargas-Hernández, A. Portillo-López, A. R. González-Ramírez, A. Huq, and R. R. Colwell. "Association of Vibrio Cholerae with Plankton in Coastal Areas of Mexico." *Environmental Microbiology* 11, no. 1 (2009): 201–8.

López Denis, Adrián. "Disease and Society in Colonial Cuba, 1790–1840." PhD diss., University of California, Los Angeles, 2007.

———. "Sugar in the Times of Cholera." *Wikiversity. en.wikiversity.org* (last modified October 27, 2009).

Lovejoy, Paul E. "The African Diaspora: Revisionist Interpretations of Ethnicity, Culture and Religion under Slavery." *Studies in the World History of Slavery, Abolition and Emancipation* 2, no. 1 (1997): 1–23.

———. *Transformations in Slavery: A History of Slavery in Africa.* New York: Cambridge University Press, 1983.

Lynch, John. *Bourbon Spain, 1700–1808.* Oxford: Basil Blackwell, 1989.

Lyotard, Jean-François. *The Postmodern Condition: A Report on Knowledge.* Translated by Geoff Bennington and Brian Massumi. Minneapolis: University of Minnesota Press, 1984.

Mannheim, Bruce, and Dennis Tedlock. "Introduction." In Tedlock and Mannheim, 1–32.

Manning, Patrick. *Slavery and African Life: Occidental, Oriental, and African Slave Trades.* Cambridge: Cambridge University Press, 1990.

Marrero, Leví. *Cuba: Economía y sociedad azúcar, ilustración y conciencia (1763–1868).* Vol. 9, 11, 12, and 13. Madrid: Editorial Playor, 1985.

Matibag, Eugenio. *Afro-Cuban Religious Experience: Cultural Reflections in Narrative.* Gainesville: University Press of Florida, 1996.

Matory, James Lorand. *Black Atlantic Religion: Tradition, Transnationalism, and Matriarchy in the Afro-Brazilian Candomblé.* Princeton, NJ: Princeton University Press, 2005.

———. *Sex and the Empire That Is No More: Gender and the Politics of Metaphor in Oyo Yoruba Religion.* Minneapolis: University of Minnesota Press, 1994.

Mbiti, John. *African Religions and Philosphy.* London: Heinemann, 1969.

McCook, Stuart George. *States of Nature: Science, Agriculture, and Environment in the Spanish Caribbean, 1760–1940.* Austin: University of Texas Press, 2002.

Mena, Luz. "Stretching the Limits of Gendered Spaces: Black and Mulatto Women in 1830s Havana." *Cuban Studies* (2005): 87–104.

Méndez, Manuel Isidro. *Bibliografía del cafetal Angerona.* Havana: n.p., 1952.

———. "Tres tipos de cafetales en San Marcos de Artemisa." *Revista Bimestre Cubana* 59 (1947): 217–24.

Miers, Suzanne, and Igor Kopytoff. "African 'Slavery' as an Institution of Marginality." In *Slavery in Africa: Historical and Anthropological Perspectives,* edited by Suzanne Miers and Igor Kopytoff, 3–81. Madison: University of Wisconsin Press, 1977.

Mintz, Sidney W. *Sweetness and Power: The Place of Sugar in Modern History.* New York: Penguin, 1986.

Mintz, Sidney W., and Richard Price. *The Birth of African-American Culture: An Anthropological Perspective.* Boston: Beacon Press, 1992.

Moreno Fraginals, Manuel. "Africa in Cuba: A Quantitative Analysis of the African Population in the Island of Cuba." *Annals of the New York Academy of Sciences* 292 (1977): 187–201.

———. *El Ingenio: Complejo económico social cubano del azúcar.* 3 vols. Havana: Editorial de Ciencias Sociales, 1978.

Murphy, Joseph M., and Mei-Mei Sanford, eds. *Oşun across the Waters: A Yoruba Goddess in Africa and the Americas.* Bloomington: Indiana University Press, 2001.

Nicholls, David. *Haiti in Caribbean Context: Ethnicity, Economy and Revolt.* New York: St. Martin's Press, 1985.

Núñez Jiménez, Antonio. *Geografía de Cuba.* 2nd ed. Havana: Editorial Lex, 1960.

Ochoa, Todd Ramón. *Society of the Dead: Quita Manaquita and Palo Praise in Cuba.* Berkeley: University of California, 2010.

Oliveros de Castro, María Teresa, and Julio Jordana de Pozas. *La agricultura de los reinos españoles en tiempo de los Reyes Católicos.* Madrid: Ministerio de Agricultura Instituto Nacional de Investigaciones Agronómicas, 1968.

Olupona, Jacob K. "The Spirituality of Matter: Religion and Environment in Yoruba Tradition, Nigeria." *Dialogue and Alliance* 9, no. 2 (1995): 69–80.

———. "The Study of Yoruba Religious Tradition in Historical Perspective." *Numen* 40 (1993): 240–73.

Olupona, Jacob K., and Terry Rey, eds. *Orisa Devotion as World Religion: The Globalization of Yoruba Religious Culture.* Madison: University of Wisconsin Press, 2008.

Ortiz, Fernando. *La africanía de la música folklórica de Cuba.* Havana: Ministerio de Educación, Dirección de Cultura, 1950.

———. *Los bailes y el teatro de los negros en el folklore de Cuba.* 2nd ed. Havana: Editorial Letras Cubanas, 1985.

———. *Contrapunteo cubano del tabaco y el azúcar.* Havana: Editorial de Ciencias Sociales, 1991. First published 1940.

———. "Felix Varela, Amigo del País." *Revista Bimestre Cubana* 6, no. 6 (November–December 1911): 478–84.

———. *Hampa afro-cubana: Los negros esclavos; Estudio sociológico y de derecho público.* Havana: Revista Bimestre Cubana, 1916.

Palmer, Colin A. "From Africa to the Americas: Ethnicity in the Early Black Communities." *Journal of World History* 6, no. 2 (Fall 1995): 223–36.

Palmié, Stephan. *Wizards and Scientists: Explorations in Afro-Cuban Modernity and Tradition.* Durham, NC: Duke University Press, 2002.

Paquette, Robert L. *Sugar Is Made with Blood: The Conspiracy of La Escalera and the Conflict between Empires over Slavery in Cuba.* Middletown, CT: Wesleyan University Press, 1988.

Parker, Andrew, and Eve Kosofsky Sedgwick, eds. *Performativity and Performance.* New York: Routledge, 1995.

Pérez de la Riva y Pons, Francisco. *El café: Historia de su cultivo y explotación en Cuba.* Havana: Jesús Montero, 1944.

Pérez de la Riva, Juan. *El barracón y otros ensayos.* Havana: Editorial de Ciencias Sociales, 1975.

———. *Cuadro sinóptico de la esclavitud en Cuba (Suplemento de la Revista Actas del Folklore).* Havana: Tipografía Ponciano, 1961.

Pérez, Louis A. *Winds of Change: Hurricanes and the Transformation of Nineteenth-Century Cuba.* Chapel Hill: University of North Carolina Press, 2001.

Perry, Mary Elizabeth. *Gender and Disorder in Early Modern Seville.* Princeton, NJ: Princeton University Press, 1990.

Pierson, William Whatley, Jr. "Francisco de Arango y Parreño." *Hispanic American Historical Review* 16, no. 4 (November 1936): 451–78.

Pineda, Baron L. *Shipwrecked Identities: Navigating Race on Nicaragua's Mosquito Coast.* New Brunswick, NJ: Rutgers University Press, 2006.

Pluchon, Pierre. *Toussaint Louverture de l'esclavage au pouvoir.* Paris: l'Ecole; Port au Prince: Editions Caraïbes, 1979.

Price, Richard, and Sally Price. *The Root of Roots; or, How Afro-American Anthropology Got Its Start.* Chicago: Prickly Paradigm Press, 2003.

Quiroz, Alfonso W. "The Scientist and the Patrician: Reformism in Cuba." Paper presented at Alexander von Humboldt: From the Americas to the Cosmos, New York, October 14–17, 2004.

Rauch, Basil. *American Interest in Cuba: 1848–1855.* Studies in History, Economics and Public Law, vol. 537. New York: Columbia University Press, 1948.

Ray, Benjamin C. *African Religions: Symbol, Ritual, and Community.* Englewood Cliffs, NJ: Prentice-Hall, 1976.

Robert, Karen, ed. *New Year in Cuba: Mary Gardner Lowell's Travel Diary, 1831–1832.* Boston: Massachusetts Historical Society; Northeastern University Press, 2003.

Rossiter, Margaret W. *The Emergence of Agricultural Science: Justus Liebig and the Americans, 1840–1880.* New Haven: Yale University Press, 1975.

Rotberg, Robert I., with Christopher K. Clague. *Haiti: The Politics of Squalor.* Boston: Houghton Mifflin, 1971.

Sartorius, David A. "Slavery, Conucos, and the Local Economy: Ingenio Santa Rosalia, Cienfuegos, Cuba, 1860–1886." MA thesis, University of North Carolina, 1997.

Scott, Julius S., III. "The Common Wind: Currents of Afro-American Communication in the Era of the Haitian Revolution." PhD diss., Duke University, 1986.

Scott, James C. *Domination and the Arts of Resistance: Hidden Transcripts.* New Haven: Yale University Press, 1990.

———. *Weapons of the Weak.* New Haven: Yale University Press, 1985.

Scott, Rebecca J. *Degrees of Freedom: Louisiana and Cuba after Slavery.* Cambridge, MA: Belknap Press of Harvard University Press, 2008.

———. *Slave Emancipation in Cuba: The Transition to Free Labor, 1860–1899.* Princeton, NJ: Princeton University Press, 1985.

Simons, Geoff. *Cuba from Conquistador to Castro.* New York: St. Martin's Press, 1996.

Singleton, Theresa A. "Slavery and Spatial Dialectics on Cuban Coffee Plantations." *World Archaeology* 33, no. 1 (2001): 98–114.

Smith, Theophus H. *Conjuring Culture: Biblical Formations of Black America.* New York: Oxford University Press, 1995.

Sogolo, Godwin. S. "The Concept of Cause in African Thought." In *The African Philosophy Reader,* edited by P. H. Coetzee and A. P. J. Roux, 177–85. New York: Routledge, 1998.

Solt, Frederick, Philip Habel, and J. Tobin Grant. "Economic Inequality, Relative Power, and Religiosity." *Social Science Quarterly* 92, no. 2 (June 2011): 447–65.

Sweet, James H. *Recreating Africa: Culture, Kinship, and Religion in the African-Portuguese World, 1441–1770.* Chapel Hill: University of North Carolina Press, 2003.

Tannenbaum, Frank. *Slave and Citizen: The Negro in the Americas.* New York: Vintage, 1946.

Taylor, Eric Robert. *If We Must Die: Shipboard Insurrections in the Era of the Atlantic Slave Trade; Antislavery, Abolition, and the Atlantic World.* Baton Rouge: Louisiana State University Press, 2006.

Tedlock, Dennis, and Bruce Mannheim, eds. *The Dialogical Emergence of Culture.* Urbana: University of Illinois Press, 1995.

Thomas, Hugh. *Cuba; or, The Pursuit of Freedom.* Updated ed. New York: Da Capo Press, 1998.

Thornton, John K. *Africa and Africans in the Making of the Atlantic World, 1400–1680.* Studies in Comparative World History. Cambridge: Cambridge University Press, 1992.

———. "African Dimensions of the Stono Rebellion." *American Historical Review* 96, no. 4 (1991): 1101–13.

Turner, Victor. *The Anthropology of Performance.* New York: PAJ Publications, 1986.

———. *The Drums of Affliction: A Study of Religious Processes among the Ndembu of Zambia.* Bath, UK: Oxford University Press, 1968.

———. "Social Dramas and Stories about Them." In *On Narrative,* edited by W. J. T. Mitchell, 137–64. Chicago: University of Chicago Press, 1981.

Van Norman, William C., Jr. "The Process of Cultural Change among Cuban Bozales during the Nineteenth Century." *Americas* 62, no. 1 (2005): 177–207.

Vélez, María Teresa. *Drumming for the Gods: The Life and Times of Felipe García Villamil, Santero, Palero, and Abakuá.* Studies in Latin American and Caribbean Music. Philadelphia: Temple University Press, 2000.

Wolf, Eric R., and Sidney W. Mintz. "Haciendas and Plantations in Middle America and the Antilles." *Social and Economic Studies* 6, no. 3 (1957): 380–412.

World Health Organization. "Cholera: Fact Sheet N° 107." *www.who.int* (accessed September 2012).

Yarini Klupffel, José Leopoldo. "Cólera en el ingenio." *Wikiversity. en.wikiversity.org* (last modified September 10, 2008). First published 1833.

Zanetti Lecuona, Oscar, and Alejandro García Alvarez. *Sugar and Railroads: A Cuban History, 1837–1959.* Chapel Hill: University of North Carolina Press, 1998.

Zuesse, Evan M. *Ritual Cosmos: The Sanctification of Life in African Religions.* Athens: Ohio University Press, 1979.

INDEX